SMASHED

Smashed

GROWING UP A DRUNK GIRL

KOREN ZAILCKAS

First published by Penguin Group (USA) Inc. 2005

First published in Great Britain by Ebury Press 2005

3 5 7 9 10 8 6 4 2

Ebury Press, an imprint of Ebury Publishing.
Random House, 20 Vauxhall Bridge Road, London SW1V 2SA

Random House Australia (Pty) Limited
20 Alfred Street, Milsons Point, Sydney, New South Wales 2061, Australia

Random House New Zealand Limited
18 Poland Road, Glenfield, Auckland 10, New Zealand

Random House South Africa (Pty) Limited
Endulini, 5A Jubilee Road, Parktown 2193, South Africa

The Random House Group Limited Reg. No. 954009

www.randomhouse.co.uk

A CIP catalogue record for this book is available from the British Library.

Cover design by Two Associates
Typeset by Carla Bolte

ISBN 0 091 90559 1

Papers used by Ebury Press are natural, recyclable products made
from wood grown in sustainable forests.

Printed and bound in Great Britain
by Mackays of Chatham plc, Chatham, Kent

For my mother,
who first made me mindful of women's issues

PREFACE

THIS IS THE kind of night that leaves a mark. When I surface, its events and the shame of them will be gone from my head, cut away as though by some surgical procedure. I will not miss the memories that were carved out of me: when my father carried me in his arms through the sliding glass doors, my head lolling the way it used to when I was the little girl who he carried to bed. When a friend, being interviewed by the doctor treating me, had to answer "vodka," which is like a curse word, in the fact that we exploit it in private but don't dare utter it in the presence of adults. When a row of people looked up from their laps because the scene of a girl, dead-drunk at sixteen, momentarily distracted them from their midnight emergencies.

I won't remember the chair that wheels me down the hospital's hall, or the white cot I am lain on, or the tube that coasts through my esophagus like a snake into a crawl space. Yet I will retain these lost hours, just as my forearms will hold the singes of stranger's cigarettes in coming years, as my back will hold the scratch of a spear-point fence, as my fingers will hold griddle scars from a nonstick grill. This is the first of many forgotten injuries that will imprint me just the same.

When I surface, there won't be any spells of shivering or gut purling, any percussion between my temples. I won't need to follow the doctor's orders: "Tylenol for discomfort." There will be no physical discomfort. My body will be still and indifferent, but mentally, the soreness of the overdose will linger.

It's strange the way the mind remembers forgetting. The fact of the blackout won't slip away like the events that took place inside of it. Instead of receding into my life's story, the lost hours will stand out. Something else will move in to fill in the holes: dread and denial that thickens with time like emotional scar tissue. In the absence of memory, the night will be even more memorable. The blackout will stay with me, causing chronic, psychic pain, a persistent, subconscious thrumming.

My INTENTION, in telling this story from the very beginning, is to show the full life cycle of alcohol abuse. I did not begin by drinking from steep glasses, viscous concoctions of rum, gin, vodka, and triple sec, and I did not start off blacking out or vomiting blood. Like most abiding behaviors, my drinking was an evolution that became desperate over time: I found alcohol during my formative years. I warmed to it instantly. Like a childhood friend, it aged with me.

I grew up in the Northeast, a white, middle-class teenager among other white, middle-class teenagers, which plunks me down in one of the highest demographics of underage drinkers. I am also Catholic, a faith that some researchers find increases the odds that teenagers—particularly girls—will drink, and drink savagely.

I started drinking before I started high school. I had my first sips of whiskey not more than a year after I first went to a gymnasium dance or first dragged a disposable razor over one knee, balancing myself on the edge of the bathtub. I had just burgeoned the new breasts I needed to shop for blouses in the juniors' department. I had only just crammed my blinking dolls and seam-split stuffed animals into a box in the attic.

I drank throughout high school, but not every weekend, not even every other weekend. It was the promise of drinking that sustained me through all of high school's afflictions: the PSATs and the SATs, report cards and driving tests, and presidential fitness exams.

In high school, I sought out booze the way boys my age sought out sex. At parties, I leered when girls unzipped their backpacks, hoping to catch the glint of a bottle; and my own sly glances reminded me of the boys who leered when girls bent forward, hoping to glimpse their breasts through the necks of their blouses. The brief encounters fed me. For weeks, I'd relive swilling rum in a graffitied bathroom stall during a Battle of the Bands, vodka in the wooded perimeters outside of a football game, tequila at a sleepover after somebody's mom fitted a nightlight into the wall and announced she was going to bed.

I drank through college, too, with an appetite that had me drinking rum by the half-liter bottle, until I couldn't squelch the impulse to unload my secrets to strangers, or sob, or pass out wherever I happened to be standing. I drank until I'd forgotten how much I had already drank, and then I drank more.

For four years, I drank aimlessly when I might have been doing things that were far more gratifying. I might have been forming real friendships, the kind that would have stretched into adulthood, and had me in ill-fitting bridesmaid dresses at half a dozen best friends' weddings. I might have been writing stories or taking pictures. I might have been sleeping a full six hours a night, or eating three square meals a day, or taking multivitamins. I might have been learning the language of affection: how to exchange glances or trace a man's fingertips with mine. I might have been reading the top hundred books of all time.

I drank after college. I drank through my first real move, my first job as an executive assistant, my first insurance forms, my first tax filing, and my first apartment where rent was due on the first of the month. I drank after the real world revealed itself to me like a magic trick, after I saw the method of adulthood, the morning commutes and mindless jobs, which shattered the illusions I had about it.

And at age twenty-three, I gave up drinking altogether once I realized how much it had cost me.

STILL, I am not an alcoholic. As far as I can tell, I have no family history of alcoholism. I am not physically addicted to drinking, and I don't have the genetically based reaction to alcohol that addiction counselors call "a disease." In the nine years that I drank, I never hid bottles or drank alone, and I never spent a night in a holding cell awaiting DUI charges. Today, one glass of wine would not propel me into the type of bender where I'd wind up drinking whole bottles. While I have been to AA meetings, I don't *go* to them.

I am a girl who abused alcohol, meaning I drank for the explicit purpose of getting drunk, getting brave, or medicating my moods. In college, that abuse often took the form of binge drinking, which for women, means drinking four or more drinks in a row at least once during a span of two weeks. But frequently, before college and during it, more time would pass between rounds, and two or three drinks could get me wholly obliterated.

I wrote this book knowing that my alcohol abuse, though dangerous, was not unprecedented. Nor were the after-effects I experienced as a result of it. Mine are ordinary experiences among girls and young women in both the United States and abroad, and I believe that very commonness makes them noteworthy.

In the past decade alone, girls have closed the gender gap in terms of drinking. I wrote this book because girls are drinking as much, and as early, as boys for the first time in history, because there has been a threefold increase in the number of women who get drunk at least ten times a month, and because a 2001 study showed 40 percent of college girls binge drink. When you factor in increased rates of depression, suicide, alcohol poisoning, and sexual assault, plus emerging research that suggests women who drink have greater chances of liver disease, reproductive disorders, and brain abnormalities, the consequences of alcohol abuse are far heavier for girls than boys.

I also wrote this book because I wanted to quash the misconceptions about girls and drinking: that girls who abuse alcohol are either masculine, sloppy, sexually available, or all of the above, that girls are drinking more and more often in an effort to compete with men, and that alcohol abuse is a life-stage behavior, a youthful excess that is not as damaging as other drugs.

You can find girls who abuse alcohol anywhere. We are everywhere. Of the girls I've known over the past nine years, the ones who took shots, did keg stands, toppled down stairs, passed out on sidewalks, and got sick in the backseats of cabs, there have been overachievers, athletes, dropouts, artists, snobs, nerds, runway models, plain-Janes, and so-called free-thinkers. Some wore oversized sweaters and lacerated jeans; more wore ballet flats and rippling skirts and fine-spun jewelry that glimmered. Even holding a pint of the headiest beer, they retained the qualities that people call *feminine*.

Girls don't drink in the name of women's liberation, for the sake of proving we can go drink for drink with the boys. We don't drink to affirm we are "sassy" or "self-confident," which newsweeklies have lately suggested. Nor is our drinking a manifestation of "girl power" or "gender freedom" or any of the other phrases so many sociologists interchange with happiness. On the contrary, most every girl I've known drank as an expression of her *unhappiness*. I too drank in no small part because I felt shamed, self-conscious, and small.

To me, it is no surprise that underage drinking has spiked, given the fact that so much of it is dismissed as experimentation or life-stage behavior. Parents tend to brand alcohol abuse as the lesser evil, as a phase that is far less actionable than drug abuse. As a drinking girl, especially a college-aged girl, I assigned happy hours and the subsequent hangovers to behavior that was expected of those my age. I believed the people who romanticized those years, the ones who told me to embrace irresponsibility before I was slapped with the burdens of corporate adulthood.

For many girls, alcohol abuse may be a stage that tapers off after the quarter-life mark. Many will be spared arrests, accidents, alcoholism, overdoses, and sexual assaults. A whole lot of them will have close calls, incidents they will recount with self-mocking at dinner parties some fifteen years later. Some of them will have darker stories, memories or half memories or full-out blackouts, that they will store in the farthest corners of their mental histories and never disclose to their families or lovers. But I fear that women, even those women who escape the physical consequences of drinking, won't escape the emotional ones. I fear some sliver of panic, sadness, or self-loathing will always stay with us.

I HAVE always loved Rainer Maria Rilke's poem "The Grown-Up," which speaks of a girl who stands bravely before the world's fear and grace. We're assured she "endured it all: bore up under / the swift-as-flight, the fleeting, the far-gone, / the inconceivably vast, the still-to-learn, / serenely as a woman carrying water moves with a full jug." I could recite that poem in my sleep, and yet I recognize that I have never been that girl. Instead of shouldering adulthood with all my young courage and strength, I dropped it after the first impossible hoist, when it all felt too unmanageable. I wrote life off as heavy cargo, and accepted it could only be mastered by masterful men. I was a coward. I grasped on to alcohol, which was the first available escape.

Nine years after I took my first drink, it occurs to me that I haven't grown up. I am missing so much of the equipment that adults should have, like the ability to sustain eye contact without flinching or letting my gaze roll slantwise to the floor. At this point in time, I should be able to hear my own unwavering voice rise in public without feeling my heart flutter like it's trying to take flight. I should be able to locate a point of conversation with the people I deeply long to know as my friends, like my memoirist neighbor or the woman in my reading group who carries the same tattered paperbacks that I do and wears the same footless tights. I should be able to stop self-censoring and smile when I feel like it. I should recognize happiness when I feel it expand in my gut.

Some of the most interesting research findings in substance abuse involve women who began drinking regularly in their preteens. Clinicians report some of these women, who seek treatment for alcoholism in their mid-to-late twenties, not only look younger, but act younger, too. Some turn up at clinics wearing kids' clothing and cradling teddy bears. Some still play the way children do, by twirling hula hoops and blowing bubbles. When faced with conflict, they just totter away. It seems some women's emotional development arrests as a result of alcohol. They stall at the age they were when they had their first drinks.

While this manifestation is extreme, it hits close to home.

As a twenty-three-year-old, I am mistaken daily for nineteen (seventeen if my hair is pulled into a ponytail and fifteen if I'm wearing Converse sneakers). Too many days, people make me aware of my own childishness. I am aware that the clerk behind the counter calls me miss instead of ma'am, telemarketers still ask to speak to my parents, and after years of financial independence, every handyman who turns up at my apartment still makes a snide remark about "Daddy paying my rent." I am aware that the fourteen-year-old girl I tutor in English is a head taller than I am; and while I craft arguments that burn my cheeks because I never spit them out, she extends her opinions even when they aren't complete. I am aware that somewhere along the line, I've subconsciously turned down the pitch of my speech, like a silencer of a gun that softens the sound of its firing. Now, even when I yell, I don't feel like I am using my full voice.

I MIGHT have waited to quit drinking. I might have kept abusing alcohol for at least five more years at the pace I was moving. I might have waited for alcoholism to fall like an axe. Or I might have tried my best to "drink responsibly," even though setting responsible limits is complicated by my physical smallness; plus the sheer fact that I'm female means the same amount of alcohol affects me differently every time.

In the end, I quit drinking because I didn't want to waste any more time picking up the pieces. I decided *smashed,* when it's used as a synonym for drunk, is a self-fulfilling prophecy.

When I stopped drinking, I never experienced the high-on-life sensation that so many people say consumes them like the Holy Spirit in their first months of abstinence. I never felt the buzz that people report feeling once they discover they can thrive without alcohol, once they dust off their sober faculties and realize everything still works. Abstinence did not help me rediscover the world with childlike awe. I never felt inspired by the simplicity of nature, by the dependability of sunup, or spring's yawning blossoms.

I didn't feel the ecstasy of returning to a life that was unaltered by alcohol because no such life ever existed for me. For nearly a decade, alcohol was the mold that shaped me. Once it lifted, I felt the immediate terror of having no framework. Without drinking, there was nothing to structure my weekends, my relationships, or my self-image. I felt my confidence cave in on itself.

For me, abstinence has been nothing but growing pains. It

has meant starting from scratch, reliving my awkward phase, and learning all over again what it means to be adult. It's meant I will act like less of an asshole, but *feel* much more like one. It's meant learning that drinking will always be more socially acceptable than abstaining. It's meant discovering I am more cautious and introspective than I ever allowed myself to be, and I will never again dance in public, which is probably preferable.

After a decade of alcohol abuse, I find myself going back over the chronology, trying to pinpoint when I might have averted it. Mentally, I go back to my university, to the row of bars that is located just across from the health center and wonder if anything could have lead me to the south side of the street, to tell my story to a man with a notepad instead of a man with a bar rag, to switch counselors. I remember the first kiss that tasted like sweet malt and then the subsequent ones, the boys whose breath held the must of wine or the ethanol of whiskey, and I wonder would my story have turned out differently if boys had played no part in it? I go back to the bite of my first drink and wonder, what if I had been sixteen or eighteen instead of fourteen? Would age have lessened my attachment?

I apply all the questions to my story that the experts employ: I wonder, What if I'd never seen an alcohol ad? What if there were no glistening bottles and bodies to catch my attention between the pages of magazines or on freeway billboards? I wonder what if the legal drinking age was eighteen? I ask myself whether any legislation might have made my drinking moderate.

My story has no real turning point. There is no critical moment that might have changed my whole narrative. My alcohol abuse, like the issue of all underage alcohol abuse, has its roots in more than one factor. Just as drinking pervades our culture, it diffused into my personality. I grew into my abuse, like the occasional tree you can find on a nature walk, its roots spilling over both sides of a boulder like outspread fingers, in spite of the rock's lack of soil, moisture, and stability. To see it only at the height of its maturity is to wonder, Why build on that?

My alcohol abuse was a seed that fell at just the right time, in just the right place, when all the conditions were just right to nurture it. To understand the outgrowth, I have to go back to the first bottle that fell out of the liquor chest and into my ready hands. I have to go back to the beginning.

INITIATION

FIRST TASTE

To THIS DAY, I can't remember when I had my first kiss. I can't tell you how old I was, if it was a moment in May, if I closed my eyes or left them open. The memory is long gone. My mind tossed it out with the bathwater of experience, with TV and takeout and chitchat, the brief intervals of time that simply never soaked in. That kiss, though historical, was in no way historic. It was a tree that fell in the forest. And I didn't make a sound.

I remember other firsts shallowly, like the type of big Broadway plays where the scenery is more moving than the spectacle. Today, any emotion that was evoked by those rites escapes me. I can only recall in detail the rows of white chiffon on my First Communion dress, or the torn vinyl seats of the school bus on my first day of school. I can't remember the trauma of my first period, or the year (was it sixth grade or seventh?), but I know that I told my mother about it in the front yard, where she was watering the hydrangea tree with a green rubber hose. The memory of the first time I drove the family Ford has been reduced to a vacant parking lot. My first sex has the solid darkness of its windowless room.

But like most women, I remember my first drink in tender minutiae.

The exact date is June 17, 1994. I am fourteen, which is the norm these days, when the mean age of the first drink for girls is less than thirteen years old.* I am a few days shy of my eighth-grade graduation. Summer vacation looms close, and just beyond it, regional high school. In the interim is public school mania, a collective chaos brought on by high temperatures and lettered report cards, when even teachers slam closed *The Metamorphosis* and let classes out ahead of the bell.

It's Friday and I'm spending the weekend at Natalie Burke's summer cottage on Lake Pleasant, which in my mind has the exoticism of St. Bart's. The cottage is small, a single-story, but we move around it as we please because Mr. and Mrs. Burke often work well into prime time. Its rooms bulge with wicker furniture, wind chimes, Bonsai trees in clay pots, framed star-fish on the walls, a thick shag carpet that always smells like sunscreen, and a china cabinet stacked with party napkins and Thai cookbooks, Natalie's old *Cosmopolitan*s, and her parents' old *Vanity Fair*s. A string of white lights on the deck, which are left to sway in the wind year-round, are a continual

*Devon Jersild, *Happy Hours: Alcohol in a Woman's Life,* 96.

reminder of the indefinite nature of our holiday. All in all, there is nothing to encourage us that the rules of our ordinary lives apply here.

It is another afternoon of Natalie and I alone, together. We spend it sunbathing on the roof and swimming unsupervised. Natalie's parents forbid us to do both, but we can't be bothered with cautionary tales while the sun is still high and motorboats skid viscously past the end of the dock.

It is seven o'clock when we towel off. A few months ago, it would have been twilight. But, since it's summer, the sky hasn't darkened past pale pink. Through the sliding glass door, the sun looks defiant. It sits bloated and orange above the lake's public beach, like another inflatable ball kids forgot in the reeds when they left for the day.

I am standing Speedo-ed in the kitchen, sliding an elastic strap down over one shoulder and examining a faint tan line. The baby oil Natalie made me rub on instead of sunscreen has left my skin feeling buttery and somehow sexy, like it's a waste that no one will touch it but me. Still, I haven't browned past the color Natalie calls "Bisque," after a tin of loose powder in her makeup chest. Bisque is a winter color, she says. I should sun myself until I can wear the same color she does—Toast—which is a warm tan she tops with Raspberry Jam blush. I tell her the oil didn't work; I'm as Bisque as ever.

I am talking too loud because my ears are stopped up from a violent plunge off the end of the dock. Water is dripping down the tips of my hair and splattering the kitchen tiles where Natalie is crouched over an open cabinet like someone searching for a spare deck of playing cards.

Only she comes up with a bottle.

. . .

THE WAY the sun is dawdling on the horizon has me feeling exposed. Pink light is filtering in through the skylight and screen doors, and the kitchen is lit up like an aquarium we are moving around in, on display.

Across the yard, I can make out Natalie's next-door neighbor, Mrs. McCree. I wonder if she can see us from where she is tipping a copper watering can into her window boxes. If she spots Natalie rooting around in the liquor chest, she'll surely tell the Burkes, the same way she did last summer, when she watched us etch our initials into the trunk of a property-line birch tree. I know enough to walk to the windows and pull the green gingham curtains closed.

I am waiting for Natalie to say something.

Mr. Burke is due home any minute to drive us to a surprise birthday party for a girl with whom we both ride the bus. We have a little more than an hour to eradicate the evidence that we've been swimming. We need to shower, blow-dry our hair, and change back into cut-off jeans. This bottle is an evident detour from the plans. It blindsides me.

On the one hand, I shouldn't be as startled as I am. It's not like I'm unfamiliar with bottles. I've seen and handled loads of them. Come Christmastime, they are lined up like toy soldiers across the marble-topped bar in the living room: bottles of different heights and shapes. The liquor is in clear or brown bottles. The wine is in green or yellow bottles. I refill my grandmother's glass when my father asks me to, and I know what kind to pour by the shape of the goblet. Whites go in the slender glasses, and reds go in the spherical ones. I know wine needs to breathe, so I fill up the glass only halfway.

I've seen all these bottles, and yet I've never seen one quite like this one. The way it is resting in Natalie's lap in this quiet house and this pale light, I sense it means something else entirely.

The difference might come from the change in context. I'm not sure what to do with the bottle *here,* where there are no parents, no relatives, and no party. All I can do is watch Natalie, and think that all the times I've poured bottles in the company of my parents, peeling back the labels and even licking the bottle caps because my mom said I could, has helped me understand drinking as much as anatomy drawings in textbooks have helped me understand sex. My eighth-grade education has taught me how liquor works: how it oozes through the walls of the intestines into the bloodstream, circulating and bleeding into body cells, making them drunk. But that's just physiology. I sense it won't help me when it comes to methodology, when I have to figure out what to do with this bottle. Its neck looks erected at me.

It's not unlike my first glimpse of male genitals, which I got while I was waiting at the fifth-grade bus stop, when a man in a brown sedan pulled up and flashed himself out the window. Natalie is holding the bottle in the same way: slanted up, with the butt of it pressed into her stomach, her fingers curled around the neck. In its presence, I feel the same hot flush of embarrassment. The same slow tingle spreads itself up the back of my neck. Years from now, I'll find myself processing the memory in the same way. I'll want to find foreshadowing in the events of the day. I'll want a sign that this presence was coming, an indication that I'd been flirting with trouble all along.

But there was no omen. Natalie is like an earthquake, the type of natural disaster that no one can predict. It is the characteristic that most draws me to her. My most exciting moments with Natalie come when I least expect them, like love.

Her attention span is short, and at any point during our afternoons together, her interest might pass swiftly from one amusement to another. A walk in the woods turns into a walk on the train tracks. A swim turns into a high dive off an old fishing bridge. I invariably find myself standing on a ledge, assessing the risk, while Natalie plunges in headfirst. She will be the blueprint for the kamikaze girlfriends I'll seek well into my twenties, the suicidal personalities who seize the day by letting go of any expectations for a tomorrow.

Inevitably, I perform many feats with Natalie that I have no real interest in doing. I hitchhike. I stuff two Hello Kitty T-shirts into my book bag while a clerk isn't looking. I let her take an X-ACTO blade to my upper arm so we can be blood sisters. I even agree to third-wheel when she goes skinny-dipping with the boy who lives down the lane; I dive down to run my hands along the lake weed, staying clear of their splashing while they do whatever makes Natalie conclude that boys' thingies float.

I don't need anyone to tell me I'm a tagalong, I know it. I operate as Natalie's sidekick. She is the magician, the one who possesses the hocus-pocus, and I see myself as her mousy assistant. It is my job to prepare her instruments and trust her magic, to stand paralyzed against the target while she throws knives at my head.

And yet, I never consider her influence to be what a decade's worth of health teachers have called "peer pressure." *Pressure* doesn't define Natalie. The word is too heavy to explain the tactics of my best friend, a girl who stands under five feet tall, who weighs less than a hundred pounds, who doesn't even have the persuasive powers to convince her mother to stop buying gallon jugs of limeade. She is not steadily compressing me under the weight of her deviance, the way the word seems to suggest.

If anything, Natalie is fragile. Too many afternoons, I walk into her bedroom and find her curled under her desk, which is the most secluded space she can find ever since her parents unhinged her bedroom door, when they decided she couldn't be trusted with that most-basic privacy. The days I find her sobbing in the same position that schoolchildren assume during bomb drills, I am all too happy to apply a five-finger discount at Cumberland Farms, or key her brother's pickup truck, or smoke a pack of cigarettes in her mother's dress closet with the intention of marring its Givenchy suits with the smell of Kools. My petty crimes are sympathy gifts, like flowers or chocolates or teddy bears. I comply with her ploys to make her laugh after a despicable world has made her cry.

I trust Natalie, which seems important. I imagine my first drink the way I imagine my first sex, and I don't think I could have either with someone I don't feel wholly comfortable with.

I anticipate that being drunk will make me feel just as vulnerable as being naked does. I expect it to strip away my inhibitions, and in my openness, I'm afraid my private confidences will come tumbling out, the way they do when women drink on sitcoms, confessing who they love or who they loathe, causing Jerry Seinfeld to declare Elaine's mental "vault" worthless because too many people know that peach schnapps is the key. I want to know that the person I drink with won't laugh if I inadvertently reveal all of me.

That was the reason I passed when Shannon Fife invited me to her house last April, to blend frozen daiquiris while her dad was at an Elk's Club meeting. We were new friends, and I had never slept over at her house before. I'd never seen her bedroom, or petted her dog, or sat at her kitchen table while her mom flipped pancakes. Drinking was too intimate an act to do for the first time with Shannon, who knew none of my secrets. I hadn't trusted her enough to show her my eighth-grade yearbook, revealing which boys' pictures I'd drawn hearts around in pink ink.

IT FEELS good to decide my first time will be with Natalie.

By now, she has deflowered me on multiple levels. The biggest milestone was two months ago, when she taught me how to smoke. We were sitting on her screened-in porch, fumbling with faulty Bic lighters amid the bite of mosquitoes and the blare of Beck, when she pulled out a pack of exquisitely thin cigarettes she'd brought back from a class trip to Rome. She'd shown me how to exhale like Audrey Hepburn in *Breakfast at Tiffany's*. Learning to smoke was like learning how to kiss, she'd said. It was all in the way you threw your head back, in the round *o* that you made with your lips.

For all her moral support, Natalie is a tough coach, too. She's quick to elbow me in the ribs in the aisles of Rite Aid, where she's pocketing tubes of lipstick and I'm staring up at the security mirror, which she says draws attention to us. When we're smoking cigarettes behind her dad's toolshed, she'll critique my technique no matter which floppy-haired boy from the neighborhood is there to hear. She'll scold me for holding the cigarette like a man or for not inhaling deep enough. She'll toss me the pack and say, "You're gonna keep lighting them until you smoke one right."

I know why I accept Natalie's lessons, but I'm not wholly sure why she offers them to me. I used to think she did it for the sole purpose of testing me. Every new task would find her with the same face a boy makes when he slides his hand up your shirt. It was an expectant look, like she was waiting to see if I leaned into the challenge or pushed it away.

It was that face that led me to believe she'd passed afternoons this way before. I thought she'd scouted out the inside of the abandoned barn on Longhorn Road before she boosted me into its hayloft. I thought she'd hitchhiked to the skate shop on Route 12 before she had me shadowing her on the road's shoulder, resting my outstretched thumb on my thigh.

Only recently have I begun to wonder if Natalie is faking her know-how. I think her expertise might be another act, a testament to what the vice principal calls Natalie's compulsive lying, and what I call her love for performance. Experienced drinker, smoker, and crook might be little more than personae she makes up at a moment's notice, like the time she convinced the ticket seller at the movie theater we were the owner's daughters and therefore didn't have to pay to see *Return of the Living Dead III*.

The liquor cabinet might be virgin territory for her, too. It might be like the haunted grove we once hiked to through streams, past tire piles, and over ravines. She might be bringing me along for company because she is too frightened to explore it alone. She might be pretending, for my sake, that she knows the way.

I KNEEL down and peer into the hole of the cabinet. It is a voyeuristic impulse, a lot like the urge to root around in someone's medicine cabinet. I can't resist. The moment Natalie pulls open its doors, she unearths her parents' answer to that age-old question, "What's your poison?" She's revealed (a) that her parents get loaded, (b) how often they get loaded, and (c) what, specifically, they prefer to get loaded on.

Of course, I am not an experienced liquor clairvoyant, as I will be in college. Now, I don't know how to interpret the information: the number of bottles (three), the names (Hiram Walker, Southern Comfort, Seagram's) and the fullness (three-quarters gone or not yet opened). I can't read them like tea leaves and predict with reasonable accuracy who poured them, when, and under what circumstances.

I sense that these bottles are leftovers. They are probably remnants from past parties, the type of midsummer cookouts where the beer and wine goes first. The triple sec evokes margaritas that were never made. The whiskey has probably been there for years, opened but rarely poured, allowed to linger as a last resort. And as for the sealed bottle of vodka, I have no doubt that Mrs. Burke bought it in preparation for a party, overestimating how much people would drink, the way hostesses often do.

Natalie's parents are big on throwing parties. Their annual Fourth of July bash is an event big enough to be advertised in the local newspaper's calendar of events. Every girl in town gets a new bathing suit, including me, and the local swim shop makes a small fortune selling one-piece swimsuits in size youth-14.

My parents beam each year when an invitation arrives in the mailbox, a cartoon duck in an inner tube reminding us, "It's that time again!" The Burkes' cottage means independence for all of us. My little sister sits on the edge of the dock and baits sunfish with watermelon chunks. Natalie and I help tow the neighborhood kids on a raft behind the motorboat. And my parents lounge on the pine deck, amid the bug-repellent candles and smoking hamburger buns, and drink an odd concoction of wine and fruit that I'll later learn is sangria.

There is something in that wine that lights them up from the inside like the fireflies settling around us at dusk. My mother glides from one conversation to the next as though hoisted by a great wind, while my father sags, bemused, in his lawn chair, allowing the lines around his eyes to relax and, for once, neglecting to answer the buzzing pager at his hip. They always seem so much happier then, less alone. And I wish I could preserve that feeling for them, capture them, too, in a mason jar and bring them home aglow.

When Natalie twists off the black plastic cap and hands the bottle to me, I take it as part of an implicit equation about how drinking dovetails people. The Burkes' parties have taught me how alcohol steadies strained social conditions. Summers before, in this house, a few rocks in lowball glasses seemed to balance impossible elements, people with disparate ideas and temperaments: A personal injury lawyer would pitch horse-shoes with a soccer mom; the newspaper editor would scrape hot dogs off the grill and trade stock tips with a recent college grad; a substitute teacher would dance with the police chief, shimmying her colossal hips and letting him spin her in close.

I think this bottle might level the differences between Natalie and me, too. As junior high slides into high school, I can see us becoming less-compatible best friends. She laughs more, and I've become quieter and more reluctant to speak. As her emotions become more transparent, mine become more opaque. When Natalie's aunt photographs our auras, the pictures reveal Natalie's persona as a swollen, orange puff and mine as a patch of brown haze.

Our time together is starting to feel precariously off-kilter, like a scale tipped in her favor. I'm hoping this bottle can make us flush for a while, the way my science teacher once used a vacuum to make a feather and a quarter fall three feet in the same amount of time.

I'm glad for Natalie's choice of bottle. I like the color—like iced tea—and the name, Southern Comfort, which makes me think of warm apple pie. It sounds like something you'd find folded in a red and white napkin and set out to cool on a windowsill.

I have reservations about the label. The very top of it is printed with the words ESTABLISHED 1874. The year makes it pretty darn elderly, and makes me feel extra guilty for touching it. Growing up, my mom always taught me not to touch other people's relics on the basis that old things are irreplaceable. The fact that this bottle looks antique reminds me that it is not intended to be handled by me.

Southern Comfort is 106 years my senior, and it shows. The lettering on the bottle looks like it's straight off an Old West flyer or the gag WANTED posters they print in the photo booth at the mall. Beneath them is a black and white drawing of a southern plantation as grand as the one in *Gone With the Wind*. I've always imagined my first drink would be from the bottle in the liquor ads that picture a man hoisting a giggling blonde onto his shoulders. Southern Comfort looks like something my grandfather would drink.

It smells sweet and spicy, like the hot apple cider my mother sometimes serves at Christmas, and I drink deeply before I realize what a terrible first drink it is. On my tongue, the flavor is completely foreign, a revolting combination of black licorice and antiseptic. I swallow it like a carnival freak swallows fire and can feel it glow red in my throat.

Natalie looks glad.

She says, "That wasn't bad, right?"

I lie and say, "Right."

I'm still shuddering. I can feel the shot not in my stomach, as

I had imagined, but lodged in my chest like a flickering ember. Its soft heat radiates in waves down my drowsy arms.

NATALIE IS tender afterward, the way I imagined she'd be. She lets me choose the radio station while we change for the party in her bedroom, and she doesn't breathe a word of criticism when I let the dial rest on the golden oldies station.

The liquor has made me feel sleepy, but not drunk.

Natalie falls face-first onto her bed and says she feels the same way.

I can tell the afternoon has been cathartic for her, too. We have bonded in a way that only people who have experienced tension can. I feel a conjunction with her. It's the same sensation of closeness that I feel with the family dentist after I've spent forty minutes in his chair, getting a cavity filled. I feel grateful to her even though she has made me uncomfortable, maybe even *because* she has made me uncomfortable. It's as though she brought out that bottle because she sensed I was starting to resent her, and she knew a few shots could chip away at my disloyalty.

Even though I'm grateful, I sense Natalie has also taken away a piece of me, the pure part that used to order Shirley Temples with dinner because my parents' friends thought that was dimpled and darling, like tap dancing with "Bojangles" Robinson.

Still, the loss is worth it because I have won Natalie's respect. I can tell she is proud of me for enduring the burn of the liquor and the risk of getting caught. Her esteem is worth every sip. She lets me borrow her favorite Sonic Youth T-shirt. She squirts a bottle of tangerine musk and dances with me through the mist.

Before we leave for the party, Natalie pulls two glass bottles from the recycling bin and fills them with So-Co. The bottles still have labels from the juice company Nantucket Nectars; we carry them into the backseat of her parents' minivan, imagining the amber fluid looks like apple juice.

Mr. Burke either doesn't suspect or doesn't want to suspect what we're really drinking. Every time he hangs a corner with too much gusto, I envision the worst-case scenario: We'll be pulled over for speeding and a shrewd cop will convict us on open-container laws. But Natalie looks confident. She even manages a few swigs while we circle the block, on the lookout for a mailbox pegged with helium balloons.

THE PARTY is in a basement. We're made to hide behind the sofa and yell "*Surprise.*" There is a cake, and a horror movie in the VCR. The birthday girl's mother periodically comes downstairs with more Pepsi or plastic forks, but for the most part, she simply leaves us alone. It's summer, after all. We have a ping-pong table, Sega Genesis, Slip N' Slides, a basketball hoop, MTV, a giant trampoline, and the pleasure of each other's company. If only she knew: It takes so much less to entertain us.

It doesn't take long for word to get out that I'm holding liquor in my little glass bottle.

I make the mistake of telling Casey Schiller: flat-assed, mammoth-chested, president of the dance committee, first-rate motormouth Casey Schiller. I do it because when she waves hello to me, it's the only thing I can think of to say. Casey tells Mary. Mary tells Vera. And Vera snatches the bottle from my hand and announces its contents to the girls who are watching an Aerosmith video and trying to pole dance like Liv Tyler around one of the basement's cast-iron pipes.

Natalie is on the perimeter of it all, hiding her bottle behind her back. It's clear that I've lost her admiration. She's shaking her head in the disapproving way she always does when I've acted like a real shit. For the moment, I don't even care. I put my hands on my hips and shake my head back.

Seventeen ounces of Southern Comfort is all it takes for me to make new friends. It is all I had to offer to the goddesses of my idolatry: the student council president, the captains of the girls' softball team, the girls voted "most daring" and "most talkative" in the junior-high yearbook. I give it up gladly.

I'd like to think I want to share because it means I have to drink less, but the truth is I like the attention. Now that they know I drink, girls invite me to their houses; they reach for HAPPY BIRTHDAY napkins to write down their phone numbers. In a matter of minutes, everyone has gathered around me like I am the one about to blow out the birthday candles. Every girl wants a sip. You'd think I'd bottled the cure for menstruation, the way they line up for a swig and close their eyes while they knock it back.

It is a moment that reminds me of an ad for sparkling wine I saw once in a magazine. The ad pictured three women dressed in sleek black sheaths, all laughing and gasping at their own wickedness. Below them was the slogan, "When it's just you and the girls without all the men, drink it in, drink it in, drink it in."

For the time being, it is always just us girls. We have our own gym class, our own choral group, and our own corner in the cafeteria. The occasional coed functions, mostly birthday parties or school dances, are self-segregated. The boys stake out a space that is separate from the girls' section. And even as we shoot them smiles and slow glances from the girls' side, we don't dare cross the border without a good excuse. In junior high, a wayward Frisbee is fine justification; some girls toss them into the boys' camp and blame poor depth perception. In high school, being drunk will be reason enough; girls will pitch themselves onto the boys' side under the guise of looking for a keg, and when they brush up against the school quarterback, they'll still blame bad aim.

Tonight, all the boys at the party are outside on the driveway, charging the basketball hoop with the wholehearted thrill of competition, half of them stripped of their shirts, mouths hinged open in concentration. I hate the boys the same way I hate them in algebra class, when they practically crawl out of their skins if they think they know the answer to whatever problem the teacher scrawls on the blackboard. They understand competition and anger in a way that girls don't. They take pleasure in fouling one another. They get to enjoy the rush of air on their naked chests.

More than that, they seem to understand who they are and who they're supposed to be. The only commandment that boys seem to live by is "Thou shalt be strong to the point of being cocky." That means pedaling their bikes toward three-foot-tall ramps without fearing broken ribs. It means taking a sucker punch without squealing. It means knowing how to change tires, drive nails, throw spirals, and unhook girls' bras without looking.

And while I don't think I'd be any good at being a boy, given the fact that I am constantly afraid, constantly crying, and characteristically weak, I envy the fact that boyhood's rules are consistent. Being male is not a mess of contradictions, the way being female is. It is not trying to resolve how to be both desirable and smart, soft and sturdy, emotional and capable.

It seems boys come off the assembly line finished, and we're the ones left wanting. We are huddling in the basement's dank impasse, alternately sipping So-Co and applying berry lip gloss.

We are passing the bottle at the same time and for the same reason that we pass compact mirrors. We are trying to master what our mothers have taught us about looking "put together."

Each girl swoops in eagerly when it is her turn, "drinking it in" by locking her pink nails around the bottleneck and jacking it to her lips. I get the impression that most of them have done it before, which is probably an accurate observation, as experts say half of all eighth graders have tried alcohol.* Many times, when the bottle is passed from girl to girl, there are multiple hands on it at once, the way women at weddings claw to catch the bride's bouquet.

But there are a few girls who hold back, ones who ask what the bottle is filled with and where we got it.

There is one in particular, Laurel. When we were ten, she formed a club to save the Florida manatees, and I passed many Sunday afternoons at her house with the other fourth-grade girls, covering my eyes while we watched videos of blubbery, gray beasts being chopped up by motorboats.

Laurel's older sister died when we were in the sixth grade. The newspaper said she fell into a ravine near her liberal-arts college, but we all knew she jumped. That was when we stopped writing letters to the Florida Coast Guard. Her house was filled with the white noise of sadness, and the Manatee Club stopped going there because we didn't know what to say.

Today, she creeps toward the bottle slowly and asks what it tastes like.

After a dozen girls' gulps the bottle is nearly empty. There is

*The 2003 National Youth and Anti-Drug Media Campaign.

less than one brown inch of liquid left, but I hand it over to her anyway.

"Try it," I say. "If you want, you can hold your nose." I pinch my nostrils closed between my thumb and my pointer finger, the way Natalie had showed me earlier. Doing this seems to help stop the sting of the liquor in the walls of my throat. I tell her, "Try to throw it down without even swallowing. Don't even let it touch your tongue."

She does. Good little Laurel pinches her nose and swallows a shot like it's cherry-flavored cough syrup. For a second, her eyes go watery and her cheeks pucker. I'm almost certain it's her first drink.

"That wasn't bad, right?" I know I'm mimicking Natalie, but I do it anyway.

Laurel's shoulders shiver. She says, "Right."

It occurs to me that in a matter of hours, I've gone from pupil to mentor. I feel a twinge of guilt for robbing Laurel of this last bit of innocence. At fourteen, her face already fringes on expressionless. Her ice-blue eyes look still and empty, and her jaw has a locked look about it. Like someone who is accustomed to silence, Laurel startles easily. I think I might have been wrong to teach her how to drink, given that she already seems too knowing.

But I look at her again, when she is across the room, pink-cheeked and grinning as she passes the bottle off to Liz Bacon, and change my mind. She looks happy nose-pinching and whiskey-sipping. I think, *It was only a matter of time until she took her first drink.*

The girls who are clumped in the basement's concrete corner are deeply involved in the ways in which the others drink. As one girl sips, the rest urge her to drink more or drink faster. Margo Thomas even holds the bottle while Darla Locke takes a pull from it. Margo tips it into her mouth in a way that looks ritualistic, like a priest doling out Communion wine.

We've been studying rituals in social studies class because our teacher Mr. Booth thinks it will shed some light on our forthcoming graduation ceremony. Mr. Booth says most initiation ceremonies take place in three parts. First, the initiate withdraws. Usually, she's sent away from her family and her village, which represent her old life, as a child. Next, she lives a life of solitude and confusion, in which she has to fend for herself. Then, after time passes, she is allowed to go home and rejoin her community, as a full adult, where she is presented with what he calls the *sacra,* meaning something sacred that symbolizes her transformation. Mr. Booth says our diplomas, in a way, are our *sacra.* But I'm not so sure.

When I think about what Mr. Booth says about initiations, I think drinking might have begun for me long before Natalie handed me the bottle this afternoon. It might have been a rite I embarked on two years ago, when I first started withdrawing from my family, shutting myself in my bedroom in the hours before dinner, cutting pictures from magazines or doing nothing, lettering signs to tape on the door that read DO NOT DISTURB. Like a girl who lives alone in the woods, haven't I felt lost since I began to withdraw? My CD changer plays only songs about dejection, "Creep" and "Loser" and "Losing My Religion." Even my outfits look confused: fishnet thigh-highs under baby-doll dresses or shapeless jeans paired with my dad's flannel shirts, which I amputate at the sleeves. My closet looks like the place where girlhood comes to battle boyhood, virginity comes to battle sexuality, youth comes to battle womanhood. Mornings that I dress in the mirror, I can't decide which virtue, or gender, or level of maturity is winning.

In a way, I have been waiting for something sacred to present itself. I've been expecting some sign to come like a lightning clap and tell me I can stop hating myself because this awkward period is finally over. I didn't find it in my monthly period, which has often been so shameful that I have to wear a thermal shirt tied around my waist. And even though I haven't had sex yet, I know it can't be the sacred thing I am waiting for, either. For girls sex is seen as a fall, not a triumph. When word got out that Sara Dohart messed around with Trent Cooper in the athletics closet, he rose to the status of teen heartthrob, and she was called "Sara Blows Hard" so often her parents had to put her in private school.

It only makes sense for the *sacra* to be the bottle. Natalie awarded it to me, and I awarded it to Laurel, and it marks our new status as drinkers.

AFTER WE finish both bottles, I rinse them out in the guest bathroom because the birthday girl doesn't want the garbage to smell like booze.

The girls who are tipsy go outside to topple down the Slip N' Slide. The ones who aren't walk home to raid their refrigerators for beer. Natalie plays video games because she's decided not to speak to me; I'm not sure what that means for my plans to sleep over later.

I pull open the sliding glass door and step out into the backyard.

I'm alone outside. The sky is dark, the steely dark of early summer, not the blind dark of winter. Through it, I can see gnats rising and falling in the porch lights. Crickets sing. Far off, a few girls are chasing each other through the spiny stretch of orchard that spreads off the backyard.

For once, I don't mind being all alone in public. Usually, I'd be frightened of what solitude might say about me. I'd worry that someone would trot up the walkway, see me sitting in the crabgrass, and assume that no one likes me enough to want to sit with me. Tonight, though, I don't care what anyone thinks. I watch the road for girls coming back with cans of beer. When no one comes, I lie on my back and stare at the slab of gray sky.

I don't know what being drunk feels like, but I don't think I am. I can walk straight. I can see straight. And for the first time in a long time, I can think straight. I am not exerting mental energy, trying to decide whether my mother is lying when she tells me I'm pretty. I am not thinking about a conversation I had two days ago, and rolling my eyes because I said something stupid.

I am not thinking about anything. My knees are bent in such a way that I can make out patterns of freckles on my thighs. My hair is fanned out under me. The air has the smell that fabric softener companies are always trying to capture—the breeze smells like fruit trees.

The word finally occurs to me: I am *comfortable.*

I close my eyes.

When I open them, Eric Ostrau is tickling my ear with a stray oak leaf.

Eric's father runs a snow-removal company that clears our driveway during heavy snowstorms. During blizzards, I meditate by my bedroom window, waiting for the groan of the plow against the asphalt and a glimpse of Eric's red baseball cap in its passenger seat.

Eric always wears a red baseball cap, although once in a celestial moment, he'll take it off by the brim and pet his own head as though its blond bristles are the softest things he's ever felt. There's no overestimating how badly I want to touch them myself and confirm it.

Normally, with Eric standing over me, I'd pop myself upright and try to dream up something to say. But tonight, I don't say anything. The act of drinking—and being seen drinking—has renewed my confidence. I look up at him from where I'm lying.

He asks if I feel all right.

"Why do you ask?" I know why he asks. In addition to making sure every girl in the basement knew Natalie and I brought liquor, Casey Schiller ran into a game of three-on-three and made sure the boys knew, too.

Eric kneels down next to me in the crabgrass.

"I don't know. I got drunk at my brother's wedding in April and I was sick the whole night."

I prop my weight up on my elbows in a way that doesn't just *look* natural, it *is* natural, which is a foreign feeling to me. Eric Ostrau is talking to me, and for some odd reason, I'm not hugging my own shoulders and curling into myself, like a slug being poked with a stick. I'm not fidgeting or parting the grass. I'm not even stumbling over what I'm trying to say.

I look at him over one shoulder and say, "Maybe you just couldn't hold your liquor."

"You really don't want to puke?"

"No."

"Not at all?"

"Not a drop."

"Well, what if I do *this*?"

In a brief moment he lurches forward and hoists me over one shoulder. He takes off running toward the orchard, stopping every few feet to spin in circles to dizzy me. I'm coughing and he's laughing, and with every step I can feel his hands on my thighs, clutching tighter, trying to steady me. The blood is funneling to my head. Blades of grass are brushing past me. And then Eric trips on a root, launching us both into the dirt and fallen apples. My flip-flops sail off my feet.

As payback for the fall, Eric lets me run my hands over every last glorious inch of his head. Sure enough, the soft fleece of his hair is the best thing I've ever felt.

When Eric's ride home shows up, I steal his hat. I fold it in half and tuck it into the waistband of my jean shorts without him noticing. I don't even feel bad about it. I think Natalie will be proud of me.

THE RIDE back to the cottage drags. Natalie still isn't talking to me, and I am trying hard to conceal a smile when Mrs. Burke glances in the rearview mirror and momentarily lets her eyes fall on me.

I'm sure I don't look any different to her. I'm still wearing Natalie's T-shirt over the holey cut-off jeans my mother likens to Swiss cheese. The humidity is still coiling the hair around my face. I'm just a girl, not even a high-school girl yet. I'm someone who comes over to her house to occupy her daughter by baking cookies and playing checkers and staging cannonball contests off the dock.

She doesn't know that the thing I found in her liquor cabinet has given me the capacity to be a completely different animal on the inside. Inside, I feel exotic and dangerous. I'm a cobra inside a kitty cat.

I run my hand under my shirt, over Eric's worn, cotton cap, and know what Columbus must have felt when he washed up on the American shore. Drinking has always been, but it's a New World to me. It's been waiting for me to discover it.

FIRST WASTE

I THINK IT'S NO coincidence that a shot is called a shot. You throw back that little jigger of liquor with the same urgency with which a gun fires ammunition into open space. You feel the same ringing in your ears, the same kickback in your arms and chest. The first time you drink, you don't aim to get drunk. The thrill of pulling the trigger is itself enough. If you like the crack of the rifle, you'll be back for a second go, which is when you'll pay attention to the crosshairs and fire enough shots to hit the mark.

After my first drink, I don't have an opportunity for target practice. The summer before high school is a succession of middle-class time-killers: ballet camp for a month, horseback-riding camp for a week, piano lessons every other day, CCD classes every third night. These are the things my mother was never allowed to do in her time, and the things I am never allowed *not* to do in mine.

Actually, that's not entirely fair. In grade school I begged for ballet slippers and jodhpurs. I could have spent whole afternoons at the Gym Nest, turning loops on the uneven bars. But that feels like so long ago. At fourteen, I long for unmitigated free time to spend my summers like normal kids do, watching talk shows and eating Pop-Tarts and complaining that there is nothing to do.

For now, there is too much to do. Before I know it, I'm in high school. Before I know it, I have a new bus driver and a new locker combination, and I am correcting new teachers who are butchering my name ("No, *Zel-kiss*"). And Natalie has convinced her parents to send her to a boarding school for the arts, despite the fact that she doesn't act or paint or play the cello, despite the fact that she doesn't do anything that technically qualifies as art. And I have no one to drink with, so I don't.

August turns to September, and I realize I didn't have a summer love. I didn't meet a boy while I was gathering shells on Cape Cod, or while I was leaning my elbows over the railing of the ferry en route to Nantucket. My eyes never met someone else's across a pebbled beach or a crowded room. My breath never cut short with immediate desire. The closest thing I found to a summer fling was alcohol: I was introduced to it. I loved it instantly. Then, circumstance separated us.

Tasting alcohol just once is as hopeful and as heartbreaking as kissing a boy just once. It feels like the time I kissed a boy in the coatroom at a wedding where he was on the bride's side and I was on the groom's side, and it was a sweet, singular kiss that dizzied my head and made me want to stay there among the trench coats forever. But then the cake got cut and the bouquet got chucked, and the boy's father put on his jacket and the boy's mother swung her purse over her shoulder, and my eyes followed him under the balloon arch and out the door, and I never saw him again.

I can't imagine a way to rendezvous with liquor again.

ONCE A week, Natalie calls from her dorm's pay phone to make me feel envious. She'll tell me about a party she went to in an abandoned house, where boys strummed acoustic guitars, girls read palms, and everyone drank red wine straight from the bottle. She'll say she was too drunk to walk the two miles home before midnight, when the dorm's doors get locked. It was better that way, she'll say, because a boy got locked out, too, and they slept in his car.

I listen for a long time and my cheeks burn. I say nothing.

Natalie promises to get me drunk when she comes home for winter break. But the interval seems unreasonable, and it doesn't console me. I think, *Even star-crossed Juliet got to marry Romeo and take him to bed in a single day.* Likewise, I've been through the ceremony of my first drink. Now I am ready to consummate it by drinking faster, drinking more.

Nights, before I go to sleep, I try to imagine what being drunk feels like. I'm not sure why, but I decide the sensation must have weight. After the third or fourth drink, the drunken feeling must sneak up and pin you down. It must quiet your mind, like a lover that puts one finger to your lips, saying "Shh, baby." It must crush you with the force of its embrace. It must bore into you, permeating your whole body, your whole soul.

I imagine all of this and my chest tightens with yearning. I can't wait until Christmas.

. . .

EVERYONE at my new high school drinks.

In the hallway between classes, I hear rumblings about a keg party at an upperclassman's house, or in the woods near the town quarry. I see girls drawing straws at lunch to choose a designated driver. I see one guy put another in a headlock and say, "Boy, prepare to get drunk tonight."

I try to get myself invited.

I do it during science class, when my lab partner is turned backward in her chair, telling two girls about the cookout she's throwing on Saturday. The theme is luau, she says. She's going to decorate the backyard with wading pools and inflatable palm trees. She's going to serve vodka watermelon.

I interject to say, "I love that drink."

In the space under their desks, I see one girl nudge another with her foot. All three of them stare at me for a stunned moment before they exhale small coughs.

That night, I find a recipe for vodka watermelon on the Internet. The instructions say to cut a hole in the top of the melon, funnel vodka inside, and let it sit for a day before you cut it into pieces so the fruit will absorb the alcohol. I read it over twice before I realize you eat the watermelon chunks, instead of drinking the juice. When I do, I want to walk outside and lie down in the street.

WITH NO friends and no chance of getting invited to a party, I try to drink alone one night in September. My parents are upstairs sleeping, and I am downstairs in the living room, mixing a mug of Kahlúa and milk and sipping it in front of Nick at Nite.

The drink tastes good and sweet. I nuke it in the microwave until it steams like hot cocoa, and it warms my whole chest as I drink it, like VapoRub. I sit in my father's favorite armchair, holding the glass in both hands so it scalds my palms. On TV, sitcom characters are drinking in a Boston bar, and I drink along while I listen for flipped light switches or feet on the stairs, signals that someone is coming. Bear, the golden retriever, watches me with his ears back like he knows what I'm doing.

I have little time. I am expecting some rapid change.

I have the idea that Kahlúa will make me either dizzy or giddy, but neither sensation comes. I wait for them. I wait for the TV dialogue to make me giggle, but it just rolls on in a series of one-liners and laugh-track hums. I wait for the carpet to wobble under me, but it stays beige and still. The only change I can feel is in my face. My cheeks feel as though they might be warm to the touch, but there is no one to put their hands on them to confirm it.

I don't drain the mug halfway before I get bored and dump the rest down the sink. I decide there's no point in getting drunk without having a friend like Natalie along to encourage me to drink more and faster in order to get drunk. There's no rivalry when you're drinking alone; it's like playing Battleship without an opponent.

As I'm climbing the stairs to go to bed, my mother hears me and groggily calls my name through the darkened door of my parents' bedroom.

She says, "Koren, is that you? Are you okay?"

I roll my eyes and pretend I don't hear her. I keep padding down the hallway.

MOST DAYS, I wish Anne Sexton were my mother. We study her in school, and because it's public school they don't mention that she was a sexually abusive mother.

I read "Mother and Daughter" in my ninth-grade English book and realize my own mom will never understand girlhood with the same level of clarity. I wish she had Anne's insomnia, panic attacks, addictions, her own shit to deal with, old-Hollywood looks. I wish she would call me "string bean" and stand back during my high school years like "somebody else, an old tree in the background."

During ninth grade, a mom who will not stand back is a nightmare, particularly if she's a stay-at-home mom, the type who says things like, "You are my full-time job," when you're pretty sure you're a dead-end vocation. She'll prepare for adolescence like the Y2K. She will scrutinize your grades, your friends, and your appearance, looking for headway, as though womanhood is a twelve-point plan and the big boss expects a progress report.

My mother is that type of mother. By the time I start high school she has not only read *Reviving Ophelia,* she has highlighted it, as though it were a how-to manual for dealing with me. Now, whenever I erupt in tears at the most inappropriate times, she puts on a face of quiet bemusement and I can imagine her thinking: *Ah, Koren exemplifies the process of disowning the true self. With puberty she went from being a whole, authentic person to a diminished version of herself.* And I cry harder because my private pains are so unoriginal.

Mary Pipher has fucked up my life good. She's convinced my mother that she needs to save my "self," to pull me from the undertow of fury and self-doubt that is sucking me down. Now, any hesitation on my part is a sacrifice to the patriarchal system. The patriarchy wins when I don't run for student council. It wins when I don't touch palms with a boy in the pew behind us during the hand-shaking portion of church.

"You need to get over this shyness," my mom will say with a shrill whine that sets me stomping up the stairs to my room. "Do you want to be like this your whole life? Do you? Do you want boys to ignore you? Teachers to skip over you in class? I used to be like you. Until I forced myself. And believe me, you have to *force yourself* because, I'm telling you now, the meek sure as hell don't inherit the world."

By now, I've accepted the fact that I'm meek. I accept the fact that I'll never know what to say in a group. In class, I will sit and watch everyone else chatter with great ease. And I'll think I should say something *now* because each passing second will only make it harder to speak without everyone turning to look at me with great shock, as though a chair, or a stapler, or some other inanimate object had sprung to life.

While that meekness won't help me make friends or get dates, it is favorable in other ways. Adults seem to think it makes me more feminine and, often, a little more grown-up. Teachers praise me for my cooperation. The "comments" portion of my report card always reads: "courteous," "attentive," and "well-mannered." But teachers treat the domineering girls differently. Girls like Natalie, who sit with the boys or speak out of turn, are called "disruptive" or "disrespectful," sometimes "cocksure," but even that sounds dirty.

But that's what my mother wants from me. She wants me to have everything she never had as a girl, which, on top of piano lessons and designer jeans, includes buoyancy. She wants me to rise to the top of the worst situations. She wants to raise a modern woman: someone who is cool and collected, a vixen, a man-eater, hell-on-wheels in heels.

Unlike Anne Sexton, she cannot accept that she has given me her "booty, her spoils, her Mother & Co. and her ailments." I have swallowed her immunities and her maladies, and now I can't help feeling skittishness deep in the coils of my DNA, a genetic predisposition like cystic acne, something that will not clear up no matter how many times she warns me to keep my hands off my face.

Years from now, I'll pick up her copy of *Reviving Ophelia* and notice a paragraph about parents who "taught their children that only a small range of thoughts, emotions, and behaviors would be tolerated," who "because of their own childhood experiences, regarded parts of their children's personalities as unacceptable." This section will not be highlighted.

I THINK my mother wants me to be like Billie Jankoff.

Billie is a girl. As far as I can tell, her name isn't even short for Beverly or Belinda or anything. Later, she will tell me she was named for Billie Holiday, and I'll insist on calling her Miss Brown.

Billie and I have assigned seats at the same round table in English class. She sits at twelve o'clock and I sit at three, and every time she flips a page in *The Yearling* her scent drifts clockwise. She smells like cigarettes and a woody perfume that reminds me of my mother's cedar chest. Her key lime–colored cowboy boots tap the table legs with a jumpy energy that shakes my notebook.

I constantly stare at her out of the corners of my eyes.

Billie is ghostly white, the way only chronically ill people and The Cure are, and her skin darkens the rest of her features by comparison. Her blonde hair has a fringe of ebony where it parts, where her unprocessed, natural color is growing in. Her blue eyes are so deep-set they look black, and when she outlines them with a charcoal pencil, her irises look bottomless. I'm compelled to look deeper into them to find her pupils, the way I'd lean over a wishing well to look for its floor.

Billie is the type of girl teachers love to hate. For one thing, she writes with a ballpoint pen shaped like a syringe. It is 1994 and Kurt Cobain is four months dead, and the administration is sensitive to heroin innuendo. She also dresses entirely in black, which teachers interpret as a sign of mutiny. Some days, she wears skirts of layered black chiffon, which wave when she walks. Other days, she wears tight black leggings under an oversized sweater with thumbholes cut into the cuffs. I love the days that Billie wears T-shirts that say things like TO DIE FOR, phrases that are provocative but too ambiguous for the dress code to ban outright.

Our English teacher, Mr. Coffee, seems to hate Billie because she's quick to pick fights with him, and not about late assignments and absences, the inconsequential things. No, Billie's fights are the kind where she stands up during a discussion of *The Great Gatsby* and says, "This is stupid, Daisy is stupid, all the girls in all the books we read are brain-dead," and then storms down the hall in a flutter of black chiffon. When she's gone, Mr. Coffee apologizes for the interruption, and I'm left wondering what I am missing. I've been thinking I'd like to be Daisy; I'd like to have someone like Gatsby stare at my house for whole years and never stop dreaming of me.

One day during English, Billie spots the spine of a fat spellbook poking out of my backpack, and I want to hide my face behind my hands. In the absence of alcohol, I've resorted to the power of real magic to transform my life. I've been lolling in the library during lunch period, combing the card catalog for *Charms, Spells, and Formulas* and *Practical Candle Burning*

Rituals. I've been tying ribbons on fence posts for happiness, sticking pins through candlewicks for friendship, and sleeping with a glass of water under my bed for love.

I take a deep breath because I know what is coming. I know Billie is going to say "Spells are stupid, that book is stupid, and you must be brain-damaged."

Instead, she leans in and whispers, "I love that shit."

I feel a rupture of joy for the first time in months. I can't stop from widening my eyes.

BILLIE LIVES in the bordering town of Clinton. Though our towns share a school, a wildlife reserve, and a waste-disposal center, their commonalities end there. Whereas my town is rural and secluded, the type of place where you can live seven years and never catch a glimpse of your neighbors, Clinton is the kind of old mill town that is common in Massachusetts. It is spotted with vinyl-sided duplexes, pool halls, Dairy Queens, and auto-body repair shops. The boys from Clinton ride dirt bikes and smoke Marlboros, and if they take you out to look at the stars, they drop the *r,* with the accent that most people attribute to the Bay State— *stahs.* To me, everything about the place sounds like freedom.

Billie lives with her divorced mother, a position that fills me with envy. I know that is stupid, that I should be grateful that my parents are still happily wed, both of them tuned into my every ballet recital or parent-teacher conference like it's Super Bowl Sunday. And I am. But our nuclear nest also makes divorce look exotic, like the stuff that art is made of. After all, this is shortly after *Newsweek* declared, "Grunge is what happens when children of divorce get their hands on guitars."* Divorce seems

*Newsweek—April 18, 1994, "The Poet of Alienation" by Jeff Giles.

like a beautiful truth, a stark contrast to my own two-parent household, which at times feels stickier, more deceptive.

What's more, divorce creates the possibility of independence, for which I am desperate. The dissolution means train rides and plane rides alone, en route to Mommy's house or Daddy's condo. And keys. I long for house keys; I want to wear them on a satin string around my neck. After school, I want to unlock the door to a quiet house and, consequently, a quiet mind.

Billie's house is like an Egyptian tomb, like it ought to be named Valley of the Queens. It is still and soundless when we take the bus there on Friday afternoons. Snapshots hang on the walls: There's one of Billie and her sister carving a pumpkin, another of Billie and her mom wearing pointed party hats. The medicine cabinets are lined with lipstick. The refrigerator is stocked with Snack Packs and mummified microwave dinners, ample provisions for the afterlife. Everything seems easy—easy to find, easier to make, easiest to clean up.

Mrs. Jankoff works odd hours as an emergency-room nurse and spends most days dressed in rose-colored scrubs and orthopedic shoes, her blonde hair fastened in a nest of loose curls. But twice a week she undergoes a magical transformation. After her shift ends, she goes out for drinks at Watson's, a pine-paneled neighborhood bar. She has single friends, loads of them, and at Watson's they meet men in droves. The following day, she describes to us whatever lawyer, welder, or real-estate agent she met, and in our own vernacular. "Joe was hot," she'll say over the kitchen stove, where she is standing in a terrycloth bathrobe and cooking scrambled eggs. "But at some point I realized he was a little messed up in the head."

When Billie's mom goes out to Watson's, she even dresses like one of us. She wears army boots, flannel skirts, and baby-doll

T-shirts with broken hearts ironed on. She refuses to wear a bra because, she says, they're just another way in which the world keeps women down. So her breasts sway like water balloons when she walks, and I love the way they make my mother wince.

As much as I love Mrs. Jankoff, I know Billie spars with her, too. She fights with her mom the same way I fight with my mom, but for opposite reasons. I want to be independent from my mom, and Billie wants to be dependent on hers. Billie loves my mother's involvement, while I love Mrs. Jankoff's detachment. We both have the magnetic properties that attract us to each other's mothers, and repel us from our own. I want to drive my mother away from me by being deceptive; Billie tries to lure her mother home by proving she's trustworthy.

THE MORE time I spend with Billie, the more I realize I have her pegged all wrong. Sure, she smokes. She also wears satin bras and smeared eyeliner, and in school, she is all too happy to scream at Mr. Coffee or skip gym class on the days that we are forced to run a mile. But when it comes to her real assets, the things Natalie would have considered *no doy,* like the fact that she has the house without chaperone for hours on end, complete with access to her mother's cherry schnapps, she pleads bankrupt. In her own house, she is quiet and reserved.

Friday nights, while Natalie is in some boy's dorm room burning incense, listening to way-hip post-rock Brit-pop, and drinking Boone's Farm Strawberry Hill wine, Billie and I do nothing. We stretch out on the kitchen counters, where we can watch headlights stream by on Water Street, and half-think we see someone we know coming or going, then speculate as to where. We eat chocolate chips from the bag and listen to FM radio until "Love Songs After Dark" turns into "Marty in the Morning."

Some nights we work on our witchcraft, but even that is dull. We want to draw baths filled with rose petals, but we can't afford to buy a dozen roses from the farmer's market, and Billie won't let me steal them. We also long to do love spells, but there is no way for us to gather boys' toenail clippings. There are no stores within walking distance that sell orrisroot.

Instead of making me calm, Billie's immobility makes me restless.

Afternoons at her house, I feel fidgety. I am incapable of being still. I have an urge to scratch my nails down my cheeks, tear the skillets down from the pot rack, strip off my clothes, and run bare-assed and shrieking through the condo's parking lot. I want to turn on the stove and press my palms into the burners just so I can test my synapses. I need to know I can still react, still feel terrified, still feel.

At the same time, I am so thankful to have Billie for a friend that I don't know how to tell her I'm bored. I don't know how to say I'm not used to a friend like her. I am used to Natalie's antagonism, the rhythm of combat and truce that could easily pass an afternoon. I miss the best friend who mows me over with her moods and her will. I miss being cut down, in the name of being forced to grow.

One night, Billie is fishing in the kitchen cabinets for something resembling a clear glass goblet to fill with salt water and dip our beaded necklaces into, in order to make them Poseidon protection charms. The closest thing she can find is a German beer stein, which we both agree will work just fine.

She is about to turn the cold knob on the kitchen sink when I say, "Wait a minute."

I lunge for the refrigerator, where I know a big, round jug of

Chardonnay occupies a large portion of the wire shelf. Its green glass feels cold in my hands.

"What do you think?" I ask. "It's a diversionary spell."

Billie wears a horrified look, like I just suggested doing one of the black-magic hexes that involve torching chicken bones. It's a look that says every good quality she's ascribed to me has been wrong.

I should get used it. I will see this look many times in the years to come. I'll see it later in high school, when a month after an alcohol overdose, someone sees me taking shots of tequila. I'll see it in college, when someone sees me drinking beer before noon to alleviate a hangover. I hate this look, but I should get used to it. It's the look you'd give a pregnant woman who orders a rum and Coke. It is people cocking their heads and wondering if they're seeing me right.

Billie looks frozen. She is still holding the stein in such a way that it looks like she might burst into an old German drinking song at any moment: swinging the glass back and forth, a frothy stout slopping out. Instead, she slams it down in the sink with a small crash.

I am mortified. I didn't think alcohol could ruin this moment so completely. I haven't met a girl yet who hasn't been interested in drinking. Every time I've seen a bottle emerge, girls have followed it the way children follow Browning's Pied Piper of Hamelin: with small feet pattering, wooden shoes clattering, little hands clapping, and little tongues chattering.

I slide the green jug back into its spot beside the Chinese food takeout containers and try to figure out how to pass it off as a joke.

I lie and say, "I didn't really mean it."

The wall clock ticks once.

Billie says, "Fine."

I should feel relieved, except she's making the same face she'd made once in English class, when Mr. Coffee said there was no way that she read *A Tale of Two Cities* in a single Saturday.

She plucks the stein from the sink, and I fill it a quarter full with Chardonnay. My shaky hand makes the blond stream come out in fits and bursts.

She sips slowly. The cup's wide rim covers half of her face, and I can't gauge her reaction. When she brings the stein down to the counter, she says, "It almost tastes like water." Under any other circumstances this would be an extraordinary lie, but everything in Mrs. Jankoff's cabinet has only a slightly higher alcoholic content than mouthwash.

We'll mix drinks during our sleepovers from this moment on. We'll sit on the tiles in front of the refrigerator or the liquor cabinet, shift bottles around, read their labels, and try to figure out what we have to work with. When it comes down to it, we have no idea how to tend bar. We mix gin with Coke and zinfandel with orange juice. Every drink we make tastes too sweet or too bitter, repellent. They are concoctions we can't bring ourselves to drink, and therefore don't ever get drunk on.

BILLIE AND I book Halloween as the night we will officially get drunk. It falls on a Monday, and Billie is spending the week with her dad in his four-bedroom town house in downtown Salem. I manage to convince my mother to let me sleep over even though it's a school night.

We enlist Billie's stepbrother Mac to help us. At eighteen, he looks old enough to buy bottles from Market Wine & Spirits, and he can procure harder liquor than Billie's mom's schnapps.

While Mac roves the aisles at the liquor store, we wait for him behind a hedgerow in the Salem graveyard. The night is cold as an icebox, with the kind of chill that gets into your skin and sticks there. After a half hour of waiting, I know nothing but a hot bath will be able to restore the feeling to certain body parts. Billie and I are wearing fingerless gloves and smoking Mild Sevens because we don't yet know how cliché that is. In plots all around us, we can hear whistling bottle rockets, dropped flashlights, someone's ill attempt at the ghoulish *oo-haa-haa*. People are tripping over their costumes, and a paranormal tour guide is leading a group toward the haunted jail, urging them to stay close because "People faint all the time."

It occurs to me that Halloween is the perfect date to get first-time drunk. It is the single day of the year on which you can shield your flaws with a layer of latex, the way Lucy Grealy did in her memoir *Autobiography of a Face*. She'd survived cancer and an endless bout of surgeries to reconstruct her jaw, and yet the only time she ever felt free was on October 31, when she could hide in a costume and feel confident, knowing no one knew what she looked like inside.

Externally, I'm not perfect, but I'm healthy. In fourteen years, I've never once fallen down stairs or caught my hand in a car door. I've never had stitches. I've never so much as twisted an ankle. It's my insides that I need to hide. Privately, I *feel* disfigured. I am ashamed of my gnarled soul, which is something no surgeon can correct. Were my inner workings exposed, I feel certain they would make children stare, and adults avert their eyes. Like Lucy, I, too, want a mask, the type Dylan Thomas talks about: "to shield the glistening brain and the blunt examiners." I want to get shit-faced, a term itself that connotes camouflage.

Mac shows up at the gravesite with his friend Phil and a bottle of Captain Apple Jack 100-proof brandy. When Billie asks if it will get us drunk, Mac says, "More like *Exorcist*-possessed," and I secretly hope he doesn't mean projectile puking.

Now that the boys are with us, I wish I hadn't worn a costume. It was my idea for Billie and I to come dressed as Wayne and Garth from the movie *Wayne's World*. I'm Wayne. Billie got to be Garth because she's the blonde. Our "costumes" aren't much different from the flannel button-ups and diaphanous T-shirts we usually wear. Even so, I have to look up at the boys from under the rim of my black *Wayne's World* cap, which makes me feel silly.

Mac has a skeleton T-shirt on. Phil is in everyday clothes, but he's looped nylon rope into a noose around his neck.

We position ourselves in a circle around an old camping lantern and the bottle of brandy. If anyone comes up through the headstones behind us, they'll probably assume we're conducting a séance. Billie in particular is staring at the bottle like she is trying to channel its energy.

Billie told Mac that we've never been drunk before, so he knows this is serious business. He twists off the brandy's plastic top and apologizes for not bringing cups. He asks if we're ready, and looks at us one at a time, waiting for a response.

Billie says, "Yeah."

Phil says, "Fuck yeah."

I nod, and pull my leather jacket tighter around me. I'm nervous. My sternum is shivering the way it does when I have to give a class presentation, but I know I am prepared for this. I like the idea of getting drunk in a group of four.

Before, when I drank by myself or with Billie, I think I held back. I didn't drink as much or as fast as I should have because I was afraid of entering new territory while I was all or mostly alone. As a girl, after all, you are taught to be fearful when you're alone. In the park or at the drugstore, you're a target. You can be abducted, scooped up by any number of unforeseen dangers, molested, tortured, left for dead. But in a group, you are taught to feel stronger, like the sum of your parts. Gradually, you forget your anxieties and reservations. You practice "The Buddy System." You falsely believe that tragedy cannot single you out.

Drinking brandy with Billie and the boys feels like booking a passage on the *Titanic*. The thought that we are all going down together consoles me.

Somebody comes up with the drinking game "Have You Ever," which basically involves the boys shouting out offensive questions like, "Have you ever seen one?" and Billie and I sipping brandy if we have. In my case, this game is perversely embarrassing; which is to say, I'm not embarrassed by what I've done, but by how little.

Phil asks, "Have you ever smoked pot?"

He and Mac drink.

Billie asks, "Have you ever done it?"

Mac and Phil drink.

Billie says, "Yeah, right, on both accounts."

Mac asks, "Have you ever given anyone a hickey?"

He and Phil and Billie drink.

Phil asks me, "Have you ever done anything?"

Mac hands me the bottle and says, "Just drink already."

I avert my eyes when I take it.

All night, I have been afraid to look directly at the boys, and I don't know why. It's not because they're handsome. They have scarred skin and sneering lips, and their eyes are small and squinty. It must be something else that's intimidating me, something in Phil's broad shoulders that reminds me of his strength, or in the stubble on Mac's chin that reminds me of his age. I'm startled by the way they both lean in to light my cigarette, as though the Zippo were too unwieldy for me. When I glance into either boy's eyes, I feel a jolt like static electricity.

Apple brandy rolls over my tongue and past my tonsils, and doesn't leave me time to process the taste. After one sip, all I can think about is a movie I saw once, in which a man torched a house that was the sight of a murder. I'm imagining the film frame by frame: the striking of the match, its slow-motion drop onto the gasoline-soaked floorboards, the line of fire that creeps up the stairs and down the hall until the house is one big fireball with blown-out windows.

That's what apple brandy does. One gulp of the plum-colored stuff kindles my tonsils, starting a fire that knocks down my esophagus like a trail of dominoes. The fumes fill my sinuses. I feel flammable. I'll combust if Phil lights another cigarette.

A new sensation follows this drink. After the brandy's initial blaze, I feel dead calm, like a shot of novocaine to my chest has set numbness spreading. I feel like it's in preparation for something, as though a tooth is about to be pulled. I take a few more sips while Mac looks me dead in the eyes. I suddenly don't care if he's watching.

The anesthetic is in my brain. All my worries fall over and die like canaries in a mine shaft. I put both hands on my hat to make sure my head is still there.

Five sips later, I start to feel like I'm watching a home movie. The camera is moving too quickly, panning from one person to the next with amateur dexterity and minimal focus. I have to close my eyes every few minutes, when the rapid motion makes me woozy. My life, at this moment, feels like *The Blair Witch Project.*

Billie is standing on the steps that lead up to somebody's hulking, granite tomb. She uses her hands to make a megaphone around her lips and screams, "Rest in peace, Salem!"

Phil is wearing her Garth glasses and crooning the Billie Holiday lyrics, "A kiss that is never tasted forever and ever is wasted."

And I am accidentally snapping my lit cigarette in half and then trying to smoke the filterless stub, while Mac talks about the band Crash Test Dummies and the plight of the human individual.

Everyone is talking at once, bruiting irrelevant stories, but brandy holds us together with a strange harmony like a doo-wop group, where each voice rises and halts with its own stray *ooh waah ooh.*

THE VERY next thing I know, I'm lying faceup on the ground with my head propped against a headstone engraved with the name CLYDE BARKER. I imagine Clyde's corpse directly under me, like we are two parallel lines spaced six feet apart. Overhead, the sky is huge and domed like the screen at the Boston Planetarium, where we went on a recent class trip.

Mac is over me, too, saying "Barker, Barker," and barking like a deranged poodle. In the lantern light, his pumpkin face looks distorted, as though he's holding a flashlight under his chin. The wind rattles the trees and leaves tumble everywhere, like it's snowing foliage.

Mac is heavier than he looks. When he lowers his skinny skater frame on top of me, I feel like I'm being buried alive. I think of Madeline in the "The Fall of the House of Usher," which we just read in school, and wonder at what point she stopped scratching the lid of the coffin and just fell into death, the way I let Mac fall into me. He is holding my head with both hands, the way I might hold an open book. My hat slides off and falls at the foot of Barker's tombstone, where someone bereft would place a bouquet.

Under any other circumstances, I would be afraid. Mac is four years older, and he is probably a bum the way my dad says "All boys are bums." He has a pierced eyebrow and a Chevy Camaro, and Billie says he sells pot. He may or may not have had sex before. He may or may not want to have sex with me right now.

At this moment I am not one bit chicken. I like the anonymity, the fact that I don't know who I'm kissing beneath his skeleton suit. Mac isn't kissing me, either. He's kissing my shit face, which makes me feel less vulnerable. I imagine it's the way Elijah Wood felt, wearing that Nixon mask, while Christina Ricci had sex with him in *The Ice Storm*. Mac is pressed smack into me. He is closer than any boy has been before, but I feel like there is a protective layer between us, a type of atmospheric safe sex.

His tongue parts my lips. His breath is potent, the way I imagine mine must be, and his cold, wet lips remind me of a bowl of eyeballs (they were really skinned grapes) I stuck my hand into once, when I was blindfolded at a Halloween party. I kiss him back because out of the corner of my eye I see that Billie is kissing Phil, and that seems like as good a reason as any.

Mac's hands are on me, too, latching on to me in places I myself don't dare touch. One curled hand is wrapped around the bantam bulge of my bra, the other kneading my upper, upper thigh like he is trying to give me a charley horse. I see where he's touching me more than I can feel it. My synapses are bootless beneath layers of thermal underwear and the deadening effects of brandy. I could be thumbed and needled and barely feel a thing.

I try to will myself to reciprocate, but I can't find my hands. Thanks to apple brandy, I can only gauge my general position. I can see the outline of my body as though I am watching myself from far away, the way people who've come back from the brink of death claim they watched doctors resuscitate them from high above their own operating tables. My body is there in the dirt, tucking one Herculean hand under the back of his T-shirt (it must be cold because it makes him shiver), while my essence is someplace much higher, far above the cigarette butts and the stone rows and the longest-reaching flashlight beam.

In college, we'll describe this as dead drunk. It's the kind of drunk where your eyes roll back in your head and your friends, smiling, say, "She's gone to a better place."

THE NEXT morning I feel like a corpse awakened at a funeral, which is an image I definitely read in a poem, but am far too disoriented to remember in full. I know I'm lying in my Wayne costume on an alien futon. I can vaguely remember the walk back from the cemetery, when Billie got sick on the side of the road and I lost my balance and skinned my knee.

I feel Billie's hand on my elbow, shaking me and saying, "Come on, we have to go."

I drag my revenant ass to the bathroom, where in the light of the vanity mirror, the lemon-colored wallpaper is too bright to look at. When I look at my reflection, my eyes are as bleary as they were the time I had pinkeye. The T-shirt I'm wearing feels damp, as though I had night sweats, so I change into a fresh one.

I splash cold water on my face and use my fingers to comb the knots out of my hair. I dig two aspirin out of the medicine cabinet because it seems like the right thing to do.

Billie's stepmom, Dawn, drives us to school in a silver Mitsubishi that has the new-car smell that turns my stomach. I sit in the backseat with my elbow on the sill of the child-safe window and my chin in my hand. My throat is raw and scratchy after smoking half a pack of cigarettes, and my fingers have retained the smell. Billie is in the front seat, pulling the sun visor down and mouthing *I'm so hungov-er* in its little lit-up mirror.

A few miles from school, Dawn steers the car into the drive-thru at Honey Dew Donuts as though this were some huge act of generosity. She leans her head out the car window to shriek into the talk-box, saying, "We want two hot chocolates, two bagels, and donut holes," even though that couldn't be further from the truth. Neither Billie nor I can think of consuming a thing. The saccharine smell of doughnuts emanates from the pick-up window, and when Dawn passes a bag back to me, I have to hold it far away from my face, for fear of losing my aspirin.

Billie tosses hers in her knapsack and says, "Thanks, Dawn. We'll eat them during homeroom."

FOR THE first part of the day, my mouth tastes bad. My stomach heaves. My head is filled with the dead space of a hangover. I feel dehydrated, but every trip to the water fountain makes my stomach fizzle. I can't stand up without suffering vertigo. For the first three periods of the day, I think these symptoms could kill me, but by fourth period, I almost enjoy them.

Fourth period is earth science, where I decide I like being hungover because it gives me a focal point. The side effects of the night before allow me to focus on life's details: raising my hand, saying "Here," resisting my stomach's contractions. I am no longer worried about the big picture. I'm not paying attention to a quiz that got passed back to me with a fat red C, or to the girls who whisper when I walk by their lab table. For the time being, I feel far removed from those issues. The bad grade is like deforestation of the Amazon. The catty girls are like global warming.

As the day spins on, I am intently focused on the here and now. *Here,* my head throbs, so I ask the nurse for more aspirin. *Now,* my stomach somersaults, so I compute the number of steps to the nearest bathroom. For the first time in my life, I'm not worried about catastrophes until they arise. The discovery is almost Confucian. I feel like I've found a religion.

UNFORTUNATELY, not everyone is a believer.

Margaret Feeney is my first and last pen pal.

We met at ballet camp the summer before I started high school, and we stayed in touch. She sends me a letter every few weeks.

I love spotting Margaret's stupid pink stationery in the mailbox. I love seeing my name lettered with curlicues on an envelope that is dotted with stickers. Inside, Margaret's letters are short. Mostly, she writes to me when she has updates. She writes to say she got a boy's phone number or a Dalmatian puppy and "Can you believe it?" Sometimes she includes goofy pictures she thinks I'll appreciate. In one she wears a sequined tutu and looks resentful. In another, she kisses a moose head on the cheek.

There is something reassuring about every letter I get from Margaret. She isn't just a testament to my ability to be liked. Over time, she's become a real confidante, and I find myself telling her things I don't even feel comfortable sharing with Natalie. I write to her to say: "I'm afraid I'm ugly," or "I'm afraid I can't ever be the person my mother wants me to be," or "I'm afraid I'll never be able to bear the sound of my own voice on a message machine or the look of my own face reflected in a storefront." I even send her a few of the poems I've started to write.

But I make a mistake when I tell her about Halloween. I write, "I kissed a boy and it was liberating. We were curled up in the dirt, among dead people. I was completely smashed."

I take great care when I choose the word *smashed* as a euphemism for *drunk*. There are infinite slang terms to chose from: *bombed, blasted, capsized, toppled, clobbered, dismantled, damaged.* But they are the type of violent action verbs the boys I baby-sit use when they play with G.I. Joes. None of them have *smashed*'s fragile femininity.

Smashed reminds me of the moment Laura Wingfield's glass unicorn tumbled off a table and broke its horn in *The Glass Menagerie.* For the past few years, I've felt as though there's been a glass shield around my heart, the type of protective barrier that says IN CASE OF EMERGENCY, BREAK GLASS. Apple brandy put its fist through my isolation. I let my reticence break apart. I vowed to no longer be as emotionally delicate as spun crystal.

Five days later Margaret sends a response.

Koren, [no dear, sans stickers]
I got your letter. By "smashed," I can only assume you meant you were drunk, which is not only not cool, it is disgusting, as is the fact you thought I'd be interested in hearing about it. Do you have any idea how many people die each year from drunk driving? It's 18,000. I know because I'm in Students Against Drunk Driving here at Montgomery High

School. There was a senior here who died drunk driving. Did you know that by the time you graduate high school at least two people in your class will be dead? Do you really want to take the risk that you could be one of them? I'm crying as I write this because I can't believe that someone with all your gifts could be so selfish and susceptible to peer pressure. I think you should really think about what you are doing. In the meantime, I don't know if I want to keep exchanging letters because I just don't want to hear about it. Maybe one day I will trust you again.

Margaret

P.S. Enclosed is a poem I think you should read.

I feel like I've torn open a chain letter.

My stomach flops and my hands quake. I want to read the letter again, to make sure Margaret is really suggesting I might die, but I can't bring myself to do it. Instead of writing in her usual slanted cursive, Margaret has printed, and the word *died* looks even more menacing as a result. I want to run the letter through my dad's paper shredder, or burn it, or take it into the woods and stuff it deep into an animal's hole.

Up until this moment, I've been lucky every time I drank, in the fact that there were never any consequences. No police officer or parent happened upon the crime scene. And though I've been hungover, I've never even thrown up. I feel as though Margaret has jinxed me with this letter. From here on out, my drinking is doomed. I can feel it.

The worst part about it is that her threat is nameless. I don't know what form the bad luck is going to take. Margaret has only assured me that some inexplicable accident is coming, the way chain letters promise heart attacks, or serial murders, or freak storms that blow down houses.

The "trust" part infuriates me, I can't understand how my drinking is a betrayal of Margaret's confidence. What exactly has she entrusted me with? Just who does she trust me to be? What possible obligation has she charged me with here in Massachusetts, more than four hundred miles away from her? Her tone reminds me of a sitcom I saw once, in which a mom found her daughter hungover after a night of drinking "tornadoes" and told her that maybe, just maybe, after good behavior and a number of years, she might trust her to stay home alone again. Only Margaret isn't my mother, she is my equal. And she's supposed to be my friend.

I throw Margaret's poem away because it outrages me most of all. Initially, I decide it's the type of touchy-feely literature that S.A.D.D. airdrops over high-school proms by the thousand. Later, it occurs to me that she's written it herself.

The writing is good, certainly better than anything I've sent her, and it has just the right amount of hidden meaning. At first read, the poem seems to be about the importance of spelling and punctuation. But when I read it again, I understand the full meaning. Margaret is trying to tell me it isn't important what I say with my life. The story, the full manuscript, is ancillary. What matters, she says, is the syntax. She says it's the rules that govern a life that make that life important.

Even though I'm no wild child, I can't imagine a goody-goody world in which how closely a person adheres to rules is a measure for how well she lives.

As my final correspondence with Margaret, I send her e. e. cummings's poem "since feeling is first," without a letter of explanation:

since feeling is first
who pays attention
to the syntax of things
will never wholly kiss you:
wholly to be a fool
while Spring is in the world.

It is my only attempt at rebuttal, my way of telling her that I am ignoring the things she respects, namely risks and rules. Just as e. e. cummings disregarded syntax, I am ignoring the minimum legal drinking age in the name of beauty, fun, and an artful existence. Of course, I don't yet know about cummings's critics, the folks who say that ignoring the rules is just as restrictive as following them. And if I did, I doubt I'd care. It is springtime in my life, even though it happens to be fall. I feel fully kissed, by Mac and by liquor.

To make this point clear, I cut off the poem's last lines when I copy it to send: "for life's not a paragraph / and death I think is no parenthesis." As far as my drinking is concerned, death doesn't even warrant an afterthought.

FIRST OFFENSE

THE FIRST TIME my parents catch me drinking is during the summer of 1995, in Ocean City, Maryland. Ocean City is the perfect place to get caught red-handed, what with its miles of boardwalk and green, plastic, mini-golf turf, its snack bars smelling of crab cakes, and the saltwater breeze carrying the screams of children as they plunge down waterslides. The setting means everyone involved can write the whole mess off as situational. It makes my drinking look like the exception as opposed to the norm, a seasonal recreation only slightly more hazardous than body surfing or searing in the noon sun without Coppertone.

There are two motivations for our trip: my father's

promotion and my injury. Sometime in May, my father receives a raise at the technological corporation where he works. Around the same time, I topple down the basement stairs and tear a ligament in my knee. The sequence of the two events seems significant to me. The whole world is rising, while I fall.

After my accident, I visit two doctors and three specialists. The last of them is an orthopedic surgeon at Emerson Hospital, a man I later dub Dr. Fix-It, who schedules me for reconstructive surgery in August.

I pass out on the examining table the day I receive the prognosis. I am shifting my weight on the parchment while Dr. Fix-It is describing his plans to harvest a portion of my hamstring and insert it into my knee. He is pointing out exactly where on the X-ray board, where my bones are lit up like a slide show of his recent trip to Fiji, and yet all I can think is, *There is some mistake, that skeleton can't possibly be mine.*

The bones are just too regular, like a stock photo from *Gray's Anatomy.* I'd assumed that inside, I'd look as dark and knotty as I feel. I was hoping the X-ray board could show me the injury I feel so deeply, a hurt that justifies the framework I've been using for living. For the past year, I've told myself that I'm drinking and smoking and otherwise acting delinquent because high school has dealt me a shitty hand, that I am winning neither popularity nor academic contests, that I am unsure and insufficient—in a word, *sick.* But there on the X-ray, I'm faced with proof that, deep down, I'm sturdy; even full-grown Dr. Fix-It says so. It is the notion of health, not injury, that makes me ill. It forces me to lean over and put my head between my knees.

I spend the rest of the school year hobbling up stairs and out of cars, never certain when my knee will submit and give out under me. Without my intricate agenda of after-school activities, I give in to self-imposed quarantine. I spend afternoons paging through stolen library books in the backyard's canvas lawn chair. Evenings, I keep vigil in the living room in front of infomercials.

In an effort to cheer me up, my mother proposes a vacation. I propose Ocean City. We spent three consecutive summers there, when I was five, six, and seven, and I've retained every second of each of them. I can remember burrowing for sand crabs in the wet sand down by the surf, letting them squirm to their deaths in a pebble-filled tank because I loved them too much to liberate them. I remember the boardwalk, where my mother bought me a T-shirt with a beaded hem that jingled when I walked. I remember the length of beach where I played catch with my father, way past my usual bedtime, and the way my hands looked when they slow-motion-grasped for the glow-in-the-dark ball. I remember the name of every resort on the strip—The Golden Sands, The Palm, The Prism—and the mirrored windows that made each one look as sunny as the sky. I remember mornings that I sat on a condo carpet, eating Cabbage Patch Kids cereal, which was the type of sugary snack that was forbidden at home, and savoring each candy-coated puff on my tongue like a gemstone far too precious to swallow.

To other people, Ocean City may be a tumbledown summer town with a name that ought to be implied. But to me, it's always represented hedonism.

I imagine my parents associate Ocean City with unity, with the years before I hit adolescence and became too mean and moody to take, because they agree to my destination quickly and resolutely. My mother even suggests I bring Natalie, who is home for two months on summer break, because the condo she's rented is big enough for us to have our own room. It feels like her final attempt to coax a smile out of me.

. . .

THE BEDROOM Natalie and I share turns out to be more like our own little apartment. It has its own bathroom, a queen-sized bed under a tufted comforter, and a sitting area where yellowed paperbacks are stacked beside a transistor TV. We fold our swimsuits into the room's white dresser and spread our arsenal of curling irons across the paint-chipped surface of the nightstand. Natalie parts the window's lace curtains, and we stand for a few minutes in front of it, awed by the condominiums that shoot up thirty stories high over the Coastal Highway. My parents' room faces the beach, and ours faces the street, and we prefer it that way.

We wait three nights to push out the screen and boost ourselves out of the window.

WE STARTED sneaking out of Natalie's house a month ago. We'd spend whole days drafting our escape plans, testing to see which hinges whined, which floorboards creaked, and gathering devices we might use to prop, resist, and muffle them. At night, we'd wait for the TV to fall silent in Natalie's parents' bedroom, and we'd silently stuff Natalie's bed and my sleeping bag with stuffed animals and sweaters. Then we'd tiptoe down the staircase, roll open the garage door, and sprint to where the driveway meets the street.

Most nights, the joy of the prison break was enough. We didn't need any plans, aside from walking the culs-de-sac like two ghosts, taunting the neighbors' tied-up Labradors, kicking bits of gravel and sharing cigarettes.

We'd learned to stay in the neighborhood after the night we hitchhiked to a party near Natalie's boarding school, where we drank Heineken and listened to a band, and nearly got stuck there without anyone to drive us home. At three A.M., we'd finally agreed to pay an older boy fifteen dollars in exchange for a ride. He had a summer job as an ice-cream man, and he drove us home in his singing white truck.

Years later, when my parents ask if I used to drink and sneak out because I wanted to test their boundaries, I'll say yes, even though that was never my aim. I won't know how to tell them it was a suicidal impulse that drove me out windows. I had a curious *It's a Wonderful Life*–like compulsion to explore what my house, or my life, would look like without me in it.

NATALIE AND I find a stand in our condo closet. It's a fold-out deal with metal legs and canvas rungs, and whoever put it there probably intended it for supporting suitcases or drying beach towels. But we see its full potential. Natalie unfolds it beneath the bedroom window and steps back to whisper, "After you." I position one foot on each of the metal legs and stand there, spread-eagle, for a moment of breath-catching before I grab both sides of the window frame and hoist myself out, one inch at a time.

We don't speak a word until we hit the pavement in the condo's parking lot. That is the divide, the predetermined finish line, and once we cross it we're free. There, we slip our feet back into our sandals and let out our pent-up laughter. All around us, the strip is illuminated with neon signs and headlights. People are everywhere, in cars, leaning out of hotel windows, roaming the sidewalks as they drink from foam-sheathed beer cans.

I feel like I did when I was younger, when my sister and I would linger on the stairs in our nightgowns during my parents' adults-only dinner parties, listening to the muffled laughter and the chiming sound of my father hitting his wineglass with a spoon. Tonight, the Coastal Highway confirms that old suspicion: There is a whole world that takes shape during the hours I'm asleep.

Across the street from the condo, Natalie and I wait for the trolley car, trying to decide if the ten dollars wadded up in our pockets is enough to feed the fare machine for two round-trip tickets. It is. When the trolley pulls up, we choose seats in the far back, which we know to be the most desirable spots on a school bus. We ride for thirty minutes, and fifty blocks.

Earlier in the day we met a guy behind the counter of the Pizza Palace who directed us to the part of town where the college kids hang out. They are waiters and lifeguards, he said, who rent entire houses on their own. Listening to him, I couldn't help but envision the staff kids in *Dirty Dancing,* the way they embraced booze, sex, and rock music like life, love, and the hunt for happiness. I sit in the trolley's grooved plastic seat, imagining I'm Baby—only I won't have to carry a watermelon the way she did to get into a party; I sense that being a girl is its own free pass inside.

NATALIE AND I aren't sure where to go once we step off the trolley. It's my idea to take off our sandals and wander down the beach, past all the darkened resorts that have beach chairs stacked in the sand. We aren't walking anywhere in particular, but Natalie keeps urging me to move faster because it's her nature. I trail behind her, watching the red tip of her cigarette move to and from her mouth, and the way the wet sand erases her footprints as soon as she makes them.

Down the beach, we see a campfire. In the dark, we can spot its orange spark, like a meteor, from a long way off. As we tread closer, we can see the empty beer bottles in the sand and the keg on ice in a trash can, a web of people settled around it. It looks like any cigarette or beer ad: a tight-knit circle of strangers made friends by atmosphere alone. Girls huddle on driftwood while boys drop kelp down their blouses. Flames brighten their faces. Steely waves crash at their backs.

It feels good to give myself over to that formula. It is like the type of extra credit where you get points for just showing up. The kids on the beach don't care that they don't know Natalie and me. A boy stands to offer us his space on a blanket. Someone else brings us beer in clear plastic cups. They welcome us into their circle, no questions asked, and we don't have to work for any of it.

The funny thing about that unconditional stamp of approval is that it makes me act less like myself. For all intents and purposes, it should make me more comfortable being regular old Koren—idiosyncratic, a bit phobic in groups, but a decent girl if you get to know her. But instead, I, too, conform to a beer-ad version of myself. I kick off my shoes and pirouette in the sand. I agree to drink beer from a funnel, even though I know the boy channeling it through will pour too fast, and I will end up wearing the thick tar of beer and wet sand. When Natalie and the other girls strip down to their underwear, I do, too. I ride a boogie board in my undershirt and white cotton panties, and don't care when the salt water makes my skin show through.

At the time, I write off these behaviors as a need to adapt. I don't want to stand out as a high-school girl, the type of baby who can't keep up with buxom sorority girls from Southern universities. I want to prove that I can funnel as much beer as they can, that I can unflinchingly take the same lascivious looks in the dark.

Later, I'll be able to see that this is how it all starts. I concede to shifting my personality, just a hair, to observe the standards I think the situation calls for. From now on, every time I drink, I'll enhance various aspects of myself, willing myself into a state where I am a little bit brighter, funnier, more outgoing, or vibrant. The process will be so incremental that I'll have no gauge of how much it will change me. I will wake up one day in my twenties like a skewed TV screen on which the hues are all wrong. My subtleties will be exaggerated and my overtones will be subdued. My entire personality will be off-color.

NATALIE AND I cut and run again the next night. It's the same escape route: over the stand, out the window, and down the strip on the trolley. This time, we head for a party in a large, stilted cottage a few blocks west of the beach. At the campfire the night before, a boy wrote the address in ballpoint pen on Natalie's forearm.

When we swing open the house's screen door, there isn't a party inside. There are college guys in T-shirts and swim shorts, just loafing around. They conjure up images of half a dozen frat-boy movies. The house is a labyrinth of rooms, empty, but for a few neon beer signs, pizza boxes, and TVs paused on video games. In the den, a few girls watch boys shoot pool from a sagging couch. Some fluff their hair so it falls over their shoulders. A few eye us distrustfully.

I make wide-open eyes at Natalie that say *This is a tragedy*. But she just screws up her face and turns a corner toward the kitchen because she knows full well I'll follow her.

There, a boy introduces himself as Greg and offers us beer. Right off the bat, Natalie says Greg looks like a criminal, on account of his T-shirt's black-and-white prison stripes, which he wears with a plastic belt and jeans so tight I can make out the square of cue chalk in his pocket. He is small, nearly my size, with blue eyes that stand out behind blond bangs so long they clear the bridge of his nose. He says he studies painting at a Maryland art institute where classes like "interactive media," "experimental animation," and other things I've never heard of are required. He's spending the summer painting his senior thesis project between shifts at a local surf shop. When I ask what he paints, he says, "Come on up and see." As I turn to follow him upstairs to his studio, Natalie says she'll stay behind. She is busy sharing cigarettes with a University of Maryland boy named Wally.

Greg's canvases are scattered across the floor of the studio, and more are propped up against easels and walls. I can't find a common motif. There are paintings of cracked eggs, hands holding apples, the shriveled breasts of a woman he says is a portrait model. What catches my attention, what holds me transfixed the way a nail holds a mirror, is an oversized American flag on the ceiling. It is riddled with holes and faded from the sun, and the effect makes it look exactly like a flag (was it the original American flag?) that I'd seen hanging in a museum in Washington, D.C. I take it as a symbol of independence. I would die to be twenty, to spend summers away from my parents, painting still lifes and gluing up surfboard gashes.

I tell Greg lies, heaps of them. Actually, they aren't lies so much as they are little shifts in facts that, I think, make me appear worldly in his eyes. I tell him I am eighteen, spending a month in Ocean City with my aunt before returning home to Boston for my senior year of high school. I weave all my stories around these small substitutions: eighteen as opposed to fifteen, relatives as opposed to parents, big city as opposed to small town. The persona I create isn't terribly far from the truth, but it makes me feel safer around him, more anonymous and less exposed.

We kiss for a while amid the toxic smell of art supplies, and Greg is gentle with me. When my hair falls into his mouth, he brushes each wet thread away. When I say something he can't quite hear, he says, "I'm sorry, sweetheart?" And the word *sweetheart* sounds so tender it soothes some raw part of me, and I find myself whispering so I can hear it again.

I imagine that Greg understands me, that he has a psychic sense for how far I am from the place where I started. I think compassion drives him to hold me closer. When I speak, he concentrates like someone listening to a seashell, and I think he can hear the ocean that is pitching itself around inside me.

That's the thing about social drinking: In the end, it's the drinking that creates the scene, not the other way around. You grow to relish the buzz, regardless of the situation. Once you're there, really there inside that moment, with its neighborly warmth and conversation, it's hard to tell what's responsible for producing emotion. What's responsible for the light-headed feeling? Is it the Molson, or the boy who is running his fingers through the ends of your hair? Are you chatty because you're drunk, or because you're connecting with someone on a level that you have never before experienced? To an outsider, the distinction is an easy one to make. But when you're fifteen and female, when you experience these feelings first and later only when you are drinking, it becomes a question of which came first, the liquor or the Greg?

THREE BEERS and twelve watercolors later, I go downstairs to find Natalie. It isn't that I have forgotten about her; she has always been there in my mind, like a telephone ringing in the background. I feel guilty for neglecting her. I imagine she's downstairs on the porch, smoking a Marlboro and delivering a sermon on Kurt Cobain conspiracy theories, which is her version of small talk. Hopefully, she's done some kissing, too, with Wally, in which case she won't be fed up with waiting for me. Either way, I'm obliged to go downstairs and pick her up.

But Natalie isn't on the porch. She isn't in the TV room, the game room, or the kitchen, either. I know because I am gripping Greg's hand and tugging him from one room to the next. I can't imagine where Natalie is, or why she would leave me. That's the big thing: I don't understand how she could abandon *me* in a house full of strangers, with dawn about to break. I imagine my parents getting up in a few hours, making breakfast and going about the business of preparing for the beach; sooner or later they will discover our empty room and the towels we have stuffed between our sheets.

Greg decides we should check Wally's room, and relief washes over me. It occurs to me that the night has already been going in the direction of a double date: The boys have paired off with us, to steal whatever couple time they can.

SURE ENOUGH, there is a girl in Wally's room, but she isn't Natalie.

"Your friend left," Wally says through the crack of the door. Through it, I can see one of the blondes from the couch downstairs. She is wearing only turquoise-colored underwear and using the corner of a blanket to shield her bare chest. In the yellow lamplight she looks less intimidating, and much more freckled and angular. It occurs to me that she's probably my age.

"What do you mean she left? Did she say she was going back

to the condo?" Panic is moving in to displace my buzz, and the feeling is intoxicating in a different way. My throat tightens enough to cut off my breath. I can feel my pulse in my head.

Wally gives a puny shrug, as if to say, *Not my problem,* before he closes the door. I hear the click of it locking, and before I know what I'm doing, I am bringing my foot back over and over, pounding the rubber toe of my sneaker against the door. The wood feels flimsy, like it might be particleboard, and the door rattles in it's frame. As hard as I kick, Wally won't come back to open it.

Greg puts his hand on my shoulder to stop me.

I start screaming. At first, there are no words. I am little more than a trumpet screaming out notes. Beer has given my voice a new wind, and it makes each squeal breathe through me brassy and clear. "What did he do with Natalie? Where *the fuck* is Natalie?"

I can feel tears welling up in my eyes, and they are dangerously close to spilling out onto the folds of my cheeks. The song of my screaming is reverberating off the walls. It blows open bedroom doors and makes boys poke their heads out.

Greg is looking at me as though I am a deranged animal he is not sure how to restrain. Something in his look implies I am being irrational. It's the look I get from my mother when she remembers midway through a fight that I'm a teenage girl and therefore have no perspective. It occurs to me that he cannot empathize; he has never empathized. He has no idea why I am upset.

"Do you mean Wally? He wouldn't do anything to her. I'm sure your friend is fine. She just decided to go to another party, that's all."

I don't know how to tell him that Natalie and I don't know

about any other parties. This was the only address Natalie had printed on her arm.

The only place I can think to look for her is down on the beach, near the burned-out shell of the campfire left over from the night before.

GREG COMES with me to look for her, but I am beginning to feel uneasy around him. I feel myself shifting into confessional mode, like I might slip up and tell him everything. Each moment that I fail to find Natalie, I am more hysterical and I care less about maintaining the details of my cock-and-bull story.

The sun is starting to come up. The waves rolling over my feet look like frothy green tea, and the sand is the color of burned sugar. The world is turning seaside colors again, and it reminds me that there is little time left. I have to find Natalie and get her back through the condo window.

I decide to tell Greg I lied to him, that I am seventeen and not eighteen. It still isn't the truth, but it feels like a small admission of guilt, like I am admitting in a critical moment how inexperienced I am.

We scuffle along the sand, and this time I am the one to walk fast, and I turn around every few feet to make Greg hurry up. When we get to the site, the same fire is burning. The same keg is being pumped from the same trash can by the same people wearing alcohol-induced grins. In the light of dawn, they seem so much more loathsome than they did the night before. Everyone is too stupid or drunk or self-absorbed to help me find Natalie.

The beach is whipping up a strong wind that straightens out wind socks and sets porch chimes clanging, and it feels like a slap in the face. I lean against Greg, trying to brace myself from it, while he stops to question people on the beach.

The conversation goes like this:

"Have you seen an eighteen-year-old girl with green eyes and freckles?"

"Seventeen," I correct him, and wonder if he's been listening to me at all.

"What was she wearing?"

"What was she wearing, again?" Greg asks me.

"A green polo shirt."

"A polo shirt. Green."

Finally, someone points to a lopsided condo on the corner. I break free from Greg and take the steps to the door two at a time.

INSIDE, I find Natalie in an armchair, looking wilted. She is conscious, but barely. Her head is bowed forward and her eyes, rolled way back, divulge only the whites. It is a look she once perfected at a rock club, when she pretended to pass out in the pit so we could watch the band from a better vantage point backstage. I can't help hoping she is faking again.

Around her are guys and a few girls, jumbled around a coffee table and on a paisley sofa, playing cards and sipping beer. A joint, the first I have ever seen, burns in a scalloped clay ashtray. I don't need anyone to tell me it isn't a cigarette. Somehow the smoke just smells green.

I go to Natalie's armchair and grab one of her legs with both hands, rattling it loosely, the way I might rouse someone from an afternoon nap. With the white flesh of her thigh in my hand, I realize she is wearing someone else's clothes. Her jeans and polo shirt have been replaced with blue mesh shorts and a white undershirt.

I don't even bother asking Natalie where her clothes are

because it's clear that she can't speak. Instead, I stand up and spin around to face the people on the sofa; I ask them where the *fuck* her clothes are.

"She threw up on them," a girl with a throaty voice says. She holds the joint between the nails of her thumb and her index finger and examines it like a tiny bug she is thinking of squashing.

"Natalie?" I lean over and shake her by the shoulders, too hard now, but I can't help it. I am desperate to wake her in the way people are desperate to revive their dead lovers in made-for-TV movies. I don't care if I look melodramatic. This is the closest I've ever come to seeing a corpse.

"Natalie?" When I call her name in my trumpet scream, the green half-moons of her eyes roll in my direction.

"You fuc-king bitch," she says and leans over as if to spit on me, but drool just rolls down one side of her chin in a glistening tear.

A guy says, "This might be a good time to get her out of here."

Greg hauls Natalie out of the armchair and onto her feet. He has to hold her by the waist to keep her upright, while I hunt for her shoes. She stands there like a ski jumper, leaning her head into his chest with her legs locked too far out behind her. She lets out another string of profanities when I lean down to put on her flip-flops.

"Fuc-king bitch-ass dirty slut."

She drops to her hands and knees on the floor, and her shoulders start to tremble like she is going to be sick.

Someone says plainly, "Get her out of here."

Greg tells me to kneel down beside Natalie and wrap one arm under her shoulder and around her waist. He does the same thing on the other side, and when he says, "Ready, set, stand," we do, and my knees buckle for a brief moment under Natalie's dead weight. Together, we move emphatically for the door, like we are storming out of a movie that has deeply offended us.

"Are you okay to stand up? If I set you down, you're not going to fall, right?"

Greg tries to lower Natalie to the sidewalk beside the trolley stop. His questions are more or less rhetorical, as Natalie has been reduced to gurgling whenever we speak to her. Her limbs look too heavy for her to move. When she tries to lift her hands, they only come up an inch or two before they fall back down and roll away from her. Greg says she looks like a rag doll; I think she looks like one of my dog's dilapidated chew toys.

The second Greg lets Natalie's feet touch the concrete, her entire body folds under her. She assumes the position of a chalk outline on *NYPD Blue*: arms outstretched, with her legs wrenched one way and her neck twisted the other. We let her rest like that while we wait. All around her on the sidewalk, ants are building knolls that look like ginger.

"How did she get like this?" I cover my hand with my mouth as I speak because Natalie is emitting a sour smell that makes me think I might throw up, too. "Honestly? She wasn't drunk at your house. How do you think she got this way? Do you think she took pills or something?" Natalie has told me about kids at her school who steal prescriptions. They mostly sell downers, she says, the kind of painkillers that make you feel as weightless as an astronaut somersaulting through a spacecraft.

Greg shakes his head. I'm not sure if he means to say no, or if he is trying to clear his bangs from his face. He says, "Naw, she just had too much to drink. Once you get her home she can sleep it off."

I should believe him because his eyes are calm, in a way that suggests he has been through this scenario a million times before. But I don't. I don't see any way that this is going to be okay. In my mind, I have a very distinct picture of what is going to happen next: I will get Natalie back to the room, tuck her in to bed, and sometime during the night she will choke on her own vomit and die. That was the one unmistakable thing I learned from our alcohol unit in health class—sometimes, if people get drunk enough, they can drown in their own puke, like Jimi Hendrix. There is even a parody of "Purple Haze" that goes "excuse me while I choke and die." I think I'm going to have to resuscitate Natalie while my parents sleep, unsuspecting, in the room next door. I don't even remember how to do mouth-to-mouth. I don't know how far you're supposed to tip the head back, or how many seconds you're supposed to wait between giving breaths.

At any minute, I imagine my parents will hit the bar on their alarm clock. My mom will go to the bathroom and start the shower spray; my ten-year-old sister will turn on cartoons; my dad will go out to buy bagels. There is no way I can stuff Natalie through the window in her condition, and if we use the front door, my parents will instantly know about the beach, the boys, and the booze.

I am stuck in this situation, and the feeling that follows that realization is the same dread and shortness of breath I felt the time I got wedged behind a basement bookshelf I wasn't strong enough to move. I am trapped and there is no way out; I can't keep that knowledge to myself any longer.

I unleash a string of confessions on Greg. I tell him that I am not eighteen or seventeen, but fifteen, and that I am actually staying with my parents and not an aunt. These are small distinctions, but to me they feel indispensable, like pronouns, without which he has no hope of understanding my language.

He says, "Don't worry about your parents. They'll be mad at first, but so what? The worst they can do is ground you. It's not the end of the world."

The sun is creeping up the sky like a bug on a wall, and all around us people are climbing into their cars to go to work. I look at Greg, and notice for the first time that he is practically crawling out of his skin, anxious to go home and, presumably, sleep before his shift at the surf shop. He, too, looks younger in the sunlight, less collegiate, more like a boy I barely know.

The trolley pulls up and I thrust Natalie onto it.

THE RIDE back to the condo is unbearable. Natalie vomits twice, and each time I struggle to hide her from the bus driver, who is watching us knowingly in his rearview mirror. I lean over and pretend to tie my shoelaces while I cover the puddles with stray newspapers. Whole families get on, carting canvas bags filled with black beach towels and sunblock. Businessmen drink coffee from foam cups and peruse *USA Today*. Construction workers clutch their scuffed hard hats in their laps. Some of them look at us with disgust, and others offer commentary, like "Friend had a rough night, eh?"

No one offers to help. No one pulls the emergency brake and shouts for a doctor. To them, we are no crisis; we're a joke. Their smirks reflect my most grisly apprehensions. We are ingrates, prime examples of godless, suburban white girls, defects in the knit of society.

When we get back, Natalie is still too drunk to climb through the window. I am forced to do the unthinkable. I cringe, and carry her in through the condo's front door.

When I lead her to bed she seems to wake up a bit, as though she has amnesia and the bed is the only thing she recognizes. She barely responds when I call her by name, but somehow the sight of the lace pillowcases flips a switch in her brain that says, *Sleep, sleep here, sleep now.* I let her crawl in between the covers without even bothering to remove the heaps of towels we had skillfully sculpted only hours earlier. I change quietly into a nightgown and curl beside her. I put my head on her shoulder so I can monitor her breathing. As far as I can tell, the rising and falling of her chest seems regular.

I don't have a chance to doze off before my mother materialized in the bedroom doorway.

"Koren," she whispers. I can see she has already changed into a beach cover-up and a wide straw hat. "We're going down to the pool. Please come down after you've rested; we'd like to talk to you."

"Shit," I shout, after I hear the front door close behind her.

Hours pass, and I am filled with the same sense of doom I felt in seventh grade, when Mrs. Kent sent me to the principal's office when I refused to read aloud. Fuck Greg for telling me this isn't the end of the world. It is the end of *my* world, the one in which I am an admittedly mopey teenager, but still the firstborn daughter, a decent student but for math and science, and the apple of my daddy's eye.

Rest? Who was my mother kidding? My eyes burn with exhaustion, but I can't sleep. I keep imagining my head on a chopping block, instead of a too-thin hotel pillow. I try to evaluate the incriminating evidence. Until I decide how much my parents actually know, I can't draft a speech in my defense. My mind spins. When I close my eyes, I feel like I'm nose-diving into a spiral descent. I'm not hungover, but I run to the bathroom and throw up.

Natalie joins me a few minutes later, and we take turns holding one another's hair and heaving into the bowl. We flush, and she tries her best to tell me what happened. Alcohol has muddled the details, so she fills in the blanks as best she can. Wally brought her to his room, bolted the door, and tried to put his hands down her pants. She escaped his grasp narrowly and unharmed, but she didn't feel like waiting on the porch, and she didn't want to mount the stairs to the studio and disrupt my time alone with Greg. So she went for a walk. She walked along the beach where we had been the night before, and when a group of guys called out to her, she joined them on their deck. She chugged what she thought was a jumbo-sized plastic cup of beer, but when she was halfway finished, it occurred to her that it might have been liquor. She also smoked what she thought was a joint, but the contents were whiter, she said, and it occurred to her that it might have been angel dust.

My stomach does another revolution, and I think I might throw up again. The scenario Natalie has described is even worse than the one I imagined. In my heart of hearts, I had thought we'd both only had a few beers. I thought she had just been "a two-beer queer," which was a term she always used to describe me when I got drunk off of very little. But the truth is laced with liquor, boys, and drugs. There is no way I can relay it to my parents, who, I imagine, wait impatiently by the pool, already burning in the one o'clock sun.

I ask Natalie if she's okay, and it's a leading question. I am trying to make her agree so I can stop my own nauseous feeling, the one that tells me this is my fault. I say, "Natalie, nobody *did anything* to you, did they?"

"I don't think so," she says, and her forehead crinkles up, as though she's considering the possibility for the first time. "But then, I don't remember everything."

It will be years before I know the horror and shame that make Natalie cringe. I will have to experience it myself before I can understand that there are two parts of the mind that constrain memory after nights like this: one that wants to dig it up, and another that wants to push it deeper down. In college, I will learn about boys and blackouts firsthand, about the way the things you can't remember can terrorize you.

I lean my head over the toilet bowl and passionately ralph.

Around two o'clock I trudge in the direction of the hotel pool, like a dead girl walking, thinking I can't possibly put it off any longer. I resolve to accept my punishment. Hopefully, my parents' backlash will be quick and painless, a kind of lethal injection, my social life ended abruptly at the hands of the state.

I spot them sitting at a flimsy poolside patio table. The morning's clouds have blown off, and behind them the day is flawlessly blue. In the pool, children buoy to the surface on red foam boards. Teenaged girls, who look exactly like me, stretch out, catlike, on lawn chairs, reading fashion magazines, and applying oil to the skin beneath their bikini strings. Waiters are everywhere, carrying piña coladas in sweaty glasses. It is an unlikely location for my first lecture about drinking.

When I get to the table, I look down and see a glass of beer resting in front of chair number three.

"I hope you don't mind," my father says. "We went ahead and ordered for you."

I decide to tell a fraction of the truth. It will become something I will tell my parents for years in times of distress. I like to think of it as the-whole-truth-and-nothing-but-the-truth's second cousin; they may not share all the same physical characteristics, but there is no denying they're related.

Years later, it's hard to remember the precise story that I tell them. But it is exactly that—a *story*. I shift various facts around like squares on a Rubik's Cube, in the hope of aligning the details. They only get more jumbled when my parents ask me to repeat them.

The night sounds like a fairy tale by the time I am through reconstructing it. Natalie and I left the house at midnight because we couldn't fall asleep. We walked along the beach to tire ourselves, enjoying the mist and the moon and the damp sand under our feet. We found a party somewhere along the breaking waves, and it was not unlike the Mad Hatter's tea party: Everyone was gathered around a campfire, singing songs, raising their glasses, and switching seats. Someone offered us something from a keg, which we drank to gauge the mystical effects it would have on us.

The narrative is straight out of *Alice in Wonderland,* right down to the bottle marked DRINK ME. My father is repressing a look that says, *Off with her head.*

He asks how many beers I drank.

"Two, only two." Saying things twice always seems to substantiate them.

He asks if I've ever had a drink before.

"No," I lie. "Never."

My mother asks what Natalie drank.

Since I'll never know, I guess and say, "Four beers."

Her look is dubious.

"Koren, she smells like *hard alcohol.*" My mother is a

bloodhound. She could make a living sniffing out contraband in luggage at customs.

I shrug and say she might have had hard alcohol. I add, "It's not like I was watching her every second."

My mother gasps.

She says, "Listen, *little girl*." It is the first time in the conversation that she has raised her voice, and whenever she calls me "little girl" I know she means business. "Natalie is your friend. You two are supposed to look out for each other. *Particularly* if you're going to be drinking." She doesn't need to add that I shouldn't have been drinking. We both know, at this point, that it is extraneous to the conversation.

What she says makes sense, and ultimately, it is the one real lesson I take away from that lecture by the pool: *During times of booze, girls are responsible for nurturing one another.* When she says it, an image flashes through my mind of Jodie Foster in *Foxes,* pouring coffee and cornflakes for her girlfriends after a night of too much Scotch and too many quaaludes. If drinking is like playing grown-up or playing house, somebody has to be the mother. And the fact that my own mother says this makes the knowledge feel all the more sacred, like a bond passed down by women through the ages. I add it to my list of drinking commandments, alongside *Thou shalt select a designated driver.*

"There weren't any boys involved, were there?" I know she is really asking if there was any sex involved.

If girls need to defend each other while they drink, sex is the threat we need to protect one another from. The thing I am discovering about girldom is, in the end, nobody cares if you are a drunk, an anorexic, a runaway, a dropout, a dope fiend, or a psychotic. These things aren't regaled, but they are allowed. With the right amount of therapy or religion or pharmaceuticals, they can be remedied and passed off as life stages. That is, as long as you are still a virgin. To be a whore is to be unsalvageable.

"No. God, no," I half-mouth the words in a way that suggests the scenario is so far-fetched it doesn't merit sound. But secretly, I am wondering if something other than vomit impelled Natalie out of her clothes and into those gym shorts.

It wasn't too long ago that Natalie and I rented the movie *Kids,* and I haven't been able to forget the look on Chloë Sevigny's face when her character is raped while she is passed out on a sofa, drunk and high. The camera captures the whole horrifying scene, and it gave me nightmares for months after I saw it. I could not stop thinking of how each thrust sent the pleather couch squeaking. The boy had bent her legs so far back over her head, they looked as though they'd snap off at her hips.

MY PARENTS never say the words "get-out-of-jail-free card," but that's what this is. As a first-time offender, I escape any real punishment. They make it clear that I will be severely sorry if they catch me drinking again. They establish what addiction counselors call a "No-Use" rule. I am not, under any circumstances, allowed to drink alcohol outside of their company before I graduate from high school. They say, "If you're curious about alcohol, that's fine, but you'll drink it with us." I am more than welcome to have half a glass of wine with dinner.

My parents seem almost relieved to get the discussion out of the way. I get the sense that they've been waiting to catch me drinking, the same way they've been waiting to catch me kissing some boy in the den. To them, it is just another version of the birds and the bees, a conversation they've been waiting for years to spring on me, holding off until I was developed enough to pass for old enough. For the most part, this lesson about alcohol strikes me as more discourse to file away with panty liners and antiperspirant. It is the type of embarrassing lecture that makes all of us uncomfortable.

They are generous with my punishment. I am grounded for a week, which means little in the grand scheme of things. I routinely get more jail time for a failing a math test or harassing my sister.

Their real charity, though, is in terms of Natalie. I'd just assumed this would be one of those situations where my mother called Natalie's mother, the way she used to when we were younger and she caught us watching R-rated movies. Up until this point, it seemed to be the preferred parental way of dealing with things—everyone rehashing the events and comparing notes out of obligation, outrage, or guilt. Instead, they decide to let Natalie tell her parents herself. I think they do it because we are old enough to be trusted as active participants in our retribution. It will take me years to see it for what it is: embarrassment and the desire to pretend the whole thing never happened.

That will be the thing about my parents. From the outside, they will come off as suspicious as hell. They will dutifully set and enforce curfews. They will ask where I'm going, and with whom. They'll keep asking who'll be there, how long I'll be gone, and how I'm getting back. My father will hug me when I come home at night, as if to check my breath for alcohol. My mother will linger in my room too long when she is putting away laundry; she'll slide her fingers along the bottoms of my drawers as if she's checking for drug-filled plastic Baggies. But when it comes down to the hard evidence, the material proof sitting right in front of them in sunglasses and sweatpants, the very portrait of hungover, they will choose optimism. They'll believe in the best in me. And years later, they'll believe in the best in my sister.

Every parent would rather believe that their child abstains—from sex, drugs, booze, and violence, all the cultish impulses.

NATALIE AND I spend the afternoon on the boardwalk. I take her there because I can't have the conversation I want to have with her in the condo without wrecking the half-truths I told my parents, and because she feels too weak to lie on a beach towel in the radiant heat. In spite of the boardwalk's hundred-foot Ferris wheel and toy-sized tram, the funnel cakes and beef-pit barbecue, the men selling bags of cotton candy that look like attic insulation, it is the most depressing three-mile stretch of wood in the world.

Beside a bike-rental shop, we find a sad, green awning that advertises SAND ART and looks private. I can tell by the way Natalie lets me take out my wallet to pay for the glass bottles that she thinks I'm indebted to her.

Plastic trays that resemble kitty-litter boxes are lined up across a wooden picnic table, and each one is filled with the kind of colored sand that doesn't exist in nature. There is mint green and lavender sand, sand in lemon yellow and fire-engine red.

Natalie goes to the cobalt-blue box and starts carefully funneling the sand through the neck of the bottle I bought her. She has changed into a sleeveless black T-shirt, but she still wears the blue mesh gym shorts from the night before, rolled up four times so they fit. For some reason, the fact that she didn't bury them in her suitcase or toss them into one of the hotel lobby's wastepaper bins makes me furious.

Natalie doesn't speak to me. She concentrates on stratifying her glass bottle in meticulous layers. She pours blue, lavender, orange, and then blue again.

I ask her to tell me, again, everything she remembers. I want her to lay the facts out for me, layer by layer, the way she handles the sand.

She says, "I told you everything. I blacked out. It's happened a few times before, at school, and when it does, there's nothing you can do to remember. So don't ask me again."

I look back at my own bottle. I haven't been paying attention while I've been pouring sand into it, and the colors are as muddled as whatever happened last night. I try to contain the hot tear I can feel simmering in one corner of my eye.

I know I can't bawl because I have no real right to bawl, because Natalie's blackout belongs to her and not me. If anyone deserves to cry, it's her. Although I pray to God she doesn't cry because I won't have a clue how to comfort her. I pray she'll keep guiding her every terror into that little glass bottle. Before we leave Ocean City, I want all talk of the incident corked.

Overnight, the world around us has changed little. The sun is blistering. Seagulls are swooping down to fight over dropped French fries. Whole families are whizzing by on rented bikes. It is Natalie who is changed. She is no longer the proud girl with swaggering shoulders and scheming eyes. I know I can't rely on her for answers the way that I used to, when I used to trust her wink, when I trusted that she knew everything. That fearlessness has been emptied from her. Now, she's filled with dread and hesitation that's even heavier than mine is.

I watch her scoop up handfuls of hot-pink sand and let it run through her fingers.

I already know Natalie and I will stop seeing each other once we get home. I already know we will be like lovers who have experienced something horrible together, like a near-fatal accident, or an abortion, or a threesome. We will have too many reasons not to look at each other. There will be too much history in the way.

From now on, whenever I look at Natalie, the memory of her face last night, sheening with sweat and smeared makeup, will float to mind like a helium balloon. I will be sickened by the thought that I was responsible for losing her because I mounted the stairs to Greg's studio. The anxiety will only grow when a girl who has been vying for Natalie's friendship since junior high uses the incident as leverage. She will call me on the telephone to say, "You should be ashamed."

More than five years later, long after we've lost all contact, Natalie will still appear in my dreams. She'll come to me again and again when I close my eyes, and together we will move through parades or giant bazaars, where I know a current of people will pull me away, and then it will. Every time, my fingers will slip from Natalie's hand, and I will be filled with a heart-thumping panic that will pull me from sleep.

I will feel the dread, too, well into the waking life of my twenties. Some days, I will think I see Natalie's face in the face of a bank teller or a woman crossing the street. I'll stop cold for a moment, before I realize I am looking at a different set of green eyes. I will have to blink Natalie away, and go back to endorsing a check or dodging traffic.

I will never get over feeling like Lady Macbeth. Natalie will be the spot of blood I can't clean from my memory.

I GO HOME, and a month later I have knee surgery. Dr. Fix-It opens my leg up and sorts things out. He cuts away the deteriorated ligaments and cartilage and replaces them with other tissues. He secures it all with nuts and bolts that are better equipped for support. I feel like the faulty family VCR, sent away for repair. After surgery, I go back to being my old self, pre-injury and pre–Ocean City. I prove to my parents that I am still good, reliable.

But before the surgery, I slip up. I am sitting in an examining room with my mother and a nurse, who is taking my medical history. It is the usual stuff:

"Any family history of diabetes, heart disease, or mental illness?"

"No."

"Any drug allergies?"

"No."

I am doing fine until she asks me the fateful question: "Do you drink?"

I suddenly and impulsively say, "Sometimes."

Right away, I know it is the wrong thing to say. It is a Freudian slip. I had meant to say *No, God No, Hell No.* What's worse is, it's too late to take it back. I feel like the squirrels that so often run in front of our car and then stand paralyzed in the forward crunch of the tires. I'm torn between the compulsion to run and the urge to stand still and hope the danger will pass.

The nurse is looking back and forth between my mother and me. She is holding her pen upright, as though it's a knife and her clipboard is a T-bone steak she is thinking about stabbing. She asks, "How often is 'sometimes'?"

I can feel my mother glaring at me, snake-like, out of the corners of her eyes.

"Sometimes," I roll the word over in my mouth as though I'm trying to determine its flavor. There's nothing left to say but, "Sometimes, like on the weekends."

. . .

DURING THE ride home from the office, I get an earful from my mother. Why, she wants to know, had I said such an awful thing? Hadn't I known that the nurse meant did I drink *daily*? It's not like I get off the bus and mix martinis every day after school.

I tell her I was referring to Ocean City. I say I thought it was a crime I was obliged to disclose, like the box on an employment form that asks, *Have you ever been convicted of a felony?*

My mom says, "She didn't need to know about that."

Didn't *need* to know. In that moment, I realize what a terrible mistake I've made. I was supposed to keep what happened in Ocean City to myself, disclosing it only to God, or, in His absence, to our priest, out of absolute necessity. I should have taken a note from the spring-break coverage on MTV, all those girls wearing whipped-cream bikinis who lean into the camera and clamor, "Remember, whatever happens in Panama City *stays* in Panama City!"

What happened in Ocean City should have stayed there. I should have disposed of the memory the way people "take care of" dirty bodies. It is a menacing recollection that deserves no marker, no eulogy. I should have given it a watery grave, the way Tom Petty does in one of his music videos, when he lays his pretty, dead girlfriend down in the Pacific, and afterward only her red lips can be seen beneath the back-and-forth motion of the waves.

I push any remembrance of that night down the sinkhole. I don't know I'll be back in the same hospital one year later, nearly swimming with the fishes, just as dead in the water.

COMA GIRL

Henceforth, my mother will refer to it as the time I almost died. We'll be sitting in the kitchen, both four and seven years from now. My dad will extend the leaves of the kitchen table to accommodate whatever college boyfriend I've brought home for the weekend. And my mom, while spooning out three-bean salad, will turn and ask him, "Has Koren told you about the time she almost died?"

I'll never know how much of that assertion accounts for melodrama.

Sure enough, it feels like death. On November 9, 1996, I wake up between the Tide-stiff sheets of my childhood Banister Bed and one thought occurs to me: *I'm not wearing any underwear.*

This is all the information I need to know that something horrendous has happened. At sixteen, I am never naked, save for ten minutes a day under the stream of a morning shower, and even then, I turn away from the bathroom mirror before I drop my towel to step in. Even alone, I am ashamed of the arcs of my own pale skin, particularly in the whitest part that spans between my hips. Given my tendency to thrash in my sleep and kick down sheets, I would never sleep without underwear.

My bed looks like it's been made with me in it. There's not a wrinkle in the comforter; its patched pastel pattern is pulled smooth and tight, clear up to my neck. When I start to unroll my arms and legs from the folds of the sheets, I feel a sharp pain in my elbow, like I've been sleeping on it, and I stop for a moment, trying to decide if that position is physically possible.

I decide to fold back the comforter from one corner, the way someone might diagonally halve a dinner napkin. I do it slowly. It's like opening a hand-addressed letter with no return address; I have a feeling I could find just about anything inside.

What I find under the covers looks like someone else's nightgown. It is a thin, white, cotton smock, stippled with green, and it cuts off at my knees. I can't imagine who I borrowed it from, since my friends and I all sleep in nylon shorts and our dads' XL T-shirts. When I feel around to the breach of cloth above my own pink ass, it dawns on me: *I'm wearing a hospital gown.*

I'm immobile in the face of my panic. I'm stunned to the point that I don't dare breathe or kick my feet in a way that would make even the faintest sliding sound on the starched sheets. I don't know how many minutes I lay like this, motionless in the small sag that my body makes in the mattress, barely breathing. I can't get out of bed until I've figured out what emergency landed me in this green and white gown. My room is directly above the dining room, and the littlest thump on the carpet can shake the chandelier; I don't want anyone downstairs to see it swinging and know I'm awake.

I feel like I'm arriving at the scene of an accident, like my physical self has been creamed in a hit-and-run and my mental self is the first one to find it. All I can do is run through the basic first-aid checkpoints, the first of which is: *Can you move?*

I pull my knees into my chest and wrap both arms around them with no problem, aside from the throbbing deep in my elbow. The back of my head is tender against the pillow, and my neck moves in a succession of arthritic-like cracks. But my joints move. I'm not paralyzed.

There are no clues in the form of a cast or a bandage or stitches. Lying down, I can't even make out any discernible bruises. Later, I'll be able to make out the purple impressions of fingers around my biceps, plus a golf ball–sized bruise on one ass cheek, a sort of yellowed half-moon around a raised, blue bump. But for now, the only visible signs that I'm injured are the hospital gown and a pink, plastic wristband that reads ZAILCKAS, KOREN.

The house is filled with the sounds of Saturday morning in motion. Bear is barking to be let in through the side door. There is the sound of coffee mugs clinking on countertops, and I detect the faint smell of bagels burning in the oven. I might even hear the far-off sound of my mother's whirring laughter.

My room appears equal in its sameness. There are dirty socks on the floor and stacks of *Seventeen* on my desk. On my bureau, there are notebooks on top of snapshots, necklaces on top of notebooks, and dust over just about everything, ever since I barred my mom from my room. Fall light filters through the window blinds and casts sunny stripes across the carpet. I can see my back-to-school sweaters brushing elbows in the closet; the price tags are still stapled to some of them, and I can make out the orange half-off stickers from Filene's juniors' department.

MENTALLY, I retrace my steps from last night to try to find this dropped memory.

As far as Friday nights go, it was typical. I spent it with my new friend, Kat Caldwell. She is a girl I made friends with a few months ago for no real reason other than we both drink and we're both sensitive. The first night I'd slept over at Kat's house, I saw that her sheets were streaked with mascara, and her Laura Ashley pillowcases retained the outline of her whole face: half-moon of foundation, faint ring of lip stain, black strokes from the flurried beating of her dripping eyelashes. She'd opened the drawers of her bureau to show me the old liquor bottles she hid under her childhood ballet costumes, and I'd laughed at dozens of tiny Lycra bodices, net tutus, and loose sequins that smelled of Tanqueray.

Kat came with a silver cord to more friends, like Abby and Allen, and I'd gone with all of them, plus my childhood friend Claire, to a Friday-night get-together near the lake in the next town over.

A girl whose parents were away in Vermont for a wine-tasting weekend threw the party. Her parents must have warned her not to have friends over while they were gone because she wouldn't let any of us inside her house to mix drinks properly, in cups. Instead, about a dozen of us—friends, and friends of friends, and neighborhood kids who'd heard that someone's parents were out—were in the backyard, slugging rum, tequila, and Kahlúa straight from their bottles. At one point, when I asked the girl if I could go inside to use her bathroom, she suggested that I drop my pants behind the hedges across the street.

The whole ordeal hadn't been the least bit thrilling. I'd sat beside Kat on a splintering dock. Our bare feet dangled over the edge of the black, rippling water, where we could occasionally hear fish jump, making plopping sounds like tossed coins. The wind propelled dead leaves across the lake's surface. The clouds swirled themselves around the moon.

I started by taking small sips from the communal bottles. I knocked back a few sips of generic rum, which tasted strong and acidic, and bit my throat. I soothed it with candied gulps of Kahlúa.

I also drank from a thermos filled with vodka that Claire had filched from a bottle in her parents' liquor cabinet. It was the same gallon-wide jug of Absolut that we always stole from, and then added water to, in an effort to recover the stolen inches. After months of adding and subtracting, the vodka had reached a diluted state that rendered it tasteless. It was as cold and wet as springwater, and we drank it fast.

The last thing I remember is telling Claire about the poet Frank O'Hara, the way he'd said that after the first glass of vodka you can accept anything about life, even your own mysteriousness. After that, my own mystery opens up.

THERE ARE only so many calamities that could have warranted this hospital gown. My first thought is that I lost my footing on the path leading up from the dock and cracked my knee in the place where it still wasn't fully healed from the surgery. One would think I'd remember that kind of fall, but perhaps the pain of it blacked me out.

For one horrible moment, it also occurs to me that Allen, who had driven, might have had too many sips of straight rum and veered the car off the road on the way home. It was only a month ago that a boy in our class got drunk and drove his car into a lake, where it sunk like an old tire, and he had to unroll the window to swim out. For a moment, I think whiplash could be responsible for my lumped head and stiff neck, not to mention the amnesia. But then I decide I'd surely remember something from the moments before we crashed: gasping, blackness spreading across the windshield, the sound of pine branches scraping the flanks of the car.

I should call one of the girls who'd been with me, to see if they can fill in the gaps. But when I look for the portable phone, someone has removed it from its cradle on my bureau, as if to prevent that from happening.

I STEP SOFTLY to my full-length mirror, using the ballet-walk where you stand only on the balls of your feet.

The image reflected back at me makes me cup my mouth with both hands: I look like a woman in a zombie film from the 1950s. My hair looks like it's been replaced with a Halloween wig; it is teased into a high pile of knots and dusted with dirt and leaves, and something sticky has lacquered the ends together. From this position, I can make out a whole range of fingerprints that wrap around my forearms in shades of brownish-blue and yellow. A cat-scratch is carved into the corner of my eye; aside from that, my face looks slack and pasty, but unmarked.

I can see now that I'm wearing hospital booties with my gown. They are blue ankle-socks with plastic beads on the soles, presumably so you won't slip on the linoleum floors while you're fleeing the ward.

I add another item to the list of possible accidents: psychiatric emergency.

My alarm clock says it's 10:30. That tells me that whatever happened must be serious because no one has bothered to wake me for my poetry workshop. I was scheduled to spend the weekend at a conference for Worcester County's most promising young writers, and it started more than two hours ago. The workshop is one of those college résumé padders that my mother would send me to in any state short of death. (Just two months ago, she *forced* me to spend a week at diplomacy camp at Washington, D.C., and just to spite her, I'd skipped the lectures on youth leadership to buy forties of beer and drink them with local delinquents on the hill behind the dorm.)

I would stay in my room all day, trying to figure out what happened, if I didn't desperately need a glass of water. My throat is so parched it feels raw, and each swallow is arduous.

I keep the hospital booties on because the morning has the cold nip of fall, but I trade the gown for a sweatshirt and a pair of flannel pants. I try to brush my hair, and realize with one painful stroke that the task could take all afternoon, so instead I wind the whole snarled mess into a lopsided bun. I look at myself in the mirror and wince before heading downstairs to meet my parents with the premonition that I am fucked.

It is my first blackout.

I will never again experience one so comprehensive. I get the details first from Claire, who I find pretending to sleep on the couch in the living room. My parents will rehash them with me again later, as will Kat and Allen and Abby when I see them Monday morning at school. The remaining gaps I'll fill in years later, when I get the courage to ask my father more questions, and when I see my emergency file.

I passed out on the dock in a puddle of my own vomit. I imagine it was mostly liquor because my dad told the doctor I didn't eat dinner that night. Before that, I pulled my shirt up over my shoulders to show my bra to someone's brother because, knowing I was slipping into oblivion, he'd asked me what color it was. I'd also professed a soul-shattering love for an older boy who had taken me for a drunken walk in the woods a few months earlier—a boy who had pushed my back into the cragged banks of a stream and called me a baby when I wouldn't let him pull off my underwear.

After I tottered and fell sideways onto the planks of the dock, nobody could wake me. Allen, Abby, Claire, and Kat carried me up the hill to the road by my arms and legs, which is why my body bears what look like forty finger-shaped bruises. They dropped me a few times, too, which explains the raised bumps on my butt and the back of my head.

When they tell me this, I envision a dead body—not my body, but the body of someone in a thriller movie who has just been clubbed with a paperweight and dragged in a bloody streak across the floor by her feet. When I ask them why they didn't roll me up in a rug, no one finds it funny.

The girl whose house we were at brought out a pair of pilled sweatpants because I'd retched all over my jeans. I can't imagine that she would have let me inside, given that I was liable to puke over all manner of Venetian rugs and calico curtains, so I'll come to imagine that they pulled off my jeans outside on the porch, leaving my underwear fully exposed while they struggled to stick my feet through the sweatpants' elasticized legs. Then they draped me across the backseat of Allen's car and drove me to Abby's house.

From what I can tell from the medical records, this whole ordeal took at least an hour. It was around 12:30. Abby's parents were asleep when my friends lugged me in through the front door.

They tried to give me a shower, to clean off the combination of liquor, vomit, dirt, and leaves that was adhered to me. I'll never know if I was fully naked or if they left my under-things on because I am too embarrassed to ask. Nor will I know if Allen was there while they did it, though I don't know how they could have held me under the showerhead without his strength. Afterward, they must have put me back into the sweatpants because they are there in the plastic bag that my dad carried home from the hospital, and they are all but crusted with vomit. My mom will wash them and insist that I return them, in a most undignified moment, to the girl at school on Monday morning.

By the time I was showered, I had already missed my curfew, so Abby called my father to tell him not to worry. She said I'd fallen asleep while we were watching a movie and asked if I could stay the night.

My father hadn't believed her. He asked to speak to her parents, and when she said they were sleeping, he asked to talk to me. I was dangling over the edge of her brother's bunk bed, getting sick again. In a second-long flash of memory, I recall someone shaking my shoulders and telling me to pull it together for two minutes, probably so I could ask my dad if I could stay the night. When they held the receiver to my ear, I slurred, "I'll be home in fifteen minutes, Daddy."

Years later, he will say it was one of those pivotal moments—

he sensed that the whole world swung on whether he went back to sleep or drove to me.

CLAIRE WENT to the hospital with my father. She was an emergency medical trainee and knew how to calculate heart rates and breaths per minute, which she did throughout the thirty-minute drive.

After everything, it is the thought of Claire answering my dad's questions that makes me feel most guilty. He is intimidating when he's not trying to be, and bloodcurdling when he is. If he puts the full boom into his voice, he can make boyfriends tremble and customer-service reps cry. When he asked Claire what happened, she told him nearly the whole truth. She injected fiction only when he asked where we got the vodka—she said older boys from the neighborhood brought it, instead of admitting that we poured it from her parents' depository of Absolut jugs.

When the car pulled up in front of the emergency room, my father says, he carried me through the doors the way he used to carry me to bed.

The doctors tested my urine for drugs. According to the doctor's notes, it was the only time I showed signs of life. When the nurse was trying to insert a catheter I kept muttering, "Stop, it's embarrassing," proving that even semiconscious, I was self-conscious. In my chart, there are ten pages of lab results, including all sorts of decimal numbers and strands of letters that I don't understand, but really don't need to. Alcohol alone was responsible for knocking me out, a combination of rum and vodka and coffee liqueur. On one page there is a long list of chemical compounds for which I came up NONDETECT.

Claire tells me the doctors seemed certain they would find

some substance, besides alcohol, sweeping through my system. It is the year that everyone first read about Rohypnol, the brand name for flunitrazepam, the tranquilizer used to treat sleeplessness, anxiety, convulsions, and muscle tension. Four months earlier, two women who had been raped after someone slipped them Rohypnol testified before Congress to urge them to take action against the vast numbers of people who were smuggling the drug into the United States. One of them said of the man who raped her, "This guy could have sawed me in half and I wouldn't have known the difference." A classification known as "date-rape drugs" had emerged. And everyone in the ER thought I was on them.

My dad will say later that the doctors were far less compassionate when my test results revealed I was just another teenaged girl who'd nearly poisoned herself by drinking. I will always wonder, though, if the staff's lack of sympathy had more to do with another brief flash of a memory, in which I clawed at the tubes tethered to my arm and screamed at the faint impression of a woman, maybe a doctor or nurse, calling her a "dumbass bitch."

No one could imagine that I'd done this to myself. My dad, particularly, was convinced that someone held a gun to my head. It was beyond his comprehension that I'd willed myself to this level of past gone. I was an A student in English, psychology, and art. Sure, math and science were touch-and-go, but that just meant I was right-brained. As far as he knew, will was what I reserved for the PSATs and ballet auditions. It was what I used to solicit cash for the mall.

My charts say my skin was cold and clammy, which is one of the signs of alcohol poisoning, as is the fact that I was only semiconscious. When my tests came back they showed my blood alcohol content to be 0.25. A 0.4 BAC is considered lethal for the average person, but it can take less for young people and first-time drinkers.

At sixteen, I'm 5'2" and 105 pounds with a ski parka on, which means it would take about one hour of downing eight to ten drinks to kill me. Claire told the doctors I'd been drinking for an hour and a half. I'd had half a thermos of vodka, plus immeasurable sips of rum and Kahlúa, straight from the bottles. As the doctor told my father, a few more drinks and I'd have fell into a coma or died right there on the dock.

No matter how many ways I go over the story, I'll never know if some part of me sought that kind of close call. A good bit of it was inexperience; it was not waiting for all those gulps of liquor to absorb into my system, but just expecting to feel them right away. But I also wonder if that night wasn't the first glimmer of a budding death drive, what Freud called the instinct we all have to return to the perfect stillness we felt before birth. Other girls my age steered into that urge with starvation diets or razor blades, but I chose alcohol because it seemed far less fanatical. On nights when I felt sad, particularly, I could feel my drinking accelerate.

I'd been saddened a lot lately, and stressed. Even with new friends like Kat, high school was a nightmarish system of checks and balances. It required observing yourself constantly, making sure you distinguished yourself enough to be accepted, but not to the point where you might garner resentment. Schoolwork required inscribing index cards for hours, all the while maintaining the illusion that you didn't give a shit about the decimals of your GPA. Getting a date required acting just disinterested enough to make a boy interested in asking you. Every consideration required reconsideration. I'd begun waking up at 4:30 A.M. so I could reappraise my outfit for the school day; the fate of the next two years seemed to weigh on whether I chose suede cowboy boots or Adidas sneakers.

My parents always swore that in my childhood they had to let me win at board games. If, by the lucky stroke of the plastic wheel, my father would accidentally beat me at Candy Land, I would fly into fits of bawling that I'm told would last for hours. If I couldn't triumph, I didn't want to play. I would pack up my toys and go home. This was perhaps how I felt about being sixteen.

But I'll never know if I intended to forfeit. They pumped my stomach, and I sprung back to life that morning in my bedroom. I went directly back to homeroom. I did not pass "Go." I did not collect $200.

SATURDAY, at breakfast, my parents seem almost serene. The coffee is still steaming. The Saturday *Boston Globe* is still spread out beneath us, in sections. My dad is sitting across from me, with his elbows folded on the woven tablecloth my parents bought in Greece early in their marriage. My mom is at the head of the table, with her hands crossed on the paper's business section. Bear is pacing the floor by our feet, hoping for a dropped cube of cantaloupe. The seating arrangement makes me feel like a fox in an English hunting painting. It feels like everyone is closing in around me, and I feel the terror of being surrounded.

My mother starts the conversation and I end up turning sideways in my chair to face her. From this position, I can avoid the gaze of my father, which is sterner on account of his being at the hospital. My mom doesn't try to recap the time line. Instead, she says, "I assume Claire filled you in."

It makes me wonder if my parents had had Claire sleep on the living-room couch because it spared them the awkwardness of rehashing the gory details for me. In fact, we'd waited to have this discussion until my dad and I had driven Claire home. Even with the babble of NPR, the car was so silent I could hear the engine purring.

My mom says the problem is not that I've been experimenting with alcohol; she'd made it clear in Ocean City that I am old enough to do that. In fact, she says, it is probably a good idea for me to toy around with drinking now, while I still live at home, instead of waiting until I get to college, where the environment makes inexperience even more risky.

She says she wouldn't have cared if I'd been drinking at home last night. I could have drunk myself into a similar stupor, she says, gone upstairs, and passed out in my bed. At home, she would have known I was safe. But anything could have happened to me on that dock. She says, "What if you fell into the water and drowned? What if you had been raped?"

My dad says hardly anything. He sets his reading glasses down on top of the front page and looks at me with eyes I don't know how to interpret. I can't remember the last time he looked at me this unremittingly. The moments we spend together usually revolve around some type of project. Typically, we talk while we cook, spray-paint patio furniture, or make candles out of melted-down crayons. Those times, his eyes are focused on the peppers in the wok, or the jet from the paint can, or the bottle we fill with hot wax. He is the type of dad who expresses concern by constructing things, or cooking, or shopping for gadgets, by making sure I have a full stomach, a computer Zip drive, and Gore-Tex boots come spring thaw. I've never seen the expression he is giving me now. It's not outrage, really, or disappointment. It is the look of crude disbelief.

The only concern he voices aloud is about my missing the young writers' conference. He asks (rhetorically, of course), "Do you see how drinking makes you miss out on other fun activities?"

My mother cries a little, which always makes me cry, too. I've always been like a dog in the way that I absorb her moods. I have been listening to my parents speak with a tension like a rock in my throat. As my mother cries, I have to keep swallowing. In the end, I give up and bawl soundlessly. I use the sleeve of my sweatshirt to wipe the wetness from my face.

At the time, I think my mother cries solely because I've frightened her. But years from now, more drunken sons and daughters will surface among her relatives and friends. There will be comatose daughters on respirators, daughters laid up in hospitals with broken cheekbones, car accidents, DUI charges, and sons whose early admissions to Ivy League universities are threatened by alcohol-related suspensions. Years from now, my mother will explain more to me. She'll say, "When you choose to stay at home to rear your kids, a dead-drunk daughter makes you question an entire decade's worth of motherhood—you wonder if the career you gave up made the slightest difference in the personalities you've been shaping."

My sister is eleven. As luck would have it, she is spending the night at a friend's house, so she misses all the clues that point to this black crime. My mom won't tell her about it until she's - eighteen, when it's used as a cautionary tale to warn her off drinking, and by that time the handles of the liquor cabinet will wear a silver luggage lock. My sister will be appalled. But mostly, she'll mourn the fact that, as the youngest, she's always the last to know.

There is not much to say in my defense. There is no point in telling a fraction of the truth because there is no gray area in which to weasel. All the facts of the night are laid out on the table, like plates of fruit and toast.

While my parents talk, I nod like a dashboard Chihuahua and say, "I know, I know, I know." I certainly say I am sorry; it's the only thing I can think to say with the hospital bracelet still sliding up and down my wrist.

I am hangover-free due to the large bags of saline pumped through my forearm's thin veins. Still, I climb the stairs back up to my room and sleep for the rest of the day. It's like slipping back into the hole of the blackout—in sleep, I can forget again.

Tomorrow, I'll go for the second day of the young writers' conference, telling the tweed-jacketed director only that I've been sick. In a low-lit corner classroom, I'll try to write a poem I decide to call "Lush," but I won't be able to come up with more than a few first words, scarred by cross-outs.

I know the whole ordeal needs to be written about. But two days afterward, I am still far too close to the night to see it clearly. I am looking only at the incident, and the result is a lot like the pictures in our biology textbook, taken at microscopic range, the ones that look like billowing clouds until you read the caption and realize you are looking at magnified cotton swabs. Years will pass before I can see the night of my stomach-pumping to scale. I will need the perspective of six more years before I understand what I am looking at.

. . .

MY PARENTS ground me for the remainder of November, which is the cruelest season to be in lockdown. There are school-sponsored carnivals. There are semiformal gymnasium dances. There are evening football games, where mist levitates in the stadium lights. And there are remote keg parties afterward.

There are parties that require a two-mile hike through the thick New England woods, crunching through dead leaves, and dodging the occasional small-town cop on the prowl. There are parties like I'll never know again. The air in the clearing smells of apple orchards, Bud Light, and pine-dense bonfire smoke. The weather seems always on the verge of snow, and some boy, who is sitting on a log a few feet away, always seems to be on the verge of crossing the fire flicker to put his arm around me.

Sometime during my punishment, the guilt I feel as a result of the incident melts away. After a few days, my parents stop talking about the reason I am grounded; they reference it only with raised eyebrows when I make some complaint. Likewise, the girls in the cafeteria, who in those first few days after the accident were a flurry of whispering, direct their attention to somebody else. The alarm I felt that morning in my bedroom fades from memory. It is replaced by the agitation that comes with being restricted.

My parents have never made good wardens, and the Zailckas Home Penitentiary is notoriously low-security. Here, a prisoner is free to leaf through fashion magazines, drive to the video store, or surf Internet chat rooms 'til dawn. Phone calls are unlimited. And time off for good behavior will certainly be afforded, if such a thing ever occurs.

In fact, the only real rule in the house of correction is that I can't leave it. At least, not after prime time. This means bonfire parties are out. So is the repertoire of fictions that I regularly use to disguise them: dinner at Applebee's, movies at the General Cinema, fishing in Harvard, canoeing in Concord, hiking Mount Wachusett, throwing spares at the Bowl-A-Way.

At ten every night, my dad punches the keypad on the security system in a series of calculated beeps, to which a robotic woman's voice answers "Al-arm Sys-tem is on!" I listen to him ascend the stairs to go to bed, to Bear's dog tags jingling two or three steps behind him, and know there is no escape. The entire house stirs whenever the system announces "Al-arm Sys-tem is off!" It's enough to wonder whether it's in place to keep criminals out, or to keep me in.

These nights, the house must look picture-perfect. For a month, my parents never have to answer the question: "It's ten P.M., do you know where your children are?" My sister and I are sachets stuffed into the pockets of our beds.

Nights, the floodlights from the perennial garden splash light over our front door, where my mother has hung a grapevine wreath. Even with the blinds closed, the light gets tossed against my bedroom wall, too. It's bright enough to read by, and well suited for shadow puppets. I've long forgotten how to lace my fingers into the shape of a barking dog, and opt instead for my favorite gesture, the flipped bird. I examine the silhouette of my middle finger from every imaginable angle, saying "Fuck you" to no one in particular. I perfect all the various forms— thumb in, thumb out, with a wrist twirl—before I lie down to close my eyes, deciding that I hate just about everyone.

Our house is close enough to the high school that I can hear the noise from its football stadium. There's the low echo of my English teacher's voice, announcing the players' names; the horns from the marching band; the swell of applause after each touchdown; and the bleacher-stomping, which sounds like thunder. Somewhere past the edge of the driveway, the mailbox, the old tire swing, I can hear football season. My friends are sneaking Jack Daniel's in the school parking lot during halftime. There is a play in motion.

The days scuttle by, and I keep myself occupied. I divide my closet into a stack of sweaters to keep, and dresses to bag up for Goodwill. I play GameBoy, drop balls of cookie dough onto aluminum sheets, and watch reruns of *The Real World: Miami,* which is the equivalent of a frontal lobotomy. I go to my math tutor nightly and try to twig the cosine rule for hyperbolic triangles.

I never find the file in the birthday cake, that secret escape through the doggy door or out the guest-room window. I never slither breathless through my father's tomato plants, like Tim Robbins in *The Shawshank Redemption,* to emerge at the neighbors' swing set, rain-soaked, jovial, free! I never give my parents the opportunity to search every doghouse, whorehouse, or crack-house. I pay my debt to society because I'm guilty.

I feel confident I could escape if I wanted to; I could shoulder out a bathroom window and walk the two miles it would take to meet so-and-so at such-and-such a party. The most high-tech safeguards are no match for the sixteen-year-old mind.

But in the end, it is my friends themselves who have the authority to keep me at home. My trip to the hospital doesn't exactly cause our falling-out; we still meet at each other's lockers between classes. In study hall, we still paint our fingernails with a black Magic Marker. They still call me on Saturday afternoons to disclose the details of their Friday nights, filling me in on the party that took place in an abandoned barn or someone's unfinished basement. I am always alerted to who threw up, who was felt up, and how long it took the police chief to show up. But no one is willing to aid and abet my escape. Never comes that call to throw down thy hair.

I don't blame them. The only A I was ever afforded in biology was in the chapter on evolution. The idea of the able-bodied predator was the only concept that made sense to me. In nature, everyone roots for the marauder. That's why we'll glue ourselves to Animal Planet for hours, stoned or straight, to watch a pair of African lions descend on a gazelle as though we aren't sure how it will end. Everyone would rather be a lion. If we feel sorry for the lesser species it is only because they were sorry enough to get caught.

That night at the dock, I proved I was the weedy one. And because I couldn't handle my liquor, because that weakness endangered everyone else's drinking with the threat of getting caught, I was temporarily cast aside.

I'd managed to get Abby in trouble. Her parents had stumbled to the door when my dad turned up at her house. Since she hadn't been drunk herself, they only grounded her for a weekend, but it was enough to make Allen and Kat temporarily turn on me. They made me apologize to Abby that Monday during lunch period, and I did, because I felt sorry at the time.

But the more I think about Abby during my house arrest, the less apologetic I feel. I can't be sorry for her or her parents, who ban me from their house afterward on the basis that I'm bad company. I decide her parents are either the world's heaviest sleepers, or they've known the score all along. They've slept through infinite Saturday nights where we mixed drinks in their kitchen, or smoked a joint in their backyard, or passed out dead-drunk in their basement in a group of twenty, looking like victims of a cult mass suicide. I think they look the other way and justify it to themselves by saying that as long as Abby drinks in their house, she is under their control.

A month later, Allen will carry Kat, dead-drunk, into Abby's parents' New Year's Eve dinner party. And as much as I'll be able to empathize, the irony will be almost poetic. After it happens, I'll think her parents will retract their harsh judgment of me, realizing that this kind of thing can happen to anybody. But it won't happen that way. In the end, her parents will blame me for Kat's near-overdose, even though I wasn't there when it happened. They'll tell the other neighborhood parents, "This kind of thing is contagious," like teenage pregnancy or suicide. They will refer to me as though I were the carrier drunk that had infected their children.

For all these reasons, a month of being grounded is a blessing. It allows time to pass, and people to forget about me. I imagine myself like the junkie bound for inpatient rehab, or somebody's pregnant daughter gone to Utah to give up the baby for adoption. I can emerge sometime in December in good health. I can come back from "visiting relatives" or that "much-needed break." One month is enough time for somebody else to replace me as the scapegoat for underage drinking. Surely someone else will do something stupid, and they will be strung up as a reminder to everyone else.

It doesn't take long. I rejoin the pack when an eleventh-grade girl, drunk on whiskey, puts a cigarette out on her ex-boyfriend's face. It allows me to sneak back into the game like someone who has been tossed out of dodgeball, in spite of being pronounced officially "out." I do it while the world is distracted, hurling its ammunition at somebody else.

THE USUAL

ALL YOU CAN DRINK

THERE COULDN'T BE a better name for freshman year of college. Every year, 2.5 million Americans sally forth for their first semester, an experience that isn't just foreign, it's unsullied, like a brand-new T-shirt to push their heads through.

Four years later, when graduation impels us into some obliged nostalgia, many of us will say our first year was our favorite year of college because the fabric of experience was still vivid. Freshman year has a freshness that will be absent later, when campus life feels thick with impurities and the novelty of self-sufficiency has faded. The small acts of sovereignty that exhilarated us during those beginning months, like wearing slippers to class or eating Lucky Charms for dinner, will be old hat by graduation. Like the desktop computers we bought before we left home, it will be hard to believe there was ever a time these things looked new.

Drinking is particularly fresh at the beginning. Even if you drank every weekend in high school, to the point where you were all but sick of those frothy cups of Bud Light, college will renew your enthusiasm for them—namely because there will be an overwhelming sentiment that underage drinking is now okay. The adult universe may not extol the nights we'll spend swallowing enough rum to pass out on the tile floor of the dorm bathroom, but they accept it as a part of the college experience, a life-stage behavior as inevitable as bad eating habits and casual sex. Administrators at the University of Colorado have gone so far as to propose "drinking permits," which would allow students to drink even if they're not yet twenty-one.

As a freshman, I will quickly discover that even when I'm not drunk or hungover, adults will assume I am anyway. During a particularly silent Friday-morning class, a teacher will say, to the rows of students drooping over the kidney-shaped surfaces of their school desks, "It looks like you all started the weekend early." When I go to the emergency room with a gut-wrenching stomach virus, the doctor, refusing to believe some natural sickness landed me on his collapsible cot, will repeatedly ask, "Are you sure you're not drunk?" followed by, "Are you sure you're not pregnant?"

When Robert Frost said, "College is refuge from hasty judgment," he was undoubtedly referring to the infinite hours of class time spent debating one topic or another, but the quote can easily be used to describe the way college insulates students in regard to alcohol abuse. Before and after college, drinking oneself into a state of blissful oblivion requires a degree of secrecy. In high school, it needs to be hidden from parents. In the working world, it must be downplayed to bosses, or concerned friends, or lovers. But in college, we can wear our alcohol abuse as proudly as our university sweatshirts; the two concepts are virtually synonymous.

WE ARRIVE at Syracuse University in two cars. My dad and my sister ride in one, and my mom and I take turns driving the other. The backseats are piled high with things that are mine alone: a computer, a desk lamp, bed linens, flip-flops for the shower, hiking boots for the 115 annual inches of snow, a yellow parka that will always look too hopeful to wear. My assets are spanking-new and still creased from the box. Still, when upperclassmen, unloading freshmen luggage for credit, pile my boxes onto the sidewalk, it looks like the Pyramid of Giza, and I am disturbed by how much of the past I am carting in with me.

I DIDN'T WANT to go to S.U. But then, I didn't want to enroll in any of the schools that would have me. Years of academic ambivalence had caught up with me. Of the six schools I applied to, I was waitlisted by three and rejected outright by one. I was accepted to S.U., the school my parents were pushing for, and to a neo-hippie liberal arts school in the Finger Lakes, the one that I preferred. I waited until the night before the deadline to decide between the two. For an hour, I sat at the kitchen table with slick pamphlets spread out in front of me, comparing pictures of grinning students in lab goggles. Later, I'll suspect the university recycles these coeds; they bear a curious resemblance to the ones pictured on campus flyers that read, MOST S.U. STUDENTS DON'T BINGE DRINK!*

I finally chose S.U. for what my mom calls "the total college experience": for community darkrooms, club snowboarding, and Big East basketball tickets—things that, in four years, I will never see or do or buy.

Everything about the city of Syracuse is gray: the ancient six-story candle factories, the slate slab of monument in Clinton Square, the fog standing fast over Lake Ontario, the pale asphalt trail of Interstate 81. Even in August, everything has the color and smell of salt, residuum from the tons the city dumps on the streets and sidewalks in a vain attempt to break the ice that will never thaw away. Syracuse's official motto is "A City for All Seasons," but during the months that I'm there it will be perpetual winter.

S.U. resides, like Goblin City, above the city's duplexes and one-way streets, state fairgrounds, a Native American reservation, a metastasizing mall, and a few neighborhoods that you don't want to get lost in but do anyway. Locals refer to it as "the hill" because its Romanesque halls sit on a slope overlooking the state psychiatric hospital and a stretch of federally funded housing, exerting their out-and-out massiveness. A bird's-eye view of the city shows the six-and-a-half acre roof of the Carrier Dome like a giant bleach stain on a gray T-shirt. The sports stadium was named after its benefactor, Carrier Air Conditioning, but we will later joke it is because it "carries" Michelob during games.

Nestled less than one mile away, in the valley below, are

*In 1999, S.U. administrators sincerely thought this campaign was the best allocation of the $88,435 the school received from the U.S. Department of Education under its Alcohol and Other Drug Prevention Models on College Campuses grant competition.

thirty-two bars, six liquor stores, and twelve mini-marts that sell beer cans in brown-paper lunch bags.

I HAVE immediate trouble making nice.

My room is on a girls-only floor of Brewster Hall. The floor is an L-shaped configuration of rooms: two corridors of doors, each trimmed with daisies cut from orange construction paper and lettered with each girl's name and hometown—CAREY W., PARKERSBURG, OR. ROSE F., LAUREL, MD. TANYA C., AVENEL, NJ. I have a roommate named Wendi P., a snarl-mouthed theater major who has already traveled the length of the L, knocking on doors and shaking hands with just about everybody.

I, on the other hand, sit on the extra-long bed that my mother fussily made just a few hours ago, shielding my face behind a paperback and reading the same paragraph over and over because I can't seem to concentrate. The door to the room is open, so I won't seem overtly antisocial, and through it, I can hear half a dozen stereos clamoring in a way that strikes me as territorial. In the hallway, I can also hear acquaintances being made. Girls are speaking in the chirping tones of false enthusiasm, and I hold my breath for a moment of closer-listening, to see if I can match the voices to the names I've read on the doors. I know I could, and maybe should, poke my head into the hallway and introduce myself, but I haven't the faintest idea what I'd say beyond giving my name.

Within a few hours of our arrival, our Resident Advisor, Jana A., calls the floor's thirty residents to the lounge for an orientation meeting. I sit on the charcoal-colored carpet, cuddling my knees and trying to figure out how the twenty-nine other girls appear to be good friends already. They have paired off into cliques of five or six, based on the proximity of their dorm rooms. While Jana reviews the rules about quiet hours, fire drills, and how to handle roommate disputes, the lounge hums with the undertones of girls joking among themselves.

But by the time she gets to the drug and alcohol policy, the room is mum. The girls stop murmuring and sit upright in a solemn moment of silence. Jana says, "Oh, *now* I have your full attention." She reads aloud from the student handbook. It's the full deal about how the university is "deeply committed to providing a safe and healthy learning environment," and how "abusing alcohol interferes with one's ability to fully participate in the academic community." The doctrine is roughly as follows:

- Do not buy, drink, or hide alcohol in your desk drawers, if you are under 21.
- Do not be publicly shit-faced.
- Do not drink and drive.
- Do not make, use, or sell fake IDs.
- If you are caught in the act of any of the aforementioned sins, you will be subject to extreme brutality, also known as weekly meetings with an addiction counselor.

When Jana finishes reading, she closes the handbook and hugs it to her chest. Her arms are tan and sturdy. She is the type of girl I expect to find at S.U., but in the end will meet very few of. She has a comic, honest face that looks wholly practical. Everyone watches her with the distinct feeling that she will say more.

"Look," she says, lowering her voice and leaning down the way people do when they speak to children. "I know what goes on. I was in your shoes just one year ago. Believe me, I'm not going to go out of my way to get you into trouble. I don't want to report you any more than you want to be reported. If you drink, keep your voices down and your doors closed. What goes on behind closed doors is your business."

Someone in the back of the room makes a crowing noise that turns into a war cry. More girls clap. Jana's eyes go as big as quarters, and she looks over both her shoulders like she's checking to make sure the Resident Director hasn't crept up behind her. She presses her index finger to her lips and breathes a fierce *Shhh*.

With that, we establish our own understanding of the university alcohol policy. The guiding principle is, *Out of sight, out of mind.* That is to say, as long as we keep our drinking out of sight, the administration won't mind if we do it.

I GO TO my first party two days after I go to my first class, which feels deviant but statistically isn't, since half of all freshmen find their first binge-drinking opportunity within the first week of college, often before they've even purchased any textbooks.*

In truth, I don't even care to go. Sometime after I had my stomach pumped, alcohol, the powers of which I once held as supernatural, was pushed to my mind's periphery when puppy love materialized in the form of a boyfriend named Reed. Reed nearly repulsed me at first, with his wool sweaters, unwashed hair, and the scent of sweat and pot he wore like eau de cologne. But he came into my life like a bowling ball tossed into a birdbath, which is to say, my adoration for him displaced my passion for everything else. When Reed appeared, my desire to drink—along with my desire to spend time with family and friends—sloshed out of my consciousness in one swell.

Of course, the appearance of Reed seems unrelated to the

*The 2001 Harvard School of Public Health College Alcohol Study.

abrupt disappearance of alcohol. It will take more accidents and more men before I can discern the pattern. Only then will I be able to see that every time the consequences of drinking leave me too shaken, I break from it and bury myself in the safety of some schoolboy's arms.

For now, I am rapt with Reed, and he is six hours away at the University of New Hampshire. Instead of going to a party, I'd rather be in my dorm room, draining a calling card of untold minutes during one of our nightly talks.

I only agree to go because when Wendi and a girl named Tess invite me to go along with them, it is the first bit of dialogue I've had in three days. I go because I am already a week ahead in my class reading. I have already eaten five meals alone in the cafeteria. I have already called two other universities to inquire about transferring. I go because I have been pulled from sleep the past three nights by girls' laughter, which sang through the cinderblock walls of my room like notes played in soft repetition. I go because already I feel isolation I swear I could die from, loneliness and panic so stifling they might asphyxiate me as I sleep.

I go because a party is the only way I can think of to make friends.

The party is in the basement of a house at the far end of Euclid Avenue, which is a residential street west of campus where upperclassmen rent time-ravaged duplexes, a good three miles from my new address.

Tess got the street number from junior boys distributing fliers in the freshmen dorms, which is a weekly occurrence we will come to look forward to. The weekly barrage of pamphlets advertising off-campus parties will arrive more often than takeout menus, and in the beginning months, we will spend much of our time comparing their bills of fare, debating the merits of Jell-O shots versus mixed drinks, kegs versus all the cans you can drink.

En route to the party, we amble up the sloped sidewalks of North Campus, past the domed roof of the chapel, the university bookstore, and the alumni center, which was once a frat house. Tess shares her cigarettes with me. Wendi doesn't smoke and, I'll find out later, hardly drinks. The stroll through campus reminds me of the time I walked through a carnival after all the rides had shut down; everything looks just that ghoulish, just that sealed-off, but open.

As we walk, we compare life stories. Adult strangers do this by giving an inventory of their careers, their spouses, their children's schools; by trading names of decorators and personal trainers, recipes, and favorite brands of driveway sealant. And as girls, we do it, too, by quantifying experiences. Even as strangers, our conversations drift back to the personal stuff of drinking, sex, and drugs. Within an hour of meeting Tess, I may not be able to tell you the last book she read, what she does for exercise, or if she eats or skips breakfast; I may not even know her last name (in college, I'll end up knowing almost everyone by first name only), but I know how many boys she's slept with, whether she prefers beer or liquor, and if she does speed to study.

We don't necessarily flaunt these facts because we're *proud* of our delinquency; we do it because the confessions represent our only milestones and emotional investments as of yet. They are the only way we can think to distinguish ourselves. None of us have jobs or degrees. Many of us still live in the cities where we were born, with the families to whom we were supernaturally assigned. Without our dirty little accolades, we are the same sex, the same age, the same *kind*. In the dorm, we sleep in identical beds, in identical rooms, like rows of saplings staked in a nursery.

• • •

THE PARTY itself would not be memorable if it were not our first. At the back door we pay five dollars for red plastic cups, the big ones that I guess were manufactured for the sole purpose of serving alcohol because I can't imagine why anyone would want to drink that much of anything else. The keg is in the basement, where the music is muffled from public-safety officers who patrol the avenue on their weekend rounds. In the coming months, I will learn that the drains in the foundations make beer-sticky floors easier to hose down. The ceiling is outlined with strands of Christmas lights, which in college will qualify as atmosphere.

We each drink three beers.

The boldness that Bud Light sends rolling back to me is just what I've been missing the past few days. When I talk to Tess, thoughts diffuse through me without any of the hesitation that so often trips me up. I speak without rehearsing the words in my head beforehand, and she listens, clapping her hands and agreeing with her whole heart. When I laugh, the hum of my own happiness is astonishing.

By my fourth cup, I have decided to sit on the basement's washing machine in order to escape the brush of too many bodies hurling for a space around the keg. Nearly a hundred freshman who, in this first week, are overcome by the novelty of a five-dollar beer binge, have crammed themselves into the confines of the basement's concrete walls. The air is as moist and misted as it is in the dorm showers.

I am planning a path through the bodies to the bathroom when the basement lights blow out like candles. In the absence of music, the three boys who live here appear in the doorway with flashlights to say, "We've blown a fuse. Everyone has to go.

Everyone has to go *now*." And I follow the throng of people that inches up the basement stairs, by the light of Tess's cigarette lighter, which she holds up like someone at a concert expecting an encore.

Outside the street is blind dark: no house lights, no headlights, streetlights that I only notice now in their powerlessness. The three miles back to the dorm is a spun-out shadow. There is a drop of rain and then two, and then water plummets from the sky like an overturned bucket, soaking us through. The sky claps and ignites deep purple. Far off, I hear a sound like a chain saw cutting through wood. Branches break themselves off of tree trunks. Garbage cans wheel themselves down the street.

After a few beers, I am usually only mildly tipped. But this time, I feel deeply drunk, like I'm in a free-fall. I am Dorothy snapped up by the tornado, and the Wicked Witch is whizzing by on a stick. I inch forward, huddling together with Wendi and Tess, and it's almost fun. The gusts of wind that drive against my back feel violent enough to launch me into orbit.

When we finally pull open the dorm's front door, all three hundred residents are crouched on the floor of the lobby. A few people are praying.

Beer is still pushing into my system, and the feeling is powerful and fluid, like a river emptying itself into an ocean. Under its ether, I am insensitive to panic. My head is the quietest it has been in months. I sit cross-legged on the floor, with my back to the broad wall of student mailboxes, and let Tess lean her head against my shoulder. She is crying, and I put one hand on her rain-soaked pant leg, to tell her it is going to be okay.

The world outside is bust, but I have been salvaged. From the junk of my character, I have pieced together some courage to pull around me. I feel like a quilt made from scraps.

. . .

THE LOCAL newspapers call it a microburst, a cold Canadian air mass that rolled into a slack system of hot summer air. They say fall met summer with a bang. The world outside my window is a mess of live wires, toppled steeples, overturned tractor-trailers, and twisted highway signs. On TV, reporters interview a succession of victims, one person whose chimney collapsed on her leg, another whose toolshed blew through a McDonald's. Roofs are blown off campus apartments, and six hundred students are homeless.

The university takes four days to clean up the wreckage. With classes cancelled, we take the four-day weekend to recover and booze.

The long weekend is an unexpected delight. It is the collegiate version of a snow day, which we will never be granted at S.U. because it snows every day. I am thrilled by the idea of spending nights drinking with Tess in our dorm rooms, and days recuperating in flannel pajamas, eating sugary cereal and watching Jenny Jones reform girls like me.

As the semester progresses, I will come to depend on this cycle. A rhythm will come to pass, whereby afternoon classes will unroll into evenings of swilling cups over card games, singing along to records, and barreling down the hallways of the dorm until I stub a toe or run out of breath. Then, evenings will unroll into mornings, to ear-ringing, nausea, and hard-sleeping afternoons.

Drinking, which was once a novelty, will become the usual. Its repetition will structure my days once I realize that college, which looked like a premier destination in high school, is just another static period of time-biding. Drinking will give college a circular configuration, like a holding pattern I can navigate while I await clearance in the real world.

My class schedule accommodates the cycle of my drinking. Monday through Thursday, I have Spanish class at 8:30 A.M., which is a ghastly hour, but allows for no classes on Friday. In the coming semesters, I will learn to design my schedules with this aim in mind. I will comb the course catalog exhaustively, weighing my requirements, trying this and that combination of classes. I will happily have four, even five, ninety-minute lectures in one day if it frees up another day for pure, unadulterated slothfulness. My craftiest friends will devise hangover-free schedules, meaning no classes before 11 A.M. and fixed four-day weekends.

Tess has Fridays off, too, and together we start our weekends on Thursday nights. Tess has a friend, an older boy she knows from home, who buys us wine coolers at the One Stop convenience store. We drink the way Jana instructed us: In Tess's room, behind a locked door, we sit opposite one another on the carpet, hands curled around full bottles of hard lemonade, ashing our cigarettes into empty bottles of sparkling pineapple breeze. Halfway through a bottle of the sweet stuff I feel a headache coming on. After one, I chatter maniacally. After two, Tess tells me to keep my voice down; I am yelling bloody murder.

Sometimes, when the mini-mart runs out of Wild Island wine coolers, Tess's friend buys us tallboys of beer, and we attempt what Tess calls "power hour," which is doing a single shot of beer every minute for one hour. We usually last only thirty minutes, after which we are cockeyed and burping like sailors.

In those first few months, getting drunk is the real amusement. Like a road trip to some arbitrary place, the real fun takes place along the way, and once we get there, there is nothing to do. We usually get drunk and push bottle caps into the ceiling panels in an effort to fill every square inch, making a roof we can sleep under, the way some girls adhere glow-in-the-dark star stickers. Some nights, we get drunk and sit on the concrete ledge outside our dorm windows, where we can listen to the booming sounds of trucks on the highway overpass. Others, we ride the elevator to the second floor, where the boys buy cigarettes by the carton, or to the seventh floor, where the boys drink Aftershock and Slip N' Slide in the hall.

A big night consists of getting drunk and stealing a couch from the dorm lobby while the security guard is outside on his cigarette break. Tess is too unsteady on her feet to carry her end, and we strip the paint off the walls in a futile attempt to jam the length of it into her dorm room.

Though our Thursday nights are uneventful, they make my roommate distinctly jealous.

When Tess and I perform our cigarettes/wine coolers routine, Wendi shuts herself in the lounge alone, cracking pistachios, flipping pages in a notebook, and watching *Change of Heart* on the fingerprint-flecked TV screen. Occasionally she'll appear in Tess's doorway to see what we're up to (her knocks always send us into a fury of window-opening and bottle-hiding), the way a baby-sitter might check up on her charges only to find them engrossed in a game she can't fully understand. Her smile shivers, and she says, "You girls are insane," before she swivels like a jewelry-box figure and leaves.

In the beginning, it never occurs to me that my drinking might bother her. After all, I don't drink with her, or even near her. I don't look at her with bloodshot eyes or breathe on her with musty breath, and I never bring bottles into our room. For that matter, I've never been loaded enough to say anything mean to her face. (Which is not to say I don't think mean things;

later, my mom will remind me that I referred to my room as "theater of the absurd," and to my roommate as "an acting major bound for big roles in low-budget porn.")

Three-quarters of students may report having bad experiences due to someone else's drinking;* but from where I stand, Wendi isn't one of them. On the nights that I don't drift off to sleep on the inflatable armchair in Tess's room, I don't even flip the light switch when I come in. I feel through my drawers in the dark and change clothes quietly, so as not to wake her.

Later, I will realize that what I see as self-sufficiency, Wendi sees as exclusivity. At first, I don't think my drinking concerns her, so much as it makes her feel rejected. Wendi, who has had little experience drinking before college, is just now learning that alcohol is the tie that binds. I think she's envious of the way that drinking allies Tess and me. It secures our bull sessions, capers, and absurd inside jokes.

Wendi could join us, of course. We have certainly invited her. But every time, she says no, on account of a Friday-morning theater history class. But the excuse isn't ironclad; she could go to class hungover, the way Tess and I sometimes do, in sweatpants and a ponytail, hands trembling, eighteen-ounce cup of coffee like a paperweight on the desk.

Her inexperience, I think, keeps her at bay. The following year, the university will release an alcohol- and drug-use survey of more than three hundred students, mostly freshmen and sophomores, and more than half will say we began using alcohol sometime between ages fourteen and seventeen. Wendi is in the

*Sixty-one percent of students who live on campus and don't binge drink say they've been interrupted sleeping or studying; 50 percent say they've had to take care of a drunken student; 29 percent say they've been insulted or humiliated by one (Harvard School of Public Health College Alcohol Study).

other half. She got drunk once in high school, which I suspect is like having sex once in high school: You don't enjoy it the first time, you endure it.

However, there is one area in which Wendi's experience surpasses my own: men. Wendi has had sex, and she knows that I haven't, and soon enough she is lolling in Tess's room on Thursday nights, bent over the pages of *Cosmopolitan,* discussing It: getting It, getting into It, the best way to have It standing up.

Her maneuver works. Tess, who has a twenty-eight-year-old boyfriend, prefers sex talk with Wendi to drinking with me, a partiality that seems almost illogical, in the same way that in the game "Rock, Paper, Scissors," paper wins out over rock. After all, sex talk is just talk, whereas power hour is brute action.

I shrink away from our competitive little threesome, regardless, and chalk up the loss to a fascination that just doesn't serve me.

As a testament to my disinterest in sex, I decide to break up with Reed.

Sometime in October, Reed decides he can't see enough of me, and every few days I get an unexpected ring from the dorm security guard, saying I have a visitor, and could I come sign him in? Most often, I feel too guilty to send him home after his five-hour drive, so I let him sleep over despite the fact his mere presence breaks the continuity of my drinking cycle. I let Reed cocoon on the floor in his Polar Shield sleeping bag even though his shadow makes Wendi sigh and huff.

To complicate matters, I spent a Saturday night drinking Durango tequila with a boy from the eleventh floor and kissing him on the tall steps outside the law building, which is the only height on campus from which the city looks pretty, where the lights of Crouse Hospital carpet the incline like bits of glittering glass. I don't know whether it was the height, or the buzz, or the disorientation that came with having a strange boy's hands cup my cheeks, but my head was filled with a whirling sensation like I was about to fall. I'd sobbed on the spot for being a lousy cheat.

For months, I've known about the rumor that most high-school relationships end by Thanksgiving of freshman year. It is a warning as old as the "freshman fifteen," and probably far more imminent. It is much easier to keep fifteen pounds off your ass than it is to keep your interest in someone else's when it's six hours and four hundred miles away.

By Christmas of second semester, almost every girl on my floor unleashes her high-school beau for one of two reasons: The breakups are either reactionary or cautionary. The girls have either been drunk and adulterous, or they can't trust that they won't be. One tells me early on a Saturday morning, while doing shots of Jim Beam with some film major she just met, somebody else rolling a joint, and time spinning by like a bicycle, that she couldn't be loyal to anything except the song on the stereo, the first down comforter that bulldozed her under, the cool glass of water in the morning that tamed her cotton-mouthed throat. She couldn't be faithful to one man. This is college, after all. At a house party, you can't wait in line for the toilet without some doll-faced boy leaning in to try to kiss you.

I can't even last until Christmas. It is during Reed's next surprise visit that I decide to break things off with him. Tess and I sit in the dorm bathroom, drinking glasses of Zima she's stirred with cubes of hard candy to infuse the drinks with a sour-apple taste. For a half-hour we sit and drink, while Reed waits in my room, Tess snubs cigarettes out in the drain, and I drum my feet against the side of the bathtub and rehearse what

I'm going to say. Only after the tart-flavored malt warms my insides do I emerge and say, "Reed, we need to talk."

ONE NIGHT, at a house party being thrown by one of the university's sports teams, I meet a gymnast named Hannah, who persuades me to try out for the cheerleading team. We are sitting at the kitchen's beige plastic patio table, holding cups of viciously yellow beer and blowing smoke in one another's faces, and she is sweetly telling me what to expect: the audition space, the judges, and the stunts I would need to knock off.

Maybe it's the beer bubbling through me, but as Hannah speaks, I forget to be indifferent. I drop the brooding face that college has given me the freedom to wear openly, now that my mother isn't around to remind me to smile. The sullenness I disguise as artistic sensibility gives way, and I let Hannah convince me. She assures me that my height-to-weight ratio will make me easily throwable.

The next weekend, I drag myself to Archbold Gym, almost as a test to myself, the way people joke that the best way to curb your drinking is to follow through with the promises you make when you're drunk. Inside, the high-vaulted room is full of hopefuls, stripped down to their sports bras, orange stars glued to their cheeks.

The coach pairs us off, one girl and one guy. I'm assigned to a big fellow named Joe, a veteran. He holds me tight around the waist and says, "Stay straight as an arrow," before tossing me skyward and grabbing hold of my heels. Standing upright in his hands, I don't dare draw a breath, afraid to lose the inner lightness I never knew I possessed. When it's time for the gymnastics portion I tell Joe I can't manage the compulsory back tuck, and he says, "Don't worry, just jump and tuck your knees to your chest." I do exactly that, while Joe launches me backward into orbit and then catches me like a fly ball to left field.

When I make the team it's like winning the grand prize for acclimation. As my prize I am awarded a cheek-grazing skirt, an orange ribbon for my hair, and plastic pom-poms that shed like the dickens. I have regular five-second appearances on ESPN, clapping and smiling into the lens 'til the cameraman says, "And we're out." My mother puts a notice in the local paper. People I knew in high school email to say they saw me on TV during a game against Rutgers. By all appearances, I am a bona fide student athlete, earning college credit and everything. At football games, boys I've never met before lean over the field gate and ask for my phone number.

Privately, I feel like a phony. "Cheerleader" is a title that fast becomes a metaphor for the girl I have always tried to be, and miserably failed. On the green rubber turf of the Carrier Dome, I just can't yell loud enough. I can't smile wide enough. Without a buzz streaming through my system, I can't laugh off a fall from Joe's shoulders. I can't drum up the obligatory level of optimism.

My days course into a stream of classes followed by team practices, weight-room training, and one-on-one practices with Joe. I dread doing stunts. My stomach churns for hours before I climb onto a pyramid that's three-people high, before the coach makes me stand in the hands of two girls who are standing on the shoulders of two guys. The view from the top is appalling, and my nervous ankles can't quit shaking. I spend hours in the gymnastics room, practicing back flips that I can't seem to master, slapping my head over and over into the blue crash mat, unleashing a string of *fuck, shit, fuck*s. I am twitchy and sleep deprived. Weight falls off of me.

The only thing that eases me through the bruises from my misfired back tucks is the promise of drinking with my teammates after practice. I don't think this is avant-garde, mainly because it's not. Roughly half of college athletes, both male and female, are binge drinkers, and a 2001 study by the NCAA found that 80 percent of college athletes drink.

At S.U., the sports teams throw the most desirable weekend parties. People pack shoulder to shoulder into a basketball player's South Campus apartment, until the air inside is more humid than the gym's treadmill room and an overflow of bodies spills out through the sliding glass door and into the trodden backyard. At these parties, there are all varieties of groupies and leeches, and players move from room to room with an entourage as daunting as any tabloid star's.

THE EXPERTS say that jocks are susceptible to "group-think," a decision-making model that includes collective rationalization (i.e., "There is no *I* in *TEAM*") and the illusion that shit can't happen. I, however, am a free thinker. On my teammate's birthday, I do shots of Devil Springs, a 160-proof vodka that burns my throat like acid and makes me cry out in awe. Afterward, I collide with the coffee table while having a cake fight with the birthday boy, in which we are nailing one another in the face with fistfuls of devil's food cake. The next morning I go to Spanish class with a black welt on my knee and chocolate frosting in my hair.

By Thanksgiving, I start to realize that the drills we do in practice—the nonstop crunches, reverse triceps dips, and suicides—are diminishing my tolerance for cocktails. Lighter, I'm noticing, I have a greater margin for error.

One night, I do a few shots of Bacardi with Hannah and Joe, nothing that would have done me in when I weighed 113, but at

105 I am caught by surprise when the floor totters under me, and Hannah tells me I'm slurring my words. The next thing I know, I'm throwing up in the trash can while Joe holds my head, his giant hand pinching the back of my neck like he's lifting a kitten from a crate. When I start passing out, he carries me to my room in a trust fall.

One year later, when Joe dies in a car crash, stone sober, I won't be able to stop thinking of the boozy wrecks that he pulled me from like the Jaws of Life. I'll unearth an old photo of us drinking Rheingold and get gooseflesh. I'll be forced to flip it over.

ALSO BY November, I have profound misgivings about Wendi, an ill will that tears through my abdomen like an ulcer. I feel the first stabs of injury on the night I wake up and hear her clattering into the phone about me, telling her boyfriend she hates my clothes and my friends, not to mention the way I sleep, eat, answer the phone, and employ the word *rad*. My bile swells the day she short-sheets my bed. By the time she tries to solicit me to write her women's studies paper for fifteen dollars, odium is choking me. The sentiment cuts off all other basic functioning.

All the college-prep books that my mother ordered obsessively before I left home warned me about this. Tensions are bound to arise, the authors wrote, when you're sharing a room the size of a bus-stop shelter. They said get out of there. It's easier to keep the peace when you're both busy. Heeding that advice, I try to distance myself from the room and from the dorm itself, where Wendi, as if she senses the loner tendencies with which I constantly struggle, has used them to rally the fourth-floor girls against me.

One night, the hallway carries the sound of a conversation she is having a few rooms away. From my bed, the acoustics are good. I can hear the high whine of Wendi's voice, telling Cara P. and Julie L. that I stay away from the girls on our floor because I think I am better than they are, and that's why I go out and drink with my teammates. I feel as though Wendi has stuck a voodoo pin through my heart because that's where the ache is. She has gone right for my weakness and twisted it into misunderstanding.

For a moment, I consider running down the hall in my nightshirt and telling them the truth. I want to say, *I don't avoid you because I think I'm superior, I do it because I think I'm inferior. I do it because I think you don't want me, and that lowliness is the reason that I drink, too.* But I know I couldn't deliver that message without crying, which would only substantiate the weirdness and weakness that I think they suspect of me. So instead, I roll over to face the wall, and when Wendi comes in, I pretend to sleep.

I retreat even further from the dorm. I study in a fifth-floor cubicle at Bird Library, among poetry volumes that haven't been checked out since the early eighties. I eat sodden pizza with Hannah in the student center. I learn to lie in bed, wearing headphones, relying on the lyrics to fold me into sleep. I handle Wendi with kid gloves until light beer hinders my diplomacy.

One night, after power hour with Hannah, my dormant resentment bursts and impels a tsunami. I am staggering down the hallway to my room, dragging my hands along the walls on either side of me, when Wendi cuts me off in the doorway, hands on her hips, carping about a phone message that I wrote on a Post-it and forgot to stick to her mirror. Under any other circumstances, I would bow my head and make an apology. But on this night, I feel as shimmering and fluid as a jellyfish drifting on a wave. The words in my head are rhythmic and pulsating, and there is nothing to stop me from saying them. I tell Wendi to leave me alone because I can't handle her bullshit.

It only gets easier from there. From there, I will come home more nights, feeling as lucent as the vodka I drank, half-hoping Wendi will start a fight with me. All week, I will save up all my rage for her. I'll stockpile it like ammo, so it will be there on the weekend, when I'm drunk enough—and therefore brave enough—to retaliate. The night she makes a reference to my dirty-clothes pile, I'll throw the telephone against the wall, splitting it open to reveal a tangle of rainbow-colored wires. The night she takes me on over a cable bill, I'll slam the door in her face so hard that the force of it blows her hair back. One night, I'll come home and rip her Mariah Carey calendar off the bulletin board for no reason other than I've decided that somebody needs to do it.

I'm uncomfortable with my new capacity for drunken belligerence. I have a feeling it's the type of thing that people can use against me, the way prosecutors on TV crime shows call character witnesses to prove that the defendant is capable of committing an unspeakable crime. But I console myself with the Claude Bernard quote "Hatred is the most clear-sighted, next to genius." I praise myself for expressing malice plainly, like a man, for howling and swearing and knocking over whatever is handy, instead of employing rumors and nasty looks, the subterfuge of women.

Wendi is not so progressive. By chance, I find out that she's telephoned my parents to discuss me, to tell them that I've lost some weight and she thinks I might have an eating disorder. As an afterthought, she tells them I am drinking a lot.

My mom tells me about it on a Sunday afternoon, a few weeks after Wendi reached out and touched her. When I ask her how she responded, she says, "Please! I told her you were working out with the team four hours a day. On top of that, you eat totally normally."

When I ask her what she thinks about the drinking, she says, "I'm not delusional; I know people drink in college. Just be responsible."

My mom is right about people drinking in college. The girls on my floor scatter to a party at least once a weekend, like seeds being blown by the wind. When Saturday nights find me stuck in my dorm room, typing a paper, I am guaranteed to have at least five hours of soundlessness in which to listen to the clicking of my own computer keys. The girls wander home again in the early morning hours, when I can hear thumping, or vague hollering, or doors fluttering open and closed, despite the tube socks we've all duct-taped to our doorframes to muffle the slamming.

If I wanted to, I could go room by room down the hallway and list each tenant's drunken acts of delinquency: There is Emma M., who, after a house party, crawled buck-naked to the bathroom on her hands and knees, as though she'd regressed to the state of infancy. There is Kylie T., who, after too many gin and tonics, mistook Anna B.'s room for her own and scrambled into bed with her. And there is Danielle P., whose cast we all signed in felt-tipped pen after she got drunk and fell through a glass coffee table.

In fact, the only person who hasn't yet been humbled by alcohol is Wendi. That's not to say that she won't be, though. Before the school year ends, she will get dead-drunk on Goldschlager and keck in her sheets. I won't say a word while she's stripping her bed the next day, but I'll feel like I've won.

I GO HOME for Christmas break feeling totally unencumbered. The commuter flight into Boston is crowded with students drinking Bloody Marys and comparing plans for New Year's Eve. By the time the plane touches down on the Logan runway, everyone's face is as red as a poinsettia, and a few rowdy frat boys have repeatedly cornered the flight attendant with a sprig of mistletoe. Behind the fake-frosted glass at the arrival gate, my dad is waiting. He gives me a bear hug and says I look great.

My parents have always considered themselves European in the fact that they think the legal drinking age ought to be eighteen, and that drinking is fine for teenagers as long as it's done at home. Therefore, Christmas dinner finds me with a glass of white wine instead of my usual goblet of skim milk. I do my best to sip naturally between helpings of squash and turkey and the goopy Jell-O salad my mom calls "blueberry gunk," even though I still haven't acquired a taste for wine. We drink little of it at school, unless you count the strawberry wine coolers that come in bottles with screw-off tops.

Relatives ask me about Syracuse: "How are the parties?" Followed by, "How are classes?" And I gesture majestically with my glass, which, as the night coasts on, feels more and more like a tulip-shaped extension of my hand. The air smells like cinnamon sticks and chimney smoke. My grandma tells off-color jokes. My uncles get plastered and pound out "Werewolves of London" on the player piano.

As a Christmas present to ourselves, my family and I spend the week following New Year's in Grand Cayman, where (as a Christmas present to me) the legal drinking age is eighteen. The days are hot and stale. Time stretches out like the blue line of the ocean, and I spend it faceup on a hotel towel, watching prop planes pull ads for drink specials at a club called Next Level. My sister and I snap pictures of sea turtles in algae-crusted tanks. We snorkel with stingrays and shriek when their slippery whips brush our legs. One afternoon, I bump into a boy from my dorm on a bleached stretch of beach (in the coming years, there will never be a city remote enough to escape people I knew at S.U.). We spend a night at a sports bar called Bobo's Iguana, drinking Red Stripes and flirting shamelessly.

On our last day in the Caymans my dad rents a Jeep, and we drive it up the curved road to the botanical park, only to find that it is closed due to bad weather. The sky growls and threatens rain. We take pictures on a burned-out tree trunk: my sister sitting high on top, me at mid-level, my mom at the base. Together we look like a succession of Russian stacking dolls, spanning the continuum of womanhood.

When the temperature slips below seventy degrees, we buy sweatshirts at the gift shop and sit wearing them in a nearby canteen. My dad orders frozen mudslides, blended with Tortuga rum and topped with whipped cream. There is a glass for everyone but my thirteen-year-old sister. When my mom lets her have a sip she purses her lips and says it tastes too much like coffee.

I drink two, fast enough to get a brain freeze, and then suck on my parents' straws when they get up to go to the bathroom. On the ride back to the hotel, I fall to rum-humming sleep in the backseat.

GREEK MYTHOLOGY

Back at school, January is gelid. The roads around campus are two inches deep in slush left behind from a New Year's Day snowstorm. Even in hiking boots, the walk to and from class requires hoofing it, with your wool gloves cradling your notebooks, your turtleneck pulled over your chin, and your feet skidding this way and that. "Ice luges" start turning up at off-campus parties. Boys tip bottles over the crests of four-foot blocks of ice that they've chiseled chutes into, and we kneel at the bottom with our hot mouths on the finish line, as vodka toboggans down the fronts of our shirts.

There hasn't been a memorable party since house parties became the usual way to pass weekends. Nothing remarkable has ensued since a routine was established: the standard procedure for Saturday nights, whereby Hannah and I toddle through the snow to the address that an upperclassman has scrawled on our doors' Dry Erase boards, while the windchill stiffens our fingers and older boys zip down Euclid Avenue toward the campus bars, leaning their heads out of car windows and roaring *"Freeesh-men,"* which is the verbal equivalent of a drive-by shooting.

Since then, I've realized that house parties, which I first thought were enormously grown-up, are actually adolescent. They are a way for senior boys to make a swift eight hundred bucks, by supplying beer to freshmen who have no other way of getting it. When I look closer, I notice the way each boy has his own chore, collecting money or carrying kegs, and each one performs it with the mope of begrudged obligation. When I'm a dollar short of the admission fee, the fuzzy-haired boy at the door has to check with his superior before letting me in. When I'm in another boy's way when he comes lugging a keg through the door, he grumbles "For-christ's-sake-move." I realize parties are these boys' part-time jobs. Two a month is all it takes for freshmen like me to pay their monthly rent.

By second semester, the parties are like a hologram that looks the same from every angle. There is nothing unexpected about them; there are only lines at discreet rear entrances, cups of sour beer, floors peppered with cigarette butts, bathrooms without toilet paper, and the same familiar faces that drift from room to room. After a while, those faces are not even worth nodding at because nothing can come from that small gesture except the same old small talk and dumb silences. After a while, these parties' only variable is the street address.

I don't change, either. I still go to these parties. I still stay at them, determined to get my five bucks' worth by filling and refilling my oversized party cup with beer.

In the future, I will always be the girl who stays too long or too late. I will be the girl who holds out for aye, as though it were a contest. I will be as determined to keep drinking as people on reality shows are determined to stay, standing one-footed on a log, for six hours at a time. I will be the last girl to leave the dinner party, the one who stays after all the other girls have given their good-bye air kisses, the one who promises to catch a ride, a cab, a bus, and yes, "Call when I get home." If I'm a guest at your party, I'll be the girl who falls asleep on the bed with the coats, sleeps until nine, and accepts a cup of French roast from your mother before I go. If I'm your love interest, you, too, won't be rid of me until morning, until you find me my shirt and my socks, until you offer me a palm filled with aspirin, and walk me out the door.

Drunk, I'll never know how to go home until I'm told to. I'll stay out until two A.M. in the suburbs, four A.M. in the city, until I get a cue, like the bar's lights coming on and a bouncer saying, "I don't care where you go, but you can't stay here." And even then, I'll invite you to my place for an after-party, or I'll invite myself to your place if my freezer is fresh out of vodka, and we'll both keep drinking until I hit the floor. I'll keep taking until I'm long saturated, and even after that. I'll be parasitic that way. I'll suck blissfully on a straw for hours, like the tick that sucks until it's big as a dime, until it bursts in a bloody streak on your arm.

DURING THE time that I am a student at S.U., *The Princeton Review* will repeatedly count it among the top twenty campuses in the United States with "more to do." And the label will always confuse me because I'm not sure whether it means S.U. has more to do than other schools, or more to do aside from drinking, which seems to be the undercurrent that runs through all campus-related references. In 2001, S.U. will actually rate as the university that has "the most to do," and it will make me think chancellors ought to start addressing sympathy cards to the nation's 12 million other undergraduates, who must be bored to tears.

I know because I'm bored to tears. Just five months into college, I am jaded. I am sated with watching student films, and sledding the steep incline in front of Crouse College on green plastic lunch trays, and buying student tickets to student productions like *Leading Men Don't Dance.* If there really is "more to do" on campus aside from holing up among the dirty-clothes piles in somebody's dorm room, smoking, swigging flavored vodka, and playing PlayStation, I can't find it. The new year finds my friends and me in a state of hog-drunk hibernation. In the cold and sleet, even average outings require a cocktail. We drink screwdrivers before we ride the shuttle to the movie theater; we stir amaretto liqueur into our cups of hot cocoa at hockey games.

It's a strange moment when I realize that drinking, which used to be the single interlude that could break up high school's tedium, is becoming just as dreary as most things in college are. That is not to say that beer has become *as* dull as dining-hall food, though it will be by the time I graduate. It's just that the sensation that comes with the third or fourth bottle of it, which used to be a sudden awareness as jolting as a blow to the head, has become so familiar that I don't have to pay much attention to it. Falling into a buzz is like falling into something staunch and comfortable, like a favorite armchair. I sink into the feeling; I could drift to sleep there.

. . .

By the beginning of February, quarter-page ads for rush appear in *The Daily Orange,* saying "Tri Delt has a rush on you" or "The sisters of Alpha Phi wish you good luck with recruitment." A Greek Expo kicks off in the student center. It's just like the consumer electronics shows I used to go to with my father, but instead of demonstrations of the latest robotic arm there are booths of girls wearing sweatshirts stitched with alien letters, exhibiting "sisterhood." A slide show flips frames on a life-sized screen. Girls are everywhere, hugging one another too tightly. Their cheeks are flushed. Their mouths are spewing laughter. Everyone wears name tags that read, HI MY NAME IS, and everyone's name is KAITLYN.

Someone passes out a guidebook that contains black-and-white photos of all fourteen houses and sorority symbols: their chosen flowers, philanthropies, and color schemes. The differentiation is as befuddling to me as the splitting of the atom. For the past semester, I've thought all sororities were one unit. I had no idea that there were points of distinction. I didn't know there were so many different Alpha, Beta, and Gamma girls in orbit.

Back in the dorm, I scrawl a note on my Dry Erase board that reads, FOOLS RUSH IN. But just before the rush deadline, Hannah asks me to sign up with her, and I cave. I resolve to rush but absolutely not pledge, a choice that will later invoke the old AA idiom, "If you hang out in a barber shop, sooner or later, you're bound to get a haircut." I figure the registration fee costs little more than two house parties, and a week of waxing sap to Greek freaks will, at the very least, give me something to do.

I am immediately disappointed to discover that "rush parties" aren't really parties at all. Whereas boys rushing fraternities lounge on black pleather couches, watching televised sports and chugging beer with the brothers, girls rushing sororities are subject to much stricter rules. For starters, we are not allowed to drink at all during rush: not in the bars, not in our dorms, and certainly not in the sorority houses. Forget about accepting a cold drink; we are not allowed to accept even the most trivial items from sisters. The Panhellenic Council interprets a tissue or a spare tampon—any exchange at all—as a bribe.

Our parties are like job interviews. I have a "rush group," a herd of thirty girls with whom I shuttle from house to house, as we are required to spend thirty minutes at each of the fourteen sororities. I tour each house's succession of bedrooms, the neat little beds lined up like those of Snow White's dwarves, and dutifully whisper "Wow." I am introduced to sisters dressed in cashmere sweater sets who peek at the label of my coat when they help me out of it. I sit with them on taupe-colored sectionals, and have odd little staring matches like the ones I used to have with my sister to see who could last the longest without blinking. They grill me about my major, my hometown, and my G.P.A. One girl has the gall to ask me what my father does for a living, and I wish I had the conviction to tell her to fuck off, but I don't, so I shyly tell her about his business.

The funny thing is, rush is one of the most legitimate experiences I'll have in college, in spite of its out-and-out bogusness. For a lot of college girls, it is our most honest—not to mention our most sober—attempt at self-definition. Rush is predicated upon classification. At every house, girls line up on a staircase, clapping out harebrained rhymes, totally confident, totally convinced that

They're the Alpha Phis, they're the best in the land,
And we'll see them wherever we go.

From the Golden Gate to the Empire State,
they'll be wearing silver and bordeaux.

These are girls who are, at least in one respect, pretty damn sure of their place in the world.

College is all about compartmentalization. The university itself is divided into graduate and undergraduate, subdivided by liberal arts and science, and then split into professional schools and divvied up by departments. As a student, you lose track of how many times people ask you, "What's your major?" or "What are your career goals?" Not just academic advisors, but other students, even some friends. Everyone wants to know *what* you *are,* followed by *what* you want to *be.* You learn to refer to yourself by taxonomy, by major and minor: *communications journalism.*

Almost spontaneously, we group ourselves socially, too. At nineteen, knowing who our friends are is the closest many of us can come to knowing who and what *we* are. Even if we haven't yet committed to a major, to a hair color, or to eating three square meals a day, we know the group of people that can best tolerate us. Our posse is a label that we wear proudly: The student government knots Brooks Brothers ties; the Outing Club anchors snowboards to the roofs of their cars; and the staff members at *The Daily Orange* use hollow lingo like "off-lead" and "hammerhead." They are markers that everyone knows how to spot and read.

The Greek system is itself a signifier. And within it there are sub-signifiers. They are the letters mounted on gold brooches, embroidered on sweatshirts, and nailed to the exteriors of every house. During rush, every sorority rolls out trays of cupcakes with their codification spelled out in icing.

During rush, it is all too easy to line yourself up against a score of female stereotypes and try to figure out which one you fit. All day long girls debate—before class, in the library, on the stationary bikes in the school's gym. Do they belong in the house of funny girls, or the house of prim-and-propers? Can they imagine themselves in the stone farmhouse, or the California rambler? Do they belong with the girls who look like Courteney Cox, or the ones akin to Anna Kournikova? Choices, choices. Girls everywhere remind me of the orphaned duckling in my favorite children's book, the one that runs the streets, asking stranger after stranger, "Are *you* my mommy?" Every girl is looking for her *sisters,* total strangers with whom she expects to share some strand of genetic code.

I am not above it.

I visit Zeta Alpha Sigma just before the sky darkens on a snow-spitting Wednesday afternoon. I've heard ahead of time that they are not your average sorority girls. In a pantheon where every house has a denomination—Kappa Kappa Glamour, A Chi Ho, etc.—they are called the Zeta Alcoholics, the fun-loving, fast-living, anti-sorority girls. Whereas most of the sororities on Comstock Avenue have ivory shutters, Bombay furniture, and a fine-tuned baby grand, Zeta is as squat as a frat house, an ivy-covered stucco with crumbling walkways, a secret smoking room, and discarded cups in the potted geraniums. It is rumored that their house chef bakes pot brownies and serves them alongside chicken à la king.

Given their reputation, I imagine the Zetas will be brawny tomboys who open bottles with their teeth. For now, I buy the myth that female binge drinkers are overweight brutes with disheveled hair and sweat stains. It is the allegory I'll later call the "Drunk Girl" myth, after the *Saturday Night Live* skit. It is a convenient misconception that gives those of us habitual drunks, the ones who don't look like Jeff Richards in a crooked wig, the license to keep discounting ourselves among girls who have alcohol-abuse problems.

In reality, the Zetas are hugely feminine. The arch-top door swings open on natural beauties, waifs, lip-gloss-and-mascara girls. They wear their lettered sweatshirts over tattered jeans, vintage slips, and paint-splattered Pumas. Tiny diamonds twinkle in their pierced noses. Tattoos peek over the waistbands of their jeans. They are the hipsters, the hippies, the rock-and-roll girls, and the renegades. They come from families of sons.

Moreover, the Zeta house has the dim, haunted feeling of New York's Chelsea Hotel. Floors croak. Pipes clang. A framed portrait of a dead housemother eyes you with too much interest. The sisters float through the tour without any overblown pep, gently joking about the sloped kitchen floor and mismatched furniture. Even clean, their bedrooms are a hash of negatives, paint tubes, and scraps of fabric. Paint-smeared photo collages hang slightly crooked in the stairwells, alongside composite photos of old members, some of them dating back to the fifties, all those women with furry cardigans and sturdy-looking hairdos.

The house immediately appeals to me as a historical landmark. It is the type of place that retains the air of its past residents: the outrageous, the artistic, the self-destructive, the wounded, the anything-goes. When I move into the house one year later, I'll find out the second floor really does show signs of the macabre. The girls who live there hear wailing at night. Some see shower curtains blowing sideways, even though the windows are closed. Many report having the same dream, in which a young blonde drowns in a bathtub.

All mentions of alcohol are strictly forbidden during rush,

but when I take a seat on a slanted window bench, opposite a sister named Maya, all of our talk drifts back to drinking. She tells me she's a sophomore photography major who hangs out at a jazz bar downtown. I tell her about drinking with Tess, and then drinking with Hannah, and the string of off-campus parties that are fast becoming déjà vu. Together, we talk like sentimental fools, like girls who can't quit gushing about our boyfriends. We don't see it, but we are just as bad as the sorority girls who define themselves by family money and designer jeans. Booze is the axis our dialogue revolves around. It is our centrifugal force.

"Look," Maya says, leaning in to grip my upper arm like a railing, and making me feel for the first time like I'm built for feminine support. "During rush, a lot of sororities try to deny the fact that they drink. Talking about it can get them in big shit with the Greek council. Sororities have a lot of bad stereotypes, you know? But I'm going to tell you, here we believe in the philosophy of 'work hard, party hard.' The girls in this house are really real, and they really go for it. But we have our fun, too."

The Zeta girls consider themselves what addiction counselors call "terminally unique," which in their case is actually more like "terminally cool." I'll learn soon enough that their triumphs are pinned up like taxidermy. And their failures are felt like a cerebral hemorrhage that no one without a poet's intensity, an artist's receptivity, or a radical's planetary foresight has any hope to understand. For the next four years, they will again and again tout themselves as "real," and I will be too naive to know that anyone who uses that designation is disguising a representation of immense falsity.

Four years later, I'll meet an old sorority sister at a Manhattan restaurant, and between sips of her third artificially colored, artificially flavored sour-apple martini, she will un-ironically tell me, as though she is still wired to the same audio loop, about her postcollege quest for "something real."

It will take me years to decipher the code of the chemically dependent, to learn that "fine" implies *hammered,* "relaxed" translates to *stoned,* "normal" means *totally fucked.* Reality just is. It is the light that permeates the thin bedroom curtains on the morning of a fierce hangover, after all the nocturnal beer tears and boozy sentiments, and the self-annihilation disguised as fine art.

Anything that needs to be represented with a concept-word (e.g., *sisterhood*) is almost always a crock of shit.

Zeta is one of eight sororities that invite me back for the second round of rush. The second round is the skit round, and I am subjected to far too many tearful renditions of "Wind Beneath My Wings."

Zeta's skit is a musical review that spans the ages and includes lyrics like, "If you're smart, you'll be here, and you'll be drinking lots of beer" and "Going to M Street, Zeta's there, everyone in the bars beware!" The sisters in the audience, the ones standing on their chairs and throwing their hands up at any mention of alcohol, make my young, drunk's heart glad.

When we hear the ringing of a dinner bell, an indication that it's time to go, Maya finds me in the crowd. She is wearing a deep-blue, polyester lounge dress that is probably a costume, but in this house, one can never be sure. Her pale face is freckled with glitter. As we walk to the door, she bends in to say, "As far as I can see, you're a Zeta through and through."

Outside, snowflakes fall like confetti. I am utterly abuzz on approval.

When it comes time to place "bids" (our three favorite

sororities, ranked in order of how much we want to join them), I write down only Zeta. This is what our rush leaders call "suiciding," namely because it's Russian roulette; if you only pick one sorority and that sorority doesn't invite you to join it, it's a shot to the head. But I can't place myself anyplace else. The Zetas and I have common interests. In any other sorority, I'd be a fish out of firewater.

Maya calls me the day I receive my invitation to pledge Zeta, to say congratulations and ask, "Aren't you excited?" And even though I am excited, even though my pride swells with the idea that a group of women likes me enough to solicit me in this way, I can't get over a pledge I was forced to sign when I vowed my intention to become a sister of Zeta: It made me promise I would abstain from alcohol for the next three months.

I tell Maya how ironic it is that one of the meanings of the word *pledge* is to drink a toast to, considering our pledge leader says we can't drink as pledges. She explains that underage drinking has been the cause of a few chapters' suspension at S.U., and a few of the nearby universities have closed down their houses altogether. There's been a lot of bad press. The local news networks make Greek organizations look like one big bender. To read it in the papers, you'd think sororities drink mimosas for breakfast and draft beer for lunch, that they turn water into wine. You'd think they toss empty bottles in the driveway and make pledges run barefoot through the shards.

"A lot of freshman—not you, but a lot of others—just don't know their limits," Maya says. "A pledge could be drinking in her room, or out at a party that has nothing to do with the sorority, and if she goes too far—if she gets taken to the emergency room or something—there's nothing to keep the administration from shutting down the house. Everyone assumes she was hazed. Everyone always assumes the worst."

Sure as hell, Maya is right. The following spring, campus security will find six girls, all pledges of Alpha Omicron Pi, drunk as badgers in their dorm rooms. Two of them will be brought to the hospital for acute intoxication, after which the administration will order the sorority's S.U. chapter to close for good.

Statistically, freshman sorority girls are a liability. Whereas freshman frat boys begin college with more boozing experience than non-frat freshman, freshman sorority members are just as green as non-Greek girls are. When freshman girls drink, we are like people learning how to drive a stick shift: We either let go of the clutch too fast or too slow. We take too many shots, or not enough. When we're trying to get drunk we stall short. When we're not trying to get drunk, we mistakenly lurch into it anyway. Either way, driving the drink is never a smooth ride.

"Hang in there," Maya says. "We'll have a party sometime soon."

It is the occasional tantalizing reminders that bait you. They are the sorority's way of keeping you on the line long enough to reel you in, along with your semesterly dues. Big-sister week is the wriggling worm on the hook. It takes place just a week before hell week, apparently so we'll have a confidante for when the shit hits the fan, a Virgil to shepherd us through so much ridiculous chaos.

Big-sister week is five days of anonymous gifts: bouquets of flowers and buckets of candy, not to mention shot glasses and cigarette lighters bearing Zeta's letters. Every day, our names are lettered on envelopes lined up on the mantel. Inside them are cryptic clues that say too much without saying anything at all:

> *So here, Koren, is clue number three*
> *Soon you'll know who your big sister will be.*
> *I'm from a small town, not far away from a city*
> *I have two dogs, a bird, and a kitty.*
> *When it comes to smoking cigarettes,*
> *I pass, though occasionally I get drunk off my ass.*
> *For music, I'm into The Cars and The Ramones,*
> *As well as Dylan, Costello, The Who, and The Stones.*
> *Guess who?*
> *Your Big Sister*

The mystery is to be revealed Saturday night, when the big sisters organize a scavenger hunt on and off campus. Their identities will be unveiled at the finish line, like a whopping grand prize.

On Saturday, I show up at Zeta at 8:30 P.M. as instructed by my final clue, wearing the plastic, party-store lei that came with it. I've spent the week pretending I don't know my big sister is Maya because I don't want to spoil her fun.

There are four other pledges waiting in the foyer, variously outfitted for the occasion: One girl is wearing a pointed party hat; another is wearing striped leg warmers; and one unfortunate girl wears her bra outside of her shirt. There is the usual rumbling that happens when girls get together, the kind that I always shrink from. Girls are comparing costumes and spitting up laughter, and the volume escalates until Zeta's president comes downstairs and tells everyone to shut up.

She gives us a math problem to solve, something like 49,832

times 0.615, minus 30,000.68, plus 20, minus 42. The final answer reveals the address that we're supposed to go to, 624 Ackerman Avenue. In the driveway, two cars wait to drive us there.

NONE OF us recognizes the drivers, which is enough to send us into a fury of nervous whispering. At the house, we've been having weekly quizzes in which the sisters file into the rec room one at a time, singling a pledge out and asking her, "What's my name? You want to be a member of my sorority and you don't even know my fucking name?" Some of the high-strung pledges have fainted under interrogation.

My heart thrashes in my chest like a drowning man, until someone figures out that the drivers are alumni. They are Zetas who graduated two and three years ago. The apartment they take us to belongs to two more former Zetas, both grad students. It is much more grown-up than the off-campus apartments where we go to house parties, which are usually a mess of neon beer signs, cigarette butts in the sink, and bookshelves constructed from police barricades and raw lumber. Even in the dark, the whole room is a rainy green. There are kiwi-colored walls and pesto-colored futons. Jute rugs line the hardwood floors. The only light comes from the stairway, where there is a lit candle on every step. We sit where we're told to, around a coffee table, on velvet floor cushions the verdant shade of aloe vera.

A girl in a black ski cap carries out a tray of two dozen beer bottles and explains the rules. They are going to turn on the stereo, and every time we hear The Police sing "Roxanne" we are going to drink. One pledge cries, "Are you kidding? They repeat it a bajillion times!" In reality, I think it works out to about twenty-five gulps in two minutes.

The music kicks in like a thunderclap. I don't have time

to acknowledge the gyre of nerves in my stomach before it's *Roxanne* over the bottles clinking on and off the table, *Roxanne* over the slow giggles of the alumni who are reclining on the futons and playing along even though no one's forcing them. *Roxanne. Roxanne. Roxanne.* I usually consider myself pretty good at this, but I find myself "putting on the red light," and missing a few refrains until an alumna warns me to pick it up. Every gulp makes my stomach flop like a sunfish.

By the time the song fades out, I've drained only one Michelob, and we can't leave for the next destination until we each finish two. The alumni make me sit on the floor, drinking until both bottles are empty, the same way my parents used to keep me at the dinner table until I swallowed every last pea.

Tonight will turn out to be the only time we will ever be hazed by being forced to drink. The following year, Zeta will scratch the big-sister scavenger hunt for good when the house elects to make its pledge period totally dry, meaning no drinking whatsoever for new members because the implications are just too risky. Ironically enough, for the next three years, pledges will beg for the drinking in its absence. They'll approach sisters over and over again to say: "We *want* to be hazed. *Make* us drink. *Please,* funnel gin down our throats."

It's hard to say why so many of us crave this type of humiliation by intoxication. Maybe it's because, for some girls, drinking is a scarily intense need: if not a physiological need, then certainly a mental and emotional one.

Usually, if you *need* alcohol you can't admit it, unless you are in AA, at which point you can't proceed *without* first admitting it. And usually, once you do own up to the fact that you're powerless over Bud Light, some gruff-faced addiction counselor makes it clear that you can't have it ever again. Being hazed, however, is one of the few times you can actually admit you are powerless *while* you coat your insides with light beer. You can lean back into defenselessness, into the voices chanting "Drink, drink, drink." For a solitary moment in time, you can claim you aren't responsible for your own disasters. You have the elbow room to say: "Of course I'm a mess. I didn't have a choice in the matter."

The alumni cart us from one off-campus apartment to another, driving despite the fact that they've been drinking right along with us. When they get loaded enough, they give in and let us smoke in the car, even though they first warned us it would mean our asses. In the backseat, we fall into each other at every turn. Embers tumble everywhere, and smoke curls around us like halos.

In the future, I will come across many people who don't understand hazing. They don't understand why anyone would want to endure humiliation in order to be a part of a team, or why, for that matter, they would desire the company of such sadists to begin with. For me, hazing is more about masochism than peer pressure. For me, the alumni feel like the only friends that have the guts to say, "Yes, your ass looks gigantic in those jeans." On the inside, I feel like a real shithead. And on the outside, they confirm that I am. I respect them for that, the way Sylvia Plath says, "Every woman adores a fascist, the boot in the face."

For some of us, fear and humiliation feel honest. They ensure devotion more than reverence, more than love. The damned loves the hand of the executioner. And compassion holds more weight when it follows ruthlessness. Frankly speaking, "You've got to be cruel to be kind."

. . .

WE STOP at a Tudor, where an older girl shows me how to smoke from a ceramic water bong shaped like a serpent, and then pushes me to fill my lungs again and again. We go to a frat house where the brothers make us down screwdrivers and read *Penthouse Letters* aloud (Maya tells me later that the porn was the boys' personal touch). And then, we go to a sublevel apartment on Lancaster Avenue, where boys tie our hands behind our backs and force us to eat pot brownies off the kitchen floor, which, it's worth noting, is *not* clean enough to eat from.

By the time we make it to the beanbag chairs in somebody's attic, everyone, including the hazers, the hazees, and the hosts, is drunkity-drunk. An alumna brings home a pledge who is passed out and puking.

The rest of us are dropped off at Forty-Fours, an S.U. sports bar that got its name because eleven of the university's football players have worn that number, and three of them have earned all-American honors. The sign on the outside of the bar is printed with the slogan A SYRACUSE TRADITION, though it will always be unclear to me whether the owners mean to say that the jersey or the drinking is traditional.

I'm admitted with a fake ID that has appeared in my pocket from nowhere.

Maya is smack in front of me as I shoulder through the door. I don't have the faculties to put two and two together, to even notice that she's got a lei on, too. Instead, I just fall into her. Even if I hadn't already suspected that she was my big sister, one of the boys who forced me to read the sentence, "Her fingers danced over the material and she began unbuttoning his jeans," had told me outright. I can't even pretend to be surprised. Drunk and stoned, I'm like a turtle without a shell, just that soft and demented.

• • •

I ALREADY HAD a rapport with Maya. I like the stream-of-consciousness messages she leaves on my answering machine, the way she can wind around what she is trying to say for a full ten minutes. I like her windswept hair, and her one-armed sweaters, and her motorcycle boots. I like the way she calls out my name across the quad, no matter how many people are circulating between classes, or how far away I am when she spots me.

But the evening's hazing has secured our union. It has bonded us the same way physical fights with my real sister brought us closer when we were young, when I would accidentally knock her hard enough to make her bottom lip bleed, and if she agreed not to tell our mom, I'd feel so thankful that I wouldn't deck her again for at least a week. Maya and I have the same kind of trust in torture. I keep the confidence of the hazing, and she keeps me as her graceless namesake. She even lets me make her a wooden paddle painted with our names, the age-old Greek symbol of our sadomasochistic connection.

At Forty-Fours, someone takes a picture of the whole lot of us while we lean together, looking stunned by the flash of the bulb. I have my head on Maya's shoulder, eyes drooping. My mouth is bent into an eerie smile, lips smeared with the garish red lipstick I forgot the alumni put on me. Tomorrow, I won't remember much about this bar, which is the first I've ever been in. I will remember only how it felt to be someone's little sister, how good it felt to be relieved of the terrible burden of good judgment. I am relieved, for that matter, of the ability to make choices at all.

Already in college, the inability to be defenseless is the thing that makes me homesick. It kills me to think of all those years in high school when I lived for the idea of being on my own. The reality is exhausting and lonesome. Already, I'm finding it takes too much energy to do the things that people do to pass for competent adults. Walking in the snow to a study group, or to the student store to buy a new toothbrush, requires a valiant effort. Some days, so does getting dressed; that's why the vast majority of us go to class wearing pajamas.

Even when I'm drunk, my nights will almost always be marred by the indecision of my days. I will spend fifteen staggering minutes trying to figure out what drink to order, which knob to pull on the cigarette machine, whether or not to let some boy from my sociology class walk me home.

Tonight it is a great comfort to have Maya telling me what to do. In some ways, from here on out, alcohol will act as my power of attorney. I will drink to incapacitate myself, and then let sisters or friends decide things for me. I will enjoy delegating my authority. I've never been one to mind not having a mind of my own.

EXCESS

YOU'RE PRETTY
WHEN I'M DRUNK

BY THE TIME I am initiated into Zeta as a full-fledged member, excess is my main objective for any night. When I drink, I aim to exceed a state of being just-drunk, and enter instead into a state of consciousness that is more like annihilation of brain waves.

Of course, that word, *excess,* won't occur to me until years later. It isn't possible to exceed normal when my drinking feels normal to begin with, when geography makes it acceptable, when everybody is doing it, and when *too much* never seems to be sufficient, anyway. I won't realize until much later that every sorority function resembles a five-day meth binge in a Kansas City RV park: For however long they last, I live in my own filth. I am united with strangers solely by my interest in getting high, talking about getting high, and doing everything I can to maintain that high.

Of course, Coors isn't crank or coke or crack. And Heineken isn't heroin. And vodka isn't Valium. And nothing that's mixed with cranberry juice will score you respect with the folks who cop drugs in the public bathroom in Tompkins Square Park. But don't tell that to my brain because when I'm drunk, it purrs with the ecstasy of being thoroughly *high*.

By the time I am initiated into Zeta, I am like any other junkie left alone with her drug of choice. Amstel Light is my upper and my downer, it is my euphoric bump, my sweet nod into vagueness, the hallucinogenic that contorts my world into one that's worth living in. After two beers, there is no question as to whether I should have two more. After four, my world is the first forty minutes of a movie so moving I can't bear for it to end, or a cake so sweet I can't help but cut another, and then another, sliver. My reality is a climax so close I can't bear to pull away.

I AM FORMALLY initiated into Zeta at four A.M. on a Wednesday in March.

The ceremony proves to be the most disorienting experience I will ever undergo while sober. Sisters in hockey masks and black robes tackle and blindfold me the moment I step through the door. The soundtrack from *2001: A Space Odyssey* is screaming from a tape deck in the foyer, and someone is clanging pots and pans so loud that the neighbors call the police.

I'm dazed throughout most of the process. Zetas are covering my eyes or my ears. My skin feels weirdly wet. My senses are all discombobulated. The only part I'm really lucid for is when I'm made to drink with Maya from a ceremonial chalice, which is filled with spiced cider that tastes alcoholic but isn't. Afterward, someone pushes me down onto a folding chair inside a shower stall. I sit there for an hour, staring at the drain and cradling my elbows, until the Zetas pull back the vinyl curtain, toss me a sweatshirt stitched with the sorority's letters, and offer hugs of congratulations.

The best part about being a full sister is that, for a while, it really does give me more to do. Every Sunday night, we have "chapter," which is the Greek term for the mandatory weekly meeting at which we discuss recycling the house's milk cartons, redecorating the rec room, bake sales for elder care, Frisbee tosses for fibromyalgia, Greek Week, alumni luncheons, and other incidental babble. Zeta's secretary takes a role call and I get to cry out "Oy coy," meaning "here," when she reads my newly given Greek name, "Alcina," after the sorceress who turned her friends and lovers into trees and stones after she tired of them. Chapter closes with announcements from Zeta's social director, Robin, who plans our parties.

Robin plans a party for most weekends, and during chapter, we struggle to scribble down the dates in our day planners. Most of the parties have a theme, lest drinking until we see double gets dull. There's a kindergarten party with Gamma Psi, to which we all wear Catholic-school uniforms and suck on baby bottles filled with gin-milk punch. There's a pajama party at Sigma Tau, where the boys wear silk pajamas and serve "sleepers," and a pillow fight leaves the den littered with stray feathers and slippers.

One Saturday night, we have an "Anything for Money" party with Phi Chi Omega, where the goal is to earn as much Monopoly money as you can by lapping whipped cream off other people's navels, and performing other sex acts for currency. The girl who has the biggest bankroll when the party ends wins a bottle of tequila silver. By the end of the night, more than a few Zetas cry, when they realize there is a name for girls who earn money that way.

There are wine-and-cheese parties, beer-and-bowling parties, wake-and-bakes, casino nights, power hours with Midori sours, plus pre-parties and after-parties, in case one bender isn't enough.

But the biggest party by far is Zeta's semesterly formal.

A FORMAL is like a high school prom, but with an open bar and no chaperones. Most sororities at S.U. have them, and mostly at resorts in Canada, where across the border just four hours away, the legal drinking age is eighteen. Everyone spends the night in a three-star hotel, doing their best impression of Led Zeppelin at the Continental Hyatt by kicking over nightstands, putting cigarette burns in hotel towels, and disrupting things enough to make other guests file formal complaints.

No sister wants to go alone, but asking a date is a big deal because you have to share a hotel room with him.

I end up inviting a boy named Milton who lives on Hannah's floor in Sadler Hall. We met a month earlier, in the dorm bathroom, where I was getting sick after a night of downing 7&7s. The room felt as damp as a sea cave, and Milton found me in one of the stalls, where I was drifting to sleep with my cheek on the toilet seat and hugging the bowl like a life preserver. In memory, he was a giant sea beast that latched on to me, kissing me right there on the tiles without even bothering to help me up from my space among the stray wads of toilet paper. I hadn't resisted. Unmoored as I was, I was happy for rescue.

I don't really *like* Milton, but I don't dislike him, which is the standard by which I measure the boys with whom I drink. I figure bringing him will be better than not going at all, or going stag, in which case I'd be sure to end up alone in a corner, taking shots, while everyone else snuggled into slow dances. Since I haven't ever been to a formal, I don't know that boys interpret the invite as an open invitation for sex, on account of both the open bar and the hotel room. If I'd known, I never would have asked.

Milton and I hitch a ride up to the Canadian side of Niagara Falls with Hannah, who also joined Zeta, and her date, Perry, a platonic friend she went to high school with. It is the slow, awkward drive of people who don't know what to talk about. We wheel up Interstate 81, past the army base in Watertown and through the Thousand Islands. Hannah fiddles with the radio. Perry folds and unfolds the map. Milton says over and over that he should have brought his stash of pot. When we get to the border, a customs officer in a glass booth waves us through, despite the fact that when he asks what country we are citizens of, Perry says "Scranton, Pennsylvania."

We park the car in front of the first packaged-goods store we spot, and skitter through the aisles like contestants on *Supermarket Sweep,* amassing bottles of rum and tequila, plus a thirty-pack of beer and the stubby Canadian cigarettes called Players. It should be a thrill to be able to buy booze legally, but for some reason, I still feel sheepish, like I'm doing something wrong. I hand a few bills to Milton and let him carry my share to the counter, where a bald man knowingly rings them up.

By the time we get to the hotel, most of the sisters have already checked in. They are moving the elevator up and down, bursting in and out of rooms holding beer bottles. There are Zetas smoking a joint in the lounge chairs beside the indoor pool, and more sitting at the hotel bar like birds on a wire, picking through peanut bowls and chatting with the bartender while he pulls back the lever of the beer tap. It's the first time I've ever checked into a hotel without my parents, and I'm unsure what to do at the horseshoe-shaped front desk, where a clerk in a hunter-green blazer hands me my room key card.

Hannah and I have arranged to have adjoining rooms on the ground floor. Mine has two double beds because I don't feel wholly comfortable bunking with Milton.

The rooms have sliding glass doors that open onto a small bay, and Hannah and I jog outside without our coats on to marvel at its half-frozen finish. We sit on the broad wooden railing that divides the lawn from the water, holding bottles of Labatt's in our laps and sighing in the dippy, satisfied way the situation seems to call for. The air around us is smoky before we even light a cigarette. It's not dark yet, but we can see the moon, as though by mistake. Hannah says the clouds make its edges look serrated, like a bottle cap.

Back in the hotel room, Hannah and I drink while Perry snaps pictures. We lie under the bed's stiff paisley comforter with our backs against the headboard, like a married couple watching the eleven o'clock news. Between us are an ashtray, a bottle of Captain Morgan coconut rum, and the tiny juice glasses from the hotel bathroom that we've been using to take shots.

After a few deep dips into the bottle, I locate the inner button that can take me off mute mode. I come up with a point of conversation. I ask everyone, "What was the last ludicrous thing you did when you were drunk?" I find out that Milton passed out in his closet. Hannah accidentally penciled in her eyebrows with red lip-liner in a bar's dark bathroom. Perry peed into his refrigerator's vegetable drawer during a drunken sleepwalk.

People seem to visit our room in sixes. Girls I pledged with come by to rap on the door, as does Maya, as well as boys in rumpled dress shirts who turn out to be other sisters' dates. Everyone is chain-smoking Players and posing for pictures, asking for beer and offering pot, until our standard-sized room starts to feel like a bank with Perry playing the teller. Since he bought most of the booze, he supervises the deposits and withdrawals.

The whole time, I stay curled up in the sheets with the rum bottle, feeling too gratified to leave it. Around the room, other sisters are bear-hugging a plastic pink bong or nuzzling drinks, and it occurs to me that this formal is like our honeymoon, like the ravenous periods of early love. In Canada, we can hardly believe we can drink legally, the way newlyweds can hardly grasp that they're married. We shut ourselves up in our rooms, consummating our lust. We consume room service, our drinks, and our dates. Each taste makes our union feel a little more real.

I know I'm starting to get drunk because I can feel my eyes turn to marbles in my head. I love that about alcohol. It has a way of making my whole face relax, the way I imagine a facial must. When I'm this slack, I wonder why I always feel so tense to begin with, why I walk around with my cheeks pulled so tight they look hollow, why my mouth is always drawn tight, into a constipated-looking little *o*.

I once heard someone use *copacetic* as a slang term for "drunk," and I thought *That's me*. With a buzz on, I'm first-rate. Alcohol is my wood sealant. When I'm painted, nothing can penetrate my essence. My best friend can call me *bitch*. The boy who is brushing my thigh with the back of his hand can tell me I'm only pretty when he's drunk. In the moment, these sentiments just bead up and roll off me.

I don't even mind when Milton crosses the room to smooth my hair, as though he cared about me.

SOME TIME later, we run out of booze, and Hannah, Perry, and I go to buy more at what we don't realize is a gigantic, fine-wine store. The bottles that line the shelves from floor to ceiling are far too good for the likes of us. I tramp through the rows of labels from Portugal, Argentina, and New Zealand—all the regions I'm too uncultivated to know—with the mania of Augustus Gloop in the chocolate room.

It occurs to me that an hour has passed since my last drink, and my buzz has begun soft-pedaling. I am still drunk, but I cannot be *just*-drunk. Just-drunk will not gut my head of its worries. Just-drunk will not swat away my misgivings about Milton, anxieties that are whirring around me when I'm alone with him, like so many insects. I need a bottle of something sweet and potent to perk me back up to a state of past-gone. Champagne will do the trick. Cheap champagne, which is both romantic and lethal, will hit me like a crime of passion. I think it can help me behead myself.

Hannah is in the back of the store, inspecting the coolers stocked with chilled Korbel, as if she has read my mind. But when I approach her to help select a fat green bottle from the cooler's shelf, she doubles over with her hands on her knees, and starts dry heaving.

I'm able to grab her under one arm, and get her out of the store before the store owner has to run for a mop. The door chimes, and the cold Canadian air hits us hard and blue. I tug

Hannah just around the corner of the storefront, where we're out of the cashier's view, and I hold her blonde curls while she throws up on the sidewalk. I grit my teeth when I hear the splashing sound vomit makes when it hits concrete.

We're standing on the edge of the town's main street, and traffic is heavy. Every few minutes, a car whizzes by. The drivers, mostly men, lean against their car horns, and the blares are mocking. Hannah wipes her mouth with the pink sleeve of her sweater and says, "We're such goddamn Americans."

WHEN WE make it back to the Crown Princess Hotel, Hannah is still down for the count, so Perry and I haul her to bed and go about the business of changing for the dance.

In what will become a mythic recovery, Hannah will wake up stone-sober two hours later, wriggle into her black satin gown, loop her hair into an updo, and come downstairs to resume drinking. As college continues, we will all build up this level of stamina, which may be the truest measure of excess. Sorority sisters who are drunk enough to have eyes swiveling around in their heads will learn to tickle their throats with their fingers, hurl, and reel back to the party to pick up drinking where they left off.

In spite of the scene at the liquor store, I still managed to net a bottle of champagne. Perry pops the cork out the sliding glass door, where it cracks like a gunshot. Milton has been lost for hours, and I'm glad because I don't have to think about him. I can just drink champagne from a bathroom glass with Perry, whom I feel comfortable with on account that he isn't my love interest, or even Hannah's.

Each sip of champagne tastes like honey. I love the whispering sound its bubbles make, as though the drink itself is trying to tell me something. After a few glasses, I am too unsteady on my feet to slip into my new floor-length gold dress without stepping on the hem and half-falling over.

Getting ready is the most challenging part about formal weekend. After five hours of pre-parties, a mascara brush is just as dangerous to operate as heavy machinery, and when we develop the film from our disposable cameras, everyone's makeup looks like Tammy Faye's. High on champagne, my biggest challenge is scooping out my suitcase. After twenty minutes of pawing through my clothes, I still can't locate two high heels. When the time comes, I go downstairs to the ballroom wearing Milton's rubber flip-flops.

The dance itself is the least interesting part of the weekend. For a few hours, there's an open bar, and we drink screwdrivers garnished with orange wedges through tiny plastic straws. As a sorority, we were too cheap to have the event catered, so the white tablecloths are covered with confetti but no food, and our empty stomachs make us even more drunk. On a banquet table are a few cheese plates, sticky glasses that are half-full or half-empty of cocktails, and ashtrays smoking with forgotten, unmashed cigarettes. The deejay we hired was detained at customs, so there's a Canadian one, spinning the culturally offensive music that's usually reserved for terrorist interrogations.

Zeta's president requests Crosby, Stills, and Nash, which is something that someone will do at every formal henceforth. When it comes on, the sisters make a ring on the dance floor, linking arms and slurring the words to "Our House." I join in, wrapping my arms around the synthetic material of two peoples' dress waists, and chirping about how life used to be hard, but now everything is easy because of Zeta. I tilt my head against the sister standing next to me and let my eyes well up.

The words zing out of me because I don't yet know what a Greek myth they are.

The rest of the night flickers on like a movie that you watch while you're nodding off to sleep, and catch only pieces of. The vodka I drank in the ballroom omits some scenes, but I manage to pay attention to the important events in the plot. Milton materializes during a slow song, when he tows me onto the dance floor by my elbow, and I let him twirl me a few times before I flip-flop back to the bar. Perry finds a piano in a hallway and thumps out a labored rendition of something truly campy, maybe "You Are So Beautiful." Someone snaps a picture of me standing beside him, listening, with one hand on the piano's lid. In it, my eyes look blank, and my skin is as white as chicken meat.

Sometime after midnight, Hannah and I get the idea to climb onto the slick roof of a ferry that is tied up in the bay. The red letters painted on the ferry's side read SEA FOX, though Hannah keeps calling it SEX FOX. We plunk ourselves down on top of the boat's bridge, smoking a joint and shouting "All aboard" as loud as we can, to see if the ice will toss our voices back in an echo.

Sometime after that, I slide back through the door of my hotel room and pass out alone in the sheets.

THE ROOM is as dark as first darkness, the way only hotel rooms can be. In my sleep I can hear the old-fashioned clock on the nightstand flip its numbers. I know I will not be able to sleep soundly here, knowing Milton still remains at large, and that he might tear through the door at any minute with his plastic key. Beyond that, I can never fully doze off when I am this loaded with hard liquor. Vodka, especially, lulls me into a state of delirious half-sleep, in which I talk and laugh out loud.

I'm lying on my side, facing the blank white wall, when

Milton comes in. I can tell he is wasted by the way he falters onto the bed, clasping me from behind and wiping his wet mouth on my collarbone. I can feel his penis pressed between my shoulder blades like I'm being robbed at knifepoint.

I feel stalled between consciousness and sleep, the way I used to on the mornings when my mother used to wake me up for high school. In my dreams, I'm saying *Go away go away go away,* but in reality I'm not sure I'm exhaling a damn word. My jaw feels too stiff to speak through.

Milton is kneading my rib cage like a ball of dough, hard enough to make me glad I'm this drunk—otherwise, his hands would hurt. Tomorrow, when I'm inspecting the bruises, I'll think I should have quoted the poet Milton, who said, "He who overcomes by force overcomes by half his foe." But in the moment, I can't think at all. Liquor has strained my mind. It has exhausted my heart. My only defense is my vacancy. I hope if I play dead, he'll leave me alone.

But he won't leave me alone. Instead, he continues the postmortem, and on top of it, he starts yelling. It's not intimidating, exactly, because Milton doesn't have the blustering roar of a man. He sounds more like a little boy throwing a tantrum in the supermarket checkout aisle. He keeps squealing, "What the fuck is *wrong* with you?"—not because I'm dead-drunk, but because I won't let him touch me.

I gain a little consciousness when I hear an empty rattling and realize Milton is punching the headboard with one fist. In the triangle of light that spills out of the bathroom, his eyes look like two thumbprints.

I squint to focus my gaze, while I try to concentrate on the power in my fingers. I feel like any woman in any movie that has, in order to save herself, willed her drugged or deadened digits to move. With enough meditative oomph, I finally complete the Jedi mind trick. My hand makes a swatting motion, and I hear a sloppy, smacking sound that says I've made contact. Milton rolls off the bed like a log, more because he's drunk than because of any real muscle on my part. I am finally left alone, permitted to curl back up with my drunkenness, hugging my own torso like a lover. From here on out, when anyone asks what happened, I'll say he's a brute, and he'll say I'm a prude.

For a few minutes in the early morning, I'll wake up prematurely and see Milton still sleeping on the floor where he fell, with the faded blue comforter wrapped around him like a torn fishing net. Sunlight will finger the room, and the bureau will be cluttered with cigarette butts and cigarette butt–filled bottles, and the carpet will hold the long, brown stain from somebody's rum and Coke. My lips will feel achy and swollen, and the sealed air will smell as musty as death.

I will decide I want to check out of all of this, maybe even for good.

Two WEEKS before finals, winter starts to break. Suddenly I am experiencing spring for the first time, the way you can only wholly experience something once you've forgotten it ever existed. The sun brightens like a lamp that's been screwed with a higher wattage of bulb. For once, the city looks less anemic.

In the quad, the snow melts to mud. I sit there in the grass between classes, beside the boys throwing Frisbees and the girls tonguing frozen-yogurt cones. We wear T-shirts, even though the temperature lags, and our skin blushes like it is shocked by its nudity.

For the past few months, I've been more interested in going to parties than in fixing my ongoing gymnastics glitches, which puts me in a less-than-desirable position when I have to try out for next year's cheerleading team. It is the absolute last thing I want to do given the weather and the fact that my coach has reassigned Joe to Hannah.

My new partner is a three-hundred-pound grad student named Ramon, whose main job on the team up until now has been to run the length of the Carrier Dome with the twelve-foot-tall flag that all the other boys are too small to hold. After the very first stunt I do with Ramon at tryouts, my clothes are streaked with his sweat and hair gel. To make matters worse, I fall midway through a back handspring, and rather than getting up, I lie on the mat like a crushed beer can.

I can't say I'm surprised when I don't make the team, but the elimination stings anyway. I cry on the floor of the locker room shower for forty minutes, grinding my nails up my shins and against the grout between the floor tiles. Then I decide to countervail the pain by getting drunk.

I go out with one of my sorority sisters, a girl named Grace, to a rock club on Westcott Street, which is the only stretch of Syracuse that could ever pass for cool. It is the old hippie part: a few blocks of thrift shops and pagan bookstores, acupuncturists, tapas bars, a community center walled with life-sized mosaics. Among students, the venue is famous for lousy music and accessible beer, proving that for two-dollar bottles of Labatt we'll endure untold agony.

When we get there, the club is under new management, and since we don't have fake IDs, a man at the door marks our hands with gigantic Xs. The marker is black and pervasive, the type that makes your pores look like a game of connect-the-dots and won't wash off for days. Grace and I storm the bathroom, where ten other girls are huddled at the sink, scrubbing their stubborn Xs with hand soap. The best we can do is to fade them to gray. When we leave, the counter is awash with ink-stained paper towels.

We twice try to order beer, but the bartender sees our blackened hands and threatens to 86 us. I feel despair that's even worse than the anguish of being eliminated from the team. It's worse than romantic rejection. Without a bottle to hold, I feel incomplete, the way Plato says we are each born only half a circle, and we spend our lives seeking out our other half. A drink is my beloved. Without it, I am wanting; I feel half-finished.

Fortunately a cigarette company is there, passing out free packs, which seems like a far bigger no-no than serving beer to minors. But I grab a pack, and feel happy to have something to occupy my hands. Without a public project, I am painfully aware of my detachedness. It is a sensation like riding the subway without gripping the handrail: Without a beer or a cigarette, something to hold on to, I feel doomed to fall over.

With my free pack, I sulk at a back-most table with Grace, running my fingers through my hair and *click-click-click*ing a disposable lighter. I smoke in a hungry sequence, lighting one cigarette with the tip of another until my throat feels as red as raw steak.

The minimum drinking age is an incomprehensible thing when you've been drinking for four years already. Your mind keeps coming back to the past, to the bygone beers that should make you more than eligible to drink in the present. It's like applying for a job when you have no degree but loads of experience. You tell the bartender, "But, but." And he says, "If buts were horses, then beggars would ride." You pine for a taste. A bottle is an old lover mocking you; it's across the room, being held by somebody else. Nothing else will ever hold you by the heartstrings. No man could ever fever your chest the same way, or awaken that kind of beauty in you.

Near the speaker, a boy is staring at me. It's undeniable. He is parked in reverse, with his back to the stage. His gaze spills toward me. I push my hair in front of my face every time I meet his eyes. His stare tears through me like a cleaver. It isn't the way men stare at women on the street, when they mentally strip them bare and weigh their proportions like lunch meat. Instead, it reminds me of the expression on my mother's face when I step out at the airport arrival gate. It is that tender look of recognition, the kind that makes me skittish.

Later tonight, when I am washing my face before bed, I'll decide that this boy is shockingly handsome, with sound features and eyes that hold light like a child's. But in the moment, I'm still lonesome for beer. I decide I can't stand him.

When a guitarist with dreadlocks tucked under a kerchief croons, "I want to fuck you in 3-D," I decide I can't stay another miserable minute. I kick out my chair and kiss Grace on the cheek. En route to the door, the phantom man dogs my footsteps. He is a lanky silhouette that leans down to say something. No words pass through me. I move around him the way I'd bypass a downed branch in the street.

FROM WHAT I can tell, S.U. hasn't ranked on a list of top party schools in over thirteen years. I know because one day, Tess and I do an Internet search on the subject. Rumor around campus is S.U. made the *Playboy* list in 1987. But the truth is, out of forty schools listed, mine didn't even earn a mention. And every year for the next four years, when *The Princeton Review* publishes its own list of the top twenty-five—something they've been doing since 1992, and something the American Medical Association has called for them to remove on account of its glorification of binge drinking—someone I know will sigh and say, "We didn't make the cut." No doubt the omission relieves school officials. But within the circles in which I travel, it is a blighted hope, a deficiency.

This is because college, like most life experiences, doesn't look as good in real life as it looks on TV. Specifically, it doesn't look as good as it does on MTV. The network's coverage of spring break first premiered when I was five, from which time I honestly believed that college was what I saw in their ninety-second promo spots. I thought it was all body shots and wet-T-shirt contests, girls shimmying on life rafts, and paranormally hot folks swapping underwear. I imagine that other people still do think this. Because in May 1999, when MTV brings its "Campus Invasion" to S.U., smack in the middle of the study days that precede finals, the mood on campus goes from stirred-up to manic.

It's strange the things the university does to celebrate its own year-end windup. Not only does the administration permit the MTV idiocy, the condom expo and video-game booths and second-rate performances by third-rate pop stars, it also sponsors carnivals on the lawn outside the underclassmen dorms, complete with ring tosses, animal balloons, and cotton candy circulating on sticks. Outside my dorm window, the dining hall cook flips hamburgers on a hibachi. Freshmen are bucking on a thirty-foot-high inflatable castle, the kind the rental company won't let you jump on without taking your shoes off. The environment on campus looks totally age-inappropriate, like the site of an eight-year-old's birthday party. All the girls on my floor get drunk or high, and hop on the castle in the name of irony.

. . .

THAT NIGHT I go with Hannah to the school year's real finale, an annual block party on Livingston Avenue, which students call Livingstock. It's a haphazard series of off-campus parties hosted by upperclassmen. Many of them are in houses we've haunted throughout freshman year, when we'd drop three dollars in a vase at the door in exchange for tapping the keg. But tonight's festivities are more or less complimentary; anyone is free to fill a cup.

Kegs are proudly displayed on front stoops and street corners, the way plastic Santas are set out at Christmas. No one appears to be afraid of repercussions from campus security. Half of us are finished with finals, and the school year feels as unalterable as our blue exam books and bubble sheets full of ink-shaded circles. Whether we're passing or failing or just getting by, our fate seems sealed.

Livingston Avenue is a stubby little road, less than half a mile long. And tonight, every square foot seems to be filled with human bodies. Tomorrow, the city newspaper will tally the head count at over a thousand. Hannah and I bound through them all, recognizing no one and saying "hi" to everyone, drifting in and out of houses, lifting Jell-O shots off kitchen counters, allowing guys to pry the caps off of our beers. For a change, there is live music. Behind the balustrade of a front porch, a girl with a halo of white-blonde curls coos into a microphone. Her face undulates. Her syllables, thick with breath, swell like rainwater in the street.

Normally, I keep track of how many drinks I have, if not in the interest of charting how punchy I am, then for the sake of comparing hangovers with Tess the morning after, when we sit in the dining hall, heads throbbing, and say, "I can't believe I drank five (or six or seven); I didn't know I could physically do that." But tonight I can't work out how much I've tossed back. I can't even pin it to a crude estimate. The night is warm and the beer is warm, and I feel starry-eyed. Everything I look at has a ripple to it.

Somewhere there is the sound of glass breaking against the sidewalk. In a second, I spin around and see that Hannah is gone to the crowd, to white lights and dim wailing and faces all bleeding together. I feel the way I did at age six when I lost hold of my father's hand in the L.L. Bean factory store. I'm alone at the road bend. If I weren't past-gone, I'd be panicked. I reach out for the first arm I can grab hold of. It's attached to my phantom man, the one from the rock club.

Under normal circumstances, this would be a coincidence of catastrophic proportions. But phased and plenty drunk, standing arm in arm with him feels like the most natural cosmic course of events.

I lean into him and say, "I saw you on Westcott Street."

He says, "I saw you, too."

As we stand, stock-still, there is confusion going on all around us. Flames surge up from lawn chairs piled in the street. People on the roof of a house are chanting, "Hell no, we won't go." More are running through the broad spray of a hose, the way my sister and I used to run through sprinklers in our front yard when we were young. Men in uniforms force themselves through doorways. Airborne bottles are everywhere, whizzing by us like paper airplanes.

I'll only know to call it a riot when I read tomorrow's headlines: HOW ONE S.U. PARTY TURNED STREETS AFIRE AFTER A POLICE REQUEST TO CLOSE DOWN. Reporters will call it "alcohol- fueled" and "the city's first riot in at least a decade." All in all, it will cost the city $22,000 in damages, including $700 to fix the shattered windshield of a fire truck. Thirty-nine students will be arrested and ordered to pay $2,500 fines. Livingstock will be a thing of the past.

I follow Chris (that's my phantom's name) around the corner of a duplex to a parking lot out back, where we stow away in the flatbed of a white pickup. We lie with our backs against the cargo space, kissing and watching the fray unfold like a display of fireworks. The fuss on the street has the same romantic qualities, the same loud popping and sparks of explosions.

We have the type of immediate intimacy that is brought on only by alcohol or physical danger. It is the kind that usually only happens in movies, when men and women save the world from nuclear holocaust or escape a detonating bus.

Up until tonight, in the bed of this pickup, I have always preferred booze to boys. For the most part, I've always wanted to be left alone with my buzz, to study the thoughts curving in my head like a girl admiring her own silhouette in the mirror. In the past, if I kissed boys during those drunken moments of self-wonderment, it was only because it was easier than resisting. I would let some boy put his mouth on mine because I knew no harm could come of it, because I was stoned and stony, and I felt nothing.

For the first time, with a stranger in a strange car, I *feel*. From nowhere, desire surfaces, and it swirls through my insides. The want is thrumming and it is everywhere, like a hive knocked from a tree that unfixes a squall of bees. The fluttering in my chest is as unfounded and unnerving as the riot itself. And dread follows it because I know in an instant that I would, and will, do anything in pursuit of this yearning. It will not be enough to want once. I will want to *want* a million times over, to feel this warmth where there used to be coldness, this prickling sensation where everything was once numb.

Chris is a prime example of why it will be hard to stop drinking: Drunk, I take bigger chances, and therefore reap bigger rewards. He is the polestar that I would never have found if I weren't shipwrecked, were my internal navigation not haywire. He is my temperate latitude, someone to drive me home, wearing his sweatshirt because my clothes still hold the dew of the fire hose. When I say good-bye, I write my phone number on a parking ticket. It will be void in a week, when I go home for the summer.

THE NEXT DAY, Chris calls to invite me to a barbecue at his fraternity, and I suddenly don't care about anything else. He is a buzz incarnate. Just like straight vodka, he has the capacity to quell my worries about everything else. When he calls, I forget about being cut from the cheerleading team, and about the final that I flat-out failed. I brush off the boxes I still haven't packed for home.

I bring Hannah to the barbecue for moral support, but when we get there, the throng of boys drinking beer and swinging Wiffle bats is still hard to approach. It's like the moment the door opens on a crowded elevator, and we're not sure whether we should try to squeeze in, too.

Chris is chasing a tennis ball across the yard, and he waves hello. A few brothers drag an armchair onto the front lawn for us, and Hannah and I sit, doubled up on it. Together, we smoke cigarettes like joints, lighting them and then passing them off. Boys pour us blended margaritas, and we turn ourselves in circles to lose the bees that trail our cups. We are less than fifty feet from campus, and the stony face of the chemistry building looks helpless to stop us from drinking.

Sometime after my third Catalina margarita, dusk lands like a 747, and the sudden change of light makes me wobble. The fraternity's cook calls the boys in to eat potato skins. Hannah squeezes my shoulders, then takes off for cheerleading practice, drunk as a handcart. For a moment, I sit there in the low light, pulled between the desire to stay and a compulsion to go. I breathe the sugary smell of hard alcohol and fresh-cut grass. And then Chris comes for me, the way you find your date when a slow song comes on at the prom.

Throughout college, every time a buzz comes on like sweet music, a man will seem to sense it and grab for me.

I FOLLOW THE back of Chris's T-shirt up the fraternity's stairs, all three floors of them, and then out the attic window and up a twelve-foot, wrought-iron ladder to the house roof. Three years later, a brother will attempt this climb while schloggered and break both of his legs. I feel a little like Orphan Annie climbing the train tracks at the end of the movie; my boozy-woozy feet tap dance on every rung.

When I make it to the height of the house, the view feels like the big picture. I can see all of campus—its green lawns, yellow hedges, and the white walkways that section it all off. I imagine myself streamlined. My mind and body are finally working in tandem, and there is no rift between what I want to do and what I actually will do. There are no stars, but I imagine I can sense them approaching, the way people can sense rain coming deep in their joints.

I kiss Chris in a plastic lawn chair, and let him pass his hands over me, while my hair whips sideways like a flag on a pole. I know it is more than the height that makes my heart leap into my throat, the way it does in the brief moment before a roller coaster breaks over the crest of the first big hill, the ground screaming toward me, the person next to me lifting his hands up.

ANDREA DWORKIN said most people see intercourse as a private act, but it's actually a social act because men are sexually predatory in life, and women are sexually manipulative. I think being drunk makes men even more predatory, and women more manipulative. Too often, I find myself drifting into a decanted daze when some boy like Milton swoops down like a thunder cat, coming at me with both paws and his big, whiskered face. And lately, even more often than that, I find myself employing a weird hocus-pocus that seems to appear from nowhere. Sober, I'll cross the street to avoid looking a leering man in the face, but drunk, I will talk him up for an hour, robbing him blind, extracting all the free drinks and free flattery he will give me. I'll watch his mouth move like a stock ticker and pretend to be deeply interested in the quotes. I'll even tell him that his voice reminds me of my favorite song, or that he has eyes like two blue flames, or maybe even that I'd like him to walk me home, before I'm gone to the refuge of the ladies' room, never to return. Drunk, I'm quick becoming an assassin, eager to settle an ancient score, to extricate payback for a guy's crimes, offenses I don't know but feel certain exist.

But tonight, my carousing with Chris feels like a wholly private act, even though it's in a most-public place. Maybe it is because he's more timid than I first thought, or because alcohol has made me feel more like the mountain lion than the piece of dropped meat. Or maybe it's because we are wholly self-interested, in the way that only drunkards can be.

I once heard someone say that the concept of moderation seems a little extreme, and tonight, on this rooftop, I agree.

Moderation is idiocy perpetuated by the alcohol industry, which bombards us with warnings about "drinking responsibly" in order to absolve itself from the irresponsibility that alcohol awakens in just about everyone at one time or another.

Even years from now, once I've stopped drinking, I will never stop trusting extremes. I will always believe that anything worth having is worth having in excess. The good things are worth hoarding until you have a cookie-fat ass, sex-aching loins, joy that fires through you like popping popcorn, or love, the weakness at the sight of some boy that makes your chest ache like indigestion. If it's good for you, it ought to be good for you in any amount, and you should track down every available bit of it. And if it's toxic, if it turns your liver into a hard little rock of scar tissue, or curls your memory at the edges like something burned in a fire, or makes your stomach flop, or your mind ache, or your personality contorted, you shouldn't buy the bullshit about temperance.

Alcohol, like all addictive drugs, changes the chemistry in your brain in such a way that after one drink, the brain wants another. The same thing happens after one kiss from Chris— my mouth wants another. After one graze of his fingertips, my skin yearns for another. Alcohol and attraction are addictive properties on their own, but the combination makes my blood bolt through me. I am hooked.

LOVE IN THE TIME OF LIQUOR

WHEN IT COMES to romance, my drinking is almost fetishistic. For years it will be the third wheel in every one of my romantic liaisons. Like the blonde bombshell in a passionate threesome, booze, in its near presence, will always make me feel sexier. Alone with a man, I'll get used to liquor's company. After a time, it will be hard to manufacture any affection without it. Sober, I won't be able to squeeze a man's hand or say "I've missed you." I won't be able to divulge the slightest hint of endearment.

Back at school sophomore year, my yearning for Chris persists with or without alcohol. But liquor makes it swell like one of those sponge capsules that flowers in warm water. Sometimes my tenderness for Chris has a breadth so wide that I can't see around it while I'm sober. That is the case when he stops by my dorm room on a whim, or invites me over to watch *A Clockwork Orange* with our shoes off, or drives me to the bus station to meet Kat, who is in from Cornell for a visit. Without alcohol, his glance alone can rattle me. Just hearing someone call his name across a room makes the fluff on the back of my neck stand up.

One damp Sunday in October, Chris invites me to be his date for his fraternity's date party. It's an affair that isn't all that different from a junior-high make-out party. But instead of playing Yahtzee, we gulp Martini and Rossi. And instead of "seven minutes in heaven," it's more like seventy.

When I call Hannah with the news, she runs directly over in her cotton pajamas, toting a bottle of Skyy vodka and four little black dresses, which I try on in frenzied succession, even though they're almost exactly like the five that I own. She stays even after I settle on a ruffled black one, and together we pour vodka into a carton of lemonade we find in the mini-refrigerator. Each sip from its cardboard lip tastes strong and bitter, but it slows my stomach jitters, so I keep drinking. Tess, who is my sophomore-year roommate, ties a red velvet bow in my hair and outlines my eyes with a kohl pencil. Hannah tucks a Durex condom into my purse's inner pocket because she thinks I ought to carry one, "just in case."

Throughout college, my friends carry condoms defensively, in stark contrast to some boys, who carry them offensively. It's part of a warped female thought process: When we're gutter-drunk with some boy we just met, we like to think that if we can't fend off danger, we can at least beseech safety. We learned this outrageous mode of prevention in part from the public-health officials who visit once a semester to lecture sororities on the dangers of excessive drinking. In 2002, a public safety slogan from the University of Colorado at Boulder will actually advise female students: "When you're drunk, you'll have sex with someone you wouldn't have lunch with, so bring a condom."

For better or worse, my girlfriends and I are products of Generation Safe Sex. As an age-bracket, we were inundated with condom catchphrases before we hit puberty—misogynistic slogans like "Before you attack her, wrap your wrapper" and "If you think she's spunky, cover your monkey." We've been taught to BYOC as we BYOB. We fear HIV before the unplanned or nonconsensual sex through which it's contracted, which is like not listing injured troops among casualties: The number of battle deaths is tragic, but it's only a part of the carnage.

CHRIS IS not the type of boy to make you wait, sitting on your bed for forty minutes, trying not to smear the lipstick your roommate painstakingly applied on whatever bottle you are swilling to take the edge off your tension. He turns up at ten o'clock sharp, dressed sweetly, the way boys do when they're giving in-class presentations. He is wearing crisp oxford cloth and khaki. Mini marlins leap on his tie. His skin carries hints of mint and cologne.

I'm too spooked to glance up at Chris as we walk from my dorm to his fraternity house, which is just down the street. He has brought a small black umbrella, which we have to huddle under to stay dry. In the cracked sidewalks, there are pools of rainwater and fat knots of worms to step over. My breath jerks when my elbow brushes against Chris's dress shirt, when it occurs to me, *I've never navigated these close inches without being drunk.*

I feel the same way I used to in high school, when I would have to put on my mother's panty hose and accompany some boy to a homecoming dance. The prospect of being someone's date embarrasses me as deeply as it did when I was fourteen. As far as I am concerned, the word *date* holds too much meaning. I operate in a culture that is hopelessly noncommittal. My sentences are punctuated with *like* and *whatever,* the linguistic indifference that was forged by Generation X, adopted by Generation Y, and is to every subsequent age bracket just as natural as *if, and,* or *but. Date* is too certain a word in a world that prefers vagueness. To me, it means a responsibility to be entertaining, bright, and opinionated, to adjust a man's shirt collar and dispute Medicare over vodka martinis. Being Chris's date feels like a terrible, terrifying burden.

AT TIMES like this, I wish I were a party girl, a term that I've always loved.

I know the designation is the stuff of amateur porn sites and bad cinema. And it's no wonder, considering that the term was once akin to *exotic dancer.* (In the 1958 film *Party Girl,* Cyd Charisse plays a young showgirl who works as a party girl at gangster soirees.) The byword has always suggested not only that women's fun exists solely for the benefit of men, but that it can't exist at all without the active gaze of Joe Francis, the wildly rich producer of *Girls Gone Wild,* or some other pervert in an OFFICIAL PUSSY INSPECTOR T-shirt to confirm it.

I know all of this, and yet I just can't help myself. *Party girl* always makes me think of jelly bracelets, tangerine-colored tights, and high-top sneakers, not to mention 1980s cocktail dresses—the sequined ones that are basted with bows and frills, the ones that are so bad they're good. It still makes me think of Cyndi Lauper, who was like any fantastical and slightly unnerving children's character to me at age three, when my mom says I would turn loops in my ballet tutu whenever "Girls Just Wanna Have Fun" came through the kitchen-counter radio.

The party girl has always existed, and it appears that she will simply never go away, particularly in the era of tabloid television shows in which cameramen stalk Los Angeles nightclubs in the hope of provoking a shit-faced starlet to flash the finger. The party girl will never stop running up five-thousand-dollar bar tabs, puking in the bathroom at Lot 61, or getting kicked out of Vegas nightclubs while screaming "Don't you know who I am?" She will never stop making headlines in the *New York Post* for gargling champagne and lifting her skirt. Without her, Shannen Doherty or Tara Reid or Britney Spears wouldn't have maintained some semblance of a career, and Paris Hilton wouldn't have one to begin with. The party gal is a sad and beautiful ingenue, who appears in photographs with tousled hair, smudged eyeliner, and a visible thong. And as long as she exists in real life, we will never cease to be interested in her.

We're fascinated because the party girl never stops making us feel better about ourselves. In her essay "Visual Pleasure in Narrative Cinema," Laura Mulvey suggests that films and the sexy starlets in them give our dirty thoughts free reign, which inevitably makes us feel wicked, until the only way to absolve ourselves of the guilt we feel is to blame the women onscreen. The same thing happens when I flip the channel and pause with perverse fascination while Paris Hilton pounds cocktails or pole dances, her bony legs spread like those of a newborn colt that's trying to stand up, before I say, "That's disgusting."

Deep down, I'm glad for Paris, for the same reason that I'm glad for all party girls, especially Jenna and Barbara Bush: Drunk, they are uninhibited, often sexually, which makes me feel intrigued, then repulsed, then superior. Their atrocities allow me to call them "the world's biggest assholes," and momentarily remove myself from the very same list.

On the night of Chris's date party, I wish I had a party girl's sexual spontaneity.

All the fraternity's usual party games have been cleared out for the occasion. The pool table has been repositioned against a far wall. The black lights and neon beer signs are absent, as is the rocking-chair-like contraption that the brothers manufactured for taking shots.

It's pretty obvious that the main floor has been outfitted to be *romantic,* which is another word that disquiets me. I will never get over the feeling that there is too much pressure to feel affectionate in formal attire, or in a restaurant with courses, or in proximity to candlesticks or flowers. It will always be nearly impossible for me to feel an affinity for someone unless we're both wearing unwashed jeans and unwashed hair, unless we're eating dinner at the corner diner, by the glow of a neon-blue aquarium light.

Tonight, even the furniture looks like it is canoodling. Someone has pushed the wingback chairs and leather sofas into a semicircle around a wood-burning fire. There are tea candles on coffee tables, vases wadded up with baby's breath, and Eva Cassidy's dumb devotion spilling out of surround speakers. I want to snatch my coat from the coatroom and hightail it home before anyone can tell me that I clean up nice. And I would, were it not for Chris's psychic pull. I would leave, if my want weren't a force strong enough to tie me into a chair.

Chris goes upstairs to help a brother move a table, and when he comes back down to find me, I'm in the kitchen drinking tequila with a sorority sister named Elle. We are swallowing shots from the type of thimble-sized plastic cups nurses use to serve pills at the student health center. Chris comes up behind me, so that Elle sees him first and smiles sheepishly.

When he lays his big palm flat in the hollow between my shoulder blades, I feel a fluttering spark like the moment a moth collides with a bug-zapper. I take it as proof that my synapses still need stunning. It is an electrical surge, and I know that I need to take the rum drink he's brought me, plus a few more shots with Elle, before I'll be senseless enough to let him touch me.

It's not that I don't like Chris's fingertips on the back of my neck; it's just the opposite. My desire for him is like my desire to drink: Privately, I want, enormously. I want in heaps and dizzying doses, and I want many times over; I want overkill. But publicly, I don't want my desire to look excessive. So I drink to get a handle on my hot cheeks, my jitters, and my speechlessness. The next time Chris puts an arm around me, I want to be as serene as the surface of a lake: something pretty and reflective that doesn't dare ripple.

ELLE AND I spend the next half-hour in the downstairs bathroom. As far as we're concerned, it's the best damn room in the whole house, a white mausoleum where we can sit on the edge of the claw-foot tub and smoke her French cigarettes. Chris is allergic and makes faces when I light up in front of him, but when I drink, I can't stand not smoking. A cigarette is the olive in my martini, the garnish waiting for me at the bottom of every glass.

At one point, Elle teeters backward into the belly of the tub and knocks her head against the soap dish. When I offer her my hand, she pulls me in, too, and the white room rings with our laughter. When I stand up and look down at my legs, there are all manners of snags and holes in my tights, and I don't care. I slide my fingers under the tinted nylon and tear wider gashes. Elle whoops. The tiles underneath my feet rock back and forth in a way that feels pendular, and it reminds me that Chris, my center of gravity, is upstairs.

By the time I clomp up the spiral stairway, I've quit feeling anxious and choked. Six cups of cheap liquor have washed away my outer layer, the cold surface of fear, under which there is an emotional stratum of lightness, gladness, and love. I coil beside Chris where he's sitting on a sofa in front of the fireplace, the way a cat attempts to reconcile after a hasty decision to hate you. I let my head tip onto his shoulder and watch his mouth move from close up, the same way I'd watch a movie from the front row. Every word he exhales lets my flickering fondness catch fire.

Someone snaps our photo while we're sitting side by side. It is a picture that I'll keep for too long, carting it with me through too many cities between the pages of *Of Human Bondage,* until the edges are bent and the matte is smudged and covered with crud. For a long time, I will see the illusion of emotional connection in the way we are sitting, totally tangent: shins touching, my arm sleeping quietly on his thigh, his cheek grazing my forehead, his arm folded entirely around me and clasping me as tenderly as any man ever has. It will take me years to notice the miserable truth in our body language, the fact that while he looks as wide open as a sunflower, I am closed as tight as a clam. My legs are tangled around each other. My chin darts down, and my chest crumbles inward. The only thing I'm grasping lovingly, with both hands, is a cup of rum and Coke.

ALCOHOL IS a manipulative bitch. If she were a person, I think she'd be a telemarketer or a used-car saleswoman, the type of woman who could persuade you to do just about anything. I think this because when my mind is stewing in alcohol, it prompts me to do things that I'd normally oppose, like take my bra off under my coat in the corner convenience store because I've suddenly decided it pinches. Drunk, I can seduce myself into any course of action. I can always come up with motivation to draw that proverbial line in the sand back one more inconsequential inch.

That's how I convince myself on the night of the date party that I want to lose my virginity to Chris.

The party doesn't slowly thin out, it goes directly from jam-packed to vacant, as some girls disappear to the campus bars and others sneak away behind the plywood doors of the brothers' bedrooms. Once girls follow their dates up to bed, they're gone for good, the way that once Lucy steps through the wardrobe in C. S. Lewis's books, she's vanished into the forests of Narnia.

I, TOO, TRAIL Chris up the spiral staircase to his room. It feels like a sleepwalk. My eyes ache under the weight of their lids, my feet take cautious, little strides. Thoughts rattle in my skull like odd dreams that have their own percussion.

I'm thinking, as I grip the staircase with both hands, that I ought to dig Hannah's Durex from my purse when I reach the landing. I'm thinking that there are party girls behind every door that I pass, girls who are unashamed and uninhibited, girls who are stark naked, their small voices warbling. I think of them, and I decide that I am, as always, being too square under the circumstances. I am attributing too much to sex, which in my well-liquored state suddenly means little.

I always hoped I'd have sex for the first time with a real boyfriend. I thought I'd do it with someone who took me to the three-dollar movie theater, or to the New York State Fair, where we'd buy snow cones, ride the Mind-Scrambler, and make fun of the sculpture that a local dairy company carves every year out of butter. Plus, I wanted to be clearheaded when it happened because I sense a hangover could make anyone feel extra defiled the next day.

But that ideal looks antiquated to me now, and I'm too hopelessly unlike the shiny liquor-ad girls who just go with the flow, who drink Sauza because "The tequila is pure, so your intentions don't have to be," and Frangelico because "fate" is "what happens when the unexpected becomes pleasure." These are the girls who know that you don't have to have a detailed plan for the evening, you can just drink Smirnoff Ice and "See where it takes you." I think, *I will let liquor take me to Chris's room.* There is no one to stop me; unlike my car keys, no one can take away my desire because they think I'm too far gone to control it.

But I don't stay conscious long enough to initiate so much as a kiss. Moments after Chris hoists me up the ladder to his loft bed, liquor sings its lullaby. The moment goes dark, and I fall into a bottomless, fairy-tale sleep.

The next day I wake up at noon, in my frilly party dress. My hair is matted against my cheek, and my head is positioned on one corner of Chris's pillow. My face is inches from his. His open eyes are watching me, honest and blue, and I can't tilt in the few inches to kiss him even though I ache to.

I am sober and therefore don't have the prowess to trigger even the smallest act of intimacy. I lay that way for over an hour, frozen, even after Chris has me pulled to his chest the way a kid clasps a teddy bear. In the throes of withdrawal, I feel like one of those ratty childhood bears that smells like spit-up and has one eye popping off.

But my hang-ups are even worse than my hangover. I feel like a field mouse caught in a glue trap. I am stuck fast in the sentiments I can't express without booze.

IF YOU buy the notion that alcohol improves the way you feel about yourself, you can't help but buy the message that alcohol improves the way you feel about, and during, sex. That's because the alcohol industry has spent a considerable amount of time tweaking its image of the sexy drinking woman. If you pay close attention to the alcohol ads of the past ten years, you'll notice that the women in them aren't nearly the passive objects of desire they used to be. These days, for every Miller Light girl who mud-wrestles in an itsy-bitsy bikini, there's another girl in spike heels and a sleek skirt-suit who is apt to take the beer and leave the guy who bought it for her.

With women drinking a quarter of the beer sold in the United States, it is as if the industry finally figured out the formula that attracts us: It's no longer enough for the alcohol-ad girl to *look* sexy; she needs to *act* sexy. She needs to be the sultry product of her sassiness and excessive self-confidence, the woman men want to be with and women want to *be*. Alcohol advertisers have learned that sex as an image doesn't sell anymore, that the mud-wrestling Miller girls were actually responsible for a slump in sales (including a 19-percent drop in Texas, the brand's most popular state).

What does sell, especially to women, is sex as an *idea*. Even more than men, we buy the concept that sex is a tricky proceeding. We understand that interacting on the coed level is a struggle for dominance, one that involves a million fouls and false starts, where the playing field is never level, and where one player almost always has the advantage. That's why Anheuser-

Busch advertises Tequiza using the brazen taglines "Actually, size does matter," and "They're not real, so what?" And on the Captain Morgan rum Web site, there is a "blow-off-line generator," which is presumably for women, right alongside a "pickup-line generator," which is presumably for men.

Pay close attention to the next TV beer ad you see, particularly for the light beers and malternative beverages that are marketed to women, and you'll notice that the guy hardly ever scores the babe anymore. In recent years the alcohol-ad guy has become a calculated douche bag. He is so simple that he is simpleminded, so horny that he is actually hamstrung. He is the guy epitomized by Bud Light's "Real Men of Genius" campaign, which salutes every schmuck from "Mr. Way Too Much Cologne Wearer" to "Mr. Silent Killer Gas Passer." He is the kind of man-child who says and does everything all wrong. These days, women brush him off as often as they brush up against him.

This is because the alcohol industry would have us believe that beer-ad Barbie is a modern-day gal. She doesn't have time to slow down, to sit still for too long in one place with just one guy. She is the woman embodied in Baileys commercials, the one with enough sense to laugh when a man spills a drink on her chest, but too much self-worth to let him wipe it off. We root for this girl because she seems smart but not snobby, sexy but not slutty, receptive to men's advances and yet completely in control of them. We need to believe that whatever she is seeking—be it a next great love or a next great lay—is just a few drinks away.

Really, why else would there be some seventy-odd drink recipes with the word *sex* in the title? Not to mention twenty with *screw,* and thirty with *orgasm.* Altogether, there are roughly a hundred and twenty recognized ways to solicit sex from a bartender. Just ask for a "Shuddering Orgasm" or a "Passionate

Screw." You can demand a "Blow Job," "Hot Anal Sex," or "Oral Sex on the Beach," not to mention "Sex in a Parking Lot," "Sex on the Ceiling," "Sex on a Pool Table," "Sex with Todd," or "Sex with the Captain." You can literally ask for "Sex Anywhere," and have it with just about anyone.

Like everyone else ordering "Hot Sex" at the bar, the connection between drinking and dating has been hardwired into my system. Even five years from now, once I have quit relying on booze as a mechanism to make friends or feel okay about myself, it will be nearly impossible to interact with men in the absence of liquor. A first date will feel too stiff without a drink at the table, and I will be too blank for conversation, too mortified when a fork falls off the table with a deafening clunk.

I SPEND THE rest of the semester drinking at a bar called Chubby's with Elle. In fact, we are there so often that the owner starts to call us "the twin birds" because we're always at the bar, holding shot glasses, with our heads bent together, swan-like.

"Basketball shots" become our new favorite drink. These are the flaming shooters the bartender turned us on to, though he never revealed the exact ingredients. I know only that he fills a sherry glass with a bile-colored liquid and lights it on fire. And there is something mystic in the vapors rising off the blaze that suctions the rim of the glass to his palm, so he can dribble it in midair without using his fingers, the same way someone bounces a basketball. When he slides his hand off the rim, we lean down to inhale the gaseous stuff before we swig the actual liquid.

The result is a lot like huffing household cleaning products. After just one, I look like TV news footage of mad cow disease; my eyes roll back in my head, and when I try to get up off my stool, my legs collapse under me. After two, I throw up in my bed sheets. After three, on the fateful night of November 1, I can't hoist my head off my pillow the entire next day. My head aches like I nose-dived onto it from three stories up. It's the first time that I'm old enough to elect a president, and I physically can't go to the polls. I don't need an MTV news anchor to tell me: I'm not a chooser, I'm an utter loser.

Part of the reason I start going out four nights a week is that I can't bear to stay in my room. The partial wall that splits my dorm room in half can no longer divide my mess from Tess's. Together, we live in turmoil, like animals or addicts, maintaining only enough free space to satisfy our immediate needs. Clothes blanket my floor, my desk, and my bed, and I am always too exhausted to undertake the big job of picking them up. Instead, I transfer them from station to station, depending on what I need to accomplish. I push them aside to write a paper. Sometimes I sleep on them. I pick them up to try them on, and then I take them off again. Everything I own smells like the floor of a bar.

The other reason I spend more hours at the campus bars than I do at the gym, the library, or the dining hall is that it's my only hope to run into Chris. Alcohol has set us into a cycle whereby we only get together when we're drinking. Even then, we don't sit and talk as we play cards and hold beer bottles. I usually mark time until he careens through a crowd to find me and follow me back to my dorm room. We are stuck in neutral, and alcohol has made it increasingly impossible to switch gears.

On the nights when I make a concerted effort not to get too drunk, I notice that Chris passes out as often as I do. I'll be nuzzling against his collarbone when I'll realize his chest is rising and falling too heavily, and breath is escaping from his mouth with a hiss. When I whisper his name a few times and he doesn't stir, I snatch back the covers. I'm always half-relieved and half-pissed.

To make matters worse, Chris starts leaving in the mornings before I wake up. At nine A.M. on a Wednesday, when I click awake with a hangover, he's as gone as the ancient Mayans. Books are stacked on my desk. Dirty T-shirts are heaped in the hamper. I'm lying diagonally, like a backslash, across the whole bed. I ask Tess if she heard the door close. When she says no, we dangle our heads off the edges of our beds, scanning the carpet for rolls of mints or stray socks, any artifact that might prove that he'd been there.

ONE THURSDAY night in November, Elle and I go to the Tropics, a downtown bar that's a short bus ride from campus. It is one of our favorite places to get sunk: a big split-level space with walls painted orange, tables shaped like sand dollars, and a giant aquarium teeming with googly-eyed fish. There, for seven dollars, we order gallon-deep, plastic fishbowls filled, I think, with a combination of strawberry and peach schnapps, Midori, Malibu rum, pineapple, and orange juice. The truth is, half the time we don't know what we're really ingesting. We just suck it down fast, through foot-long plastic straws.

In my experience, there is a bar and a drink for every mood. Sorrow has a certain taste, and joy has a certain atmosphere. You can't indulge your gladness anywhere that has cement floors, where people watch infomercials on the bar's lofted TV, or where two dollars buys you a shot of tequila and two tallboys. Similarly, you can't coddle your blues anyplace that has tables or single-sex bathrooms. You need to piss and get pissed with the drudge of humanity. You and your grief have to be on display, on a stool at the bar, digging through the pretzel bowl that the bartender keeps on filling, like reparation.

The Tropics is my happy space. It is predicated on denial. With the vintage sunscreen ads tacked on the walls and the red lightbulbs in beach-bucket fixtures, not to mention the fact that the furnace is cranked up so high that the front window fogs over and the bartenders have to wear tank tops, it's easy to forget that outside it is twelve degrees below zero. Here, it's easy to forget that I'm missing another study group for statistics class. I forget life can conceivably suck as much as it does.

Elle is striking and blowing out a succession of matches. I am caught up in trying to sneak maraschino cherries from the bartender's plastic tackle box, which is stocked with cocktail napkins and orange wedges. A crowd of people is milling around, and holding their bottles like Academy Awards, and when it parts, I see Chris mouth to mouth with some other girl, who clearly has no problem expressing affection. Even flat-drunk, I can feel something strain inside me. It is a wrenching pang that can only be my detonating heart.

Elle is the ideal friend to have in moments of melodrama. She will dive into conflict with you so that you'll have company, instead of pulling you out. She will smack down her MasterCard on the bar and tell whoever is listening to "Keep 'em comin'." She'll happily play the decoy so you can maintain some semblance of self-respect, making the big distracting bang that prevents people from noticing while you drink until you're gone.

Elle is not the friend who puts one hand on your cheek and coos "It will be okay." Elle is the friend who stands on the bar stools and hurls bottles, the one who understands pain so completely, even when it's not directly her pain, that she doubles over and sobs. She reminds me that this is *not* okay, that *"This* is bullshit."

I don't remember seeing Elle kick out her bar stool to go talk to Chris, nor do I remember her giving him a right hook to the temple, which is too bad in a way. And I don't remember how long I slumped at the bar with my chin in my hand, telling the whole damn story to the bartender, who offered his phone number on a napkin. Who knows how many gin-filled fishbowls I downed? I know only that the bitterness of them lasted—I could still taste it, metallic like pennies, on my tongue the next morning.

I SHOULD KNOW better than to go Zeta's fall formal alone; there's nothing like drinking alone in a room full of happily paired people to make you want to off yourself. But I do go alone because a lacy green dress has been hanging in my closet since the day I asked Chris. Plus, Hannah and Elle don't have dates, either, and an older sister named Nadine sets us up with three boys from her date's synth/prog-rock band.

The fall formal is on one of the big spade-shaped islands in Alexandria Bay. Hannah, Elle, and I hitch a ride up with a sister named Brianne, a sophomore who has a date beside her in the front seat. So we have to sneak sips of Amaretto the whole way up I-81, rolling our eyes every time they touch hands and pretending we're not jealous.

It turns out that the "charming Victorian resort" that was described to us by Zeta's president is actually a stretch of hunting cottages with wooden decks that the concierge proudly says we can fish off of. In all fairness, it probably would be breathtaking in summertime, when you could dive for antique bottles in the St. Lawrence River or roam through the stone structures of Boldt

Castle, ride a pony, race a go-cart, or eat egg sandwiches under covered pavilions. But as usual, we do everything ass-backwards. My friends and I operate only at night and in the winter, when things are dead or sleeping or frozen, and the only thing to do is haul up with a liter of citrus-flavored vodka.

After Hannah, Elle, and I check in to our room, a bald compartment with rust-colored comforters and elks stenciled on the walls, we wander down the walkway to Nadine's room to meet our dates. According to pictures, this is the only time we spent with these boys with thin arms and skewed haircuts. Clearly, liquor made us feel we knew them well enough to commit them to a good chunk of film. A dozen pictures show us pig-piled on top of each other. Everyone's face is stopped in a look of shock, lips pursed in speech like they're exhaling cigarettes. One guy is licking Hannah's forehead. Another, who is wearing a leopard-print scarf, has me hoisted like a sack over his shoulder.

Since we don't have cards or dice or coins, oddly enough, we play the verbal drinking games that I hate, the stupid tongue twisters and tests of trivia that I'm always too slow to say without slurring. We play "Sex, Drugs, and Rock 'n' Roll," the game in which everyone has to name something from one of the categories that starts with the letter A ("anal sex," "amphetamines," "Alice Cooper"), and then on down the alphabet, drinking while they think, or if they get stuck, or if they're stoned enough to repeat someone else's answer.

Then we move on to "Rhyme or Reason." Then, "Screaming Numbers." Then, "Celebrity Name Game." The whole time, we sip straight vodka until we start forgetting the rules, whose turn it is, and who just got skipped. By the time we get around to playing "Categories," I'm leathered enough to forget that the capital of New York State isn't New York City.

. . .

AT THE dance, the hotel's ballroom looks like an Elk's Club. It's hung with flannel curtains and mounted heads, including a doe-eyed deer that someone crowned with a party hat. The table centerpieces are clusters of pinecones and glitter. Overhead, strands of ribbon dangle from a hundred helium balloons. We produce our fake IDs for the doorman, and he passes them back to us with total indifference.

I'm surprised to find we're among the last few people to arrive, which makes me wonder just how long everyone has been here, snapping cameras and eating pigs-in-a-blanket, dancing so fervently that their foreheads shine. Elle and I take stools at the bar, squaring our shoulders over glasses of vodka and cranberry juice, while Hannah makes a beeline for a crowd of sisters swishing their satin gowns on the dance floor. Already I'm discovering that my two friends mix together as badly as beer and liquor, the by-product of which is *you've never been sicker.*

The bartender seems to be mixing drinks under the mode of trial and error. Everything tastes not quite right, like spoiled juice. In pictures, we are all carting around parfait glasses filled with toxic-looking, tangerine-colored fluid.

Looking through photo albums a couple of years later, I'll find it telling that we never put our drinks down when we pose for pictures. We choose instead to hold our glasses in front of us like iron shields, our cigarettes unsheathed from the pack like drawn swords. I don't have a single photo from college in which I'm not wearing this armor. In every one, I'm clasping a glass like the date I just can't keep my hands off of.

It doesn't take long before I feel a sharp pain behind my eyes. Cheap liquor always gives me this headache. It's as though my brain is recoiling from the label, like the guy who tests the wine at the dinner table by gurgling, spitting it out, and sending it back. The headache is usually followed by nausea. My stomach turns over like I've been swallowing Clorox, and it is a sickness I can both smell and taste. I feel hungover before I've even stopped drinking.

I ought to take this as a sign that something bad is about to happen, the way murderesses on soap operas get battering migraines before their dual personalities take over, before they crack heavy art-deco sculptures across the backs of their twin sisters' heads. But I never do, and I don't this time. Instead, I ask the bartender for some ibuprofen, and I wash down the tablets with rum and pineapple juice.

Elle and I take off our shoes and join Hannah on the dance floor, holding hands and shaking our heads hard from our necks. When I look around, everyone is coming undone. The boys have freed themselves of their jackets and vests, and unhitched the silk nooses of their neckties. The girls are pulling out their bobby pins one at a time, and their hair is cascading down around them like liquid. Hannah's bangs are standing up in spikes where she stuck one wet hand in them, and Elle is dancing with someone else's date, blind to the squabbling it's aroused among the sisters. She keeps moving with her hands on her hips, and her dress straps skate off her shoulders.

Somewhere in the middle of a slow song, I look up from the palms of my hands and notice that I have drawn a crowd. There are multiple arms grabbing for me, and too many faces fighting for a space inside my line of vision: first Nadine, then the house president, then Elle, urging everyone to get the hell away from me. Someone's date picks me up and carries me over to sit at a linen-covered table, so I don't cut my bare feet on the bits of broken glass on the floor.

I don't remember the glass wriggling loose from my hand, so I'll be relieved tomorrow, when Elle assures me that I dropped—and didn't throw—it. Nor do I remember exactly what slipped inside me, the eyeblink's time where I went from fine to totally fucked, precisely when the barricade around my brain broke, making it impossible to contain a private thought inside me. The fact that I'm crying doesn't fully register. I can only gauge my actions by other people's reactions, by the fact that Elle is using a towel to sponge streaks of rum off my face and legs.

When the moment's sounds come through, I can hear my voice whining at a pitch of pure pain, as if I'd just closed my hand in a car door. My breath is jerking through me like a succession of sneezes. I have no idea how miserable I am until I hear myself confess it out loud.

A HALF AN hour later, my booze-induced tantrum means nothing. It's only one of many that night. The girl whose date Elle has been dancing with has locked herself in the bathroom, where she is sobbing and scribbling on her legs with a tube of red lipstick.

Plus, whatever scene I made passes quickly, like a tropical storm that leaves you soaked and dazed, with little actual damage. Elle goes back to our room to fetch my CDs and gives them to the deejay. The moment "Rock Lobster" comes scratching through the hotel speakers, she convinces me to shut up and dance.

The real trouble with my fit is that it has distinguished me from the crowd. I've bared my emotional wounds, made myself the lame lamb of the flock, and earned the attention of any nearby predator.

Elle and I are hopscotching across the dance floor with the hems of our skirts in our hands when a boy hooks me around the waist and twirls me off like a top in another direction. A slow song has come on, and he has positioned his face precariously close to mine. He is so close, in fact, that the tips of our noses keep touching. Still, I can't make out who he is. His head looks very small and far away, like I'm looking at him through the wrong end of a pair of binoculars.

For a while, I'm fine with the idea of having someone to dance with. But after a few songs, he is nudging me in so close to him that the length of my dress is getting caught up in my legs. I push my palms against his chest, trying to eke out enough space to say *Thank you for the dance* and urge him to go back to his date. But he just keeps jouncing me up by the waist and pulling me into him, the way someone moves down the street with a big bag of laundry. Later, I'll realize he doesn't have a date because he is one of the hotel's employees.

Every time a sister walks by us, I try to open my eyes big and round, which, in my experience, is the universal code for *Please help me,* the same way that two hands around the throat is lingua franca for choking. But they just smile back, like they are happy to see that I'm feeling better. Someone flashes me a thumbs-up.

It occurs to me to say that I have to go to the ladies' room. But when I do, the big shadow of the man lurks just outside the restroom's door. I stand in front of the mirror, for a long time, washing my hands. The bathroom light is soupy, and I feel too sluggish to find an escape hatch. I decide the only ways around him are through the double-hung window or around the corner while his back is turned. I slide onto the floor beside the sink, sitting while I try to decide what to do, which is where Elle finds me. She decides to go outside and tell him that I've gone home to sleep. Once the man is gone, I follow Elle down the blacktop path to our cabin. My heels are in my hands, and I am wavering. I don't even feel the wet gravel under my toes.

Not far from our cabin, we hear the scuffing of shoes and realize that the man is padding up the path in the opposite direction. I try to adjust my eyes to get a good look at him, to see through the fog that has arranged itself on the walkway and in my head, and decide if he is as menacing in real life as he is in my mind. But I can't make out anything beyond a thumbnail sketch of a man's broad shoulders.

Elle jabs me and tells me to get down. We sprawl on our stomachs in the wet grass behind a chokecherry shrub for a long while, holding our breath until he has passed, and being so silent that I nod off with my face in the dirt. Drizzle is floating down in one sheet, like a mist of perfume. Tomorrow, our dresses will be ruined with watermarks. Hannah will say the man knocked at the door for an hour, after he pulled our room number off the hotel's computer database.

I DON'T THINK people realize that drunk girls are themselves a fetish object. The phrase itself is as porn-sensitive as *schoolgirls* or *lesbian orgies*. Type it in to an Internet search and you'll get more than 450,000 porn sites in less than twenty seconds. And I'm not only talking about sites that feature spring-break footage of "easy drunk girls flashing their tits," but also ones that highlight "dead-drunk girls passed out," and publish gritty, overexposed pictures of girls lying unconscious while anonymous male hands pull off their underwear.

Take, for example, clubdrunk.com, which advertises, "This site is not a joke! We find real drunk girls and fuck them on video. We go out all year round to bars, beaches, colleges, and wherever else drunk girls are and get them to come home with us!" Or consider deaddrunkgirls.com, which boasts 60,000 members who log on because: "We all know the situation when a girl feels shy. If you don't help her to relax, you will end up wanking off alone . . . If you get her drunk she'll do anything for you, she'll even satisfy *all* of your friends." These sites show photos of girls slamming back glasses of whiskey, right alongside the nasty close-ups of the sex acts that we're led to believe came afterward. Visitors are reminded, "Kelly was dead-drunk and I don't think she realized what was going on. But one thing is for sure, she certainly enjoyed herself!"

And the tragic part is, we can't even allow ourselves to feel sorry for girls like Kelly. Because if we follow through with Laura Mulvey's argument about visual pleasure and apply it to the modern-day party girl, if we say that Kelly, who is clattering beneath some man in the live feed of a hidden camera, exists as a passive object for the gaze and enjoyment of men at their laptops (one that intrigues us, then grosses us out, then makes us feel superior), she is already guilty. She has already been transformed into the type of fetish object that makes the guys who watch her feel reassured, rather than endangered, by her sexuality.

There is a sadistic quality in our assignation of blame to her. Once we write her off as an "easy drunk girl" (porn-site speak), we can feel comfortable that her punishment fits her crime. We can distance ourselves from the room where she is lying all but lifeless on leopard-print sheets, and chalk up her "drunken gang bang" to the fact that there were animal instincts skulking inside her, just waiting for the moment when men and tequila would draw them out. We can accept headings that suggest she had this coming. We'll buy statements like: "You are about to see three hot party girls get fucked in the VIP room. They were so drunk, they didn't even care."

. . .

By the final weeks of fall semester, I notice that the quality of men's manners seems to be directly proportional to how drunk I am. It's a fascinating relationship between variables. When I'm stone-sober at a party, I can count on a man offering me his seat (if we're in the den) or his jacket (if we're on the deck). He will shake my hand during an introduction, and offer some wrenched pleasantry like, "Weren't you in my cultural perspectives class?" On the other hand, if I'm running amok in a bar, I can bank on the fact that some gruff-faced guy will snap my bra strap while I'm swaying on my feet, en route to the ladies' room. One night in a campus dive, a man I barely know bites my armpit, leaving a vampire-like ring of teeth marks and bruises that lasts weeks.

To be fair, the boys I date after Chris might account for the decline of etiquette. They are a series of drunks and depressives. They are nocturnal boys, the kind who rarely come alive until the library has been locked for the night. They don't return phone calls or buy textbooks. They live in off-campus apartments because the administration has ousted them from the dorms for possessing drugs or booze.

I spend the final weeks of fall semester dating Jody, a boy who has a date-rape accusation to his name (although charges are never pressed). I'm not sure why I do it, except to say that he doesn't scare me. He is a musical-theater major, an elfin boy with a feminine face and scant deltoids, and I'm pretty sure I could take him in a fight. Moreover, he is always drinking Scotch or snorting coke off of my album covers, and his desire for drugs seems to displace his desire for sex. Jody is a non-threat. I can invite him to stay the night in my dorm room and swill wine the whole time. I can drink excessively with him, until I knock myself out cold, knowing he won't make any move to paw me.

Drinking and drugging, Jody is a bigger wreck than I am. On the nights that he's drunk, my phone machine bleeps with messages at five A.M., when he calls, crying, to say his car has a flat tire and he's too rat-assed to change it. And on the nights that he's high, he's a one-man production. He jogs between the phone and the stereo, calling his agent, belting out show tunes, dragging his fingers through his bleached hair, digging up old scripts, and rattling off disjointed daydreams that I think he sincerely believes—like he used to date a young indie-film star, or he was in the Broadway revival of *Annie Get Your Gun*. We lie side by side on my bed, staring glassy-eyed at a late night talk show and drinking red wine. I usually dip into sleep while Jody prattles on about which of tonight's guests he once did a play with in London, or bought weed from, or screwed in the bathroom of a five-star sushi joint.

I like having Jody around because, in contrast to him, I feel in control. Alone, my life is beginning to feel like it's running away from me, so much so that I've started to have recurring nightmares that I am driving a car with faulty brakes, skidding wildly out of control, and plowing ninety miles an hour into highway overpasses. But next to the white lines Jody cuts up on the cover of the *Tommy* LP, my bottles look as benign as lollipops. Next to the two thousand dollars he gave his dealer this month, the two hundred I dropped at the campus bars doesn't look half-bad.

Other times when I'm with Jody, alcohol feels childish. I find myself mixing drinks liberally in order to keep up with him, and to make up for the fact that booze isn't some stronger drug. I slosh vodka two inches deep into my S.U. coffee mug, and feel like a baby for refusing the rolled-up dollar bill he'll hold out for me.

For better or worse, I'm a product of Nancy Reagan's Just Say No campaign. Drugs make me fearful in a way that booze never does, probably because public service announcements have worked their magic on me: The U.S. government still spends twenty-five times as much on campaigns to fight drugs as it does on campaigns to prevent underage drinking.

Even in the moments when I'm so smashed I'm scared, when I'm lying on the bathroom tiles I can't hoist myself up from, throwing up so tirelessly that I start to cry, I can still rest assured; it's comforting to know my brain is not on drugs. I assure myself that this, too, will pass. After all, it's just rum.

ONE NIGHT, Jody gets drunk enough to talk about the girl that people say he sexually assaulted. We are sitting at his coffee table mixing Salty Dogs when he gets up and starts burrowing through an antique oak chest, tossing out weathered scripts and old *Playbill*s as he goes, until he comes up with a sheet of notebook paper. It's a letter, he says, that she wrote him during the semester that he was studying in France, which irrevocably proves he is not guilty.

I read it over twice between sips, but I'm saturated with grapefruit juice and vodka and I can't absorb anything else. The letter is penned in big, bubbly letters, and the ink is blue, and the words meld on the page. I fold it back up where it's creased, and decide it's impossible to know what actually happens when a man and a woman are alone together, particularly when they're both drunk, and when they dated both before the incident and for months after. I ignore the fact that only guilty people think to hoard evidence; I decide that Jody is harmless.

It is an opinion that I stick by through the late-night phone calls and parties at his place where a dozen people dump Baggies onto a mirrored coffee table, and I drink too much apricot brandy to care, and Hannah leaves crying because she walked in on someone snorting lines off a toilet seat.

And I keep on thinking it until the night when Jody and I are stretched out on the floor of my bedroom, and Tess is away at a sorority party. The night is muggy and motionless. On TV, women are doing leg-lifts. Jody is buffing his gums with his fingertips, and I am drinking more and more merlot, feeling the lumpish, leaden drunk that comes with wine. I am drifting to sleep with my head on Jody's stomach when I hear the crack of two hard surfaces making contact. I come around a few seconds later, when I realize the smacking sound was my head hitting the nightstand when Jody pushed me.

When my eyes adjust, I can see that he is bent over me with blue eyes as wide and dull as the designs printed on the ends of wine corks. He's got one hand pressed hard on the top of my head, and the other curled tight around my neck, so I feel like the gray slab of clay he's compressing on a potter's wheel.

He kneels down to say, "Don't you dare tell my girlfriend."

I'm amazed, not by the force of his request, but by my senses' dullness. I can't believe I could barely feel such a crash. All I do is pitch my head back to croak, "I didn't know you had one."

AFTER EVERYTHING with Jody and Chris and the man at the formal, I develop trouble sleeping. When I close my eyes, I see men as big as monsters. They are hairless and bare-chested; their arms bulge and twitch like snakes digesting mice.

In my dreams, I always run from men. I sprint through dark suburban streets, always looking over my shoulder, while my heart rate clangs and hammers. But it is never fast enough; the men always sack me from behind, and I hit the concrete under their oppressive weight. I am flattened. The wind is always knocked out of me when I wake up.

The only nights I sleep soundly are when I am excessively drunk. When I'm wasted, exhaustion drops from clear out of nowhere, like the steel combination safes that flatten people in cartoons. I can be going about my business, doing my thing, playing cards or debating partial-birth abortion or executing a handstand, blind to the shadow of drowsiness that hangs over me—that is, until it falls with the *bam* of its total molecular weight and I have to lie down wherever I am, in a restaurant booth, on a friend's couch, or on the sidewalk.

I love that kind of drunken sleep. I love that for a few brief hours after it strikes, every thought is knocked clear out of my head. That is, before sunlight drains through the window blinds and I have to peel my steamrolled body off the bed sheets and pop my brain, with its misgivings, back into 3-D.

In the quest for self-erasure, sleeping picks up where drinking leaves off. On the nights when, drunk as a drum, I still can't calm myself enough to fall asleep, if alcohol amplifies my emotion instead of silencing it, I swallow a few of the sleeping pills that Elle carries like dimes in her change purse. Those nights, permitting I make it home to my bed and don't pass out on Elle's floor, I fall asleep without setting the alarm, giving no thought to what I might need to get done in the morning, nor to anything that goes bump in the night.

BEER TEARS

IN THE FALL of my sophomore year, I am still a virgin. For someone who has been drunk enough to lose as many jackets and wallets and bits of sterling silver jewelry as I have, it's hard to believe that I haven't lost this, too. After all, one study reports that 60 percent of girls have had sex by their high-school graduation, and the majority of those who haven't will have their first sex in college. Plus, a study by the Institute of Alcohol Studies in the UK that polled a thousand women found that a third of them had had unprotected sex after drinking too much, and almost half had a one-night stand they wouldn't have otherwise considered.

Still, through all the weekend parties where I've sipped vodka straight-up and gone wobbling through strange bedrooms, whacking into door frames, and bumming cigarettes from boys, I know I've stayed as chaste as an unscooped sugar bowl. That certainty lasts until two days before winter finals, when I open one eye after the soundest sleep of my life.

THROUGH THE sting of consciousness, there is too much information to process. The time of day, for instance, is wholly undeterminable. The room is like a casino in its clocklessness. Hot, white light is spewing through the bay window, but it means nothing without a directional gauge. If the room faces east, it might be seven in the morning. If it points west, it might be midday.

I know I am on the second floor of a master suite in a fraternity house that I usually wouldn't be caught dead in. It is the Greek organization that at S.U. harbors painfully preppy boys. I am lying in the fetal position on a full-sized futon, under a patchwork quilt that looks like someone's mother might have made it. The bed is on a lofted platform, atop a wrought-iron ladder that I vaguely remember being nudged up.

Beside me is a boy I recognize as a senior, a political science major named Skip. I met Skip briefly at a party two weeks ago. The introduction is dwarfed in my memory because it was the same night that Chris stopped me in the stairwell to hold my hands and make a beer-teary apology. I'd followed Chris home that night and slept in the bow of his arm, feeling violently happy until the morning, when I felt the same old deadlock: His closeness made me tremble, and I crept out the door while he slept.

I barely know Skip, but I know I don't like him. He is smug in a distinctly male way. He has calculated facial stubble and the type of ego that is hatched from early admission to law school and a family yacht named *Never Again II,* tied up in Newport.

The one time we spoke, he made it clear that the feeling is mutual. He hates girls like me, the ones who have difficult names and thrift clothing. He hates those of us who are pale where we should be tan, dark where we should be blond, sullen where we should be smiley, and mute when we should be fawning.

I decide he even looks like he's swaggering when he's sleeping. He is facing me, with his eyes pinched closed and his lips pulled into a pout. I'm not happy that I've passed out here, but I'm not alarmed by it—not until I move my hands under the quilt to quietly roll myself away from him, and realize that I am as naked as the day I was born.

THE SITUATION is almost sci-fi. I feel like I've been reborn into a whole different reality, and whoever transported me has rubbed out my memory. My body is as sapped of energy as any screen heroine's after she has swapped realms or bodies, and I am experiencing the same wooziness. My lower back cramps. My limbs shirk orders when I tell them to move.

I try to retrace last night's steps:

The night began at a campus bar, where I didn't drink much. I had, what? two, maybe three, shallow glasses of white wine before the party filtered out. It tasted cool and thin, and it hadn't affected me at all.

Next, Elle wanted to go to a party in the basement of this fraternity house. I owed her a favor, so I came even though I call this place the Inferno because its every party is a pilgrimage into hell.

The basement is a stony cavern lit by red lightbulbs. There were fights. Boys leapfrogged onto each other's backs and started throwing punches, and one girl caught an elbow in the teeth. The air was hot as an oven, and the cigarette smoke had nowhere to filter off to. Everywhere, people were kissing like they were trying to devour each other.

I remember brooding in that lower hell, holding a beer bottle, and talking to Skip. I'd had a few beers, enough to make me feel sunny and lithe, and I was nowhere near being brutally drunk.

Then come the gaps. There is an interlude between the memory of the basement and the one where I am here, on the ground floor of this suite, sitting on the couch and being kissed by Skip.

And there is another hole, between that and a few blurred moments that I remember sitting on a toilet seat, leaning forward with my chin between my knees. The instant dissolves around the edges. The bathroom is just a small patch of floor and a toilet. My feet are bare. Under them is a pattern that seems like no real pattern at first, as though a contractor tossed tiles into the air and glued them down wherever they landed. Some are square. Some are rectangular. Some are black. Some are white. Then the floor starts to blur, and it looks like a crossword puzzle that no one bothered to fill in. I remember that I couldn't hold my torso upright without it flopping back down like a sheet of cheap poster board.

And sometime after that, I remember standing in the hallway in my underwear, staring at a succession of doors, the way a winner on *The Price Is Right* tries to decide which grand-prize display to crack open. I knew that behind one of them was the million-dollar spectacular: my clothes. I vaguely recall that a boy came along like Bob Barker and told me which one to open.

· · ·

IF THIS were a movie, this would be the point where I would lean over and ask Skip what happened. He would say, "We just passed out is all." And then we would both hide our heads under our pillows, and cringe at the close call that nearly spoiled our friendship.

Only this is real life. Skip is not my friend. He is snide and combative, and he makes me feel small. I will not ask him what happened because I do not want to know.

Instead, I collect my clothes as quietly as I can, while Skip sleeps, or pretends to. My socks, pants, and shirt are strewn across the couch like bread crumbs, but they don't lead me any further out of my blackout. I have never felt so lost. I will never find a way to MapQuest myself to this futon. I'll never know how I got here. I'll never know what intersections I crossed along the way.

I decide to hold my shoes in my hands until I make it to the hall, until I'm far enough away to risk the clomping of my cowboy boots. I can't find my bra, so I opt to leave it behind. I hate to think I might be leaving a trophy that Skip can hold up as proof of the conquest, but it is the limb I am willing to bite off to escape the steel-jawed trap.

Outside the bedroom door, it can only be early morning because the whole house is as quiet as a tomb. I confront the same conundrum I must have faced last night: Every stone hallway seems to lead me back to where I started. My legs are shuddering, and I try every possible direction. I go right instead of left. I go up and down different sets of stairs. Yet all routes are circular; they all lead back to Skip's door.

Were I in my right mind, this house with its mural towers, Canterbury windows, and spiral vaults would make me mad as hell. And it will later, when I think about the way these swaggering shitheads live here, insulated as shining knights in a stronghold. But right now, I feel like a drugged rat in a maze during a clinical trial. I'm so desperate to leave that I am willing to wake Skip just so he'll show me the way.

Later, I won't remember how I roused him from sleep. I won't know whether I climbed the stairs to the loft, or if I called out his name and stayed very far away. I know that I must have averted my eyes because I can't conjure a clear picture of him getting up from the bed. I have no idea what he was wearing, if he had on anything at all. Only the sight of him forcing his feet into unlaced sneakers will stay with me. The laces make little tapping noises as we move across the floor of the pantry, which is the one avenue I didn't try.

When we make it to the garden-side entrance, Skip swings back the door and bleached light courses over him. He is so blond that sunlight mirrors off him, the same way light gets reflected off the three-foot-high mounds of snow on the sides of the street. He wears blue cotton shorts and a white polo shirt. I can't help but wonder what he plans to do after I leave, if he'll go back to bed or sit down with jellied toast and the newspaper's sports section. I can't imagine that any other news could possibly matter.

He stuffs one hand in his shorts' pocket and says, "See you around."

Outside, nature is indifferent. Birds are actually chirping the way they do in Disney movies. I only make it a few steps toward home, before I have to double over to rest. I crouch on the curb, where I can hear Skip close and bolt the storm door behind me.

THERE'S ONLY one thing to do when you're not sure what happened during a blackout, and that's to keep on not being sure. G.I. Joe had it ass-backwards in those public service announcements from the 1980s when, in between commercials for Combos and Robo Strux, he taught us to put reflectors on our bikes and test doorknobs during a fire because "Knowing is half the battle." In terms of denial, it's the opposite: *Not knowing* is half the battle.

Doctors at Duke University say blackouts happen when alcohol totally shuts down the hippocampus, the chunk of the brain's temporal lobe that churns out new memories—the same one that is damaged by Alzheimer's disease and epilepsy. Experts used to think blackouts were an early sign of alcoholism, but today they are finding that mind erasures are common among nonalcoholics, too. Plus, girls needed far fewer Long Island Iced Teas to blow the fuse. On average, girls black out after five drinks. It takes guys nine.

The only upshot of a blackout is that you're spared the emotional effort it takes to repress whatever happened in the midst of it. The night in question forever exists like the train scene in a silent movie, the one where the screen goes dark the instant the train charges the tunnel, and when it emerges a few seconds later with two long whoops of its whistle, the audience never really knows what happened in the tunnel's obscurity. Who made love in the first-class compartment? Who stabbed the man in the club car? You can guess, but you'll never know for sure.

After a blackout, all you have to do is keep on not knowing. If you can't remember, you hope you never remember. You indulge your selective amnesia. You operate under the philosophy *I don't think, therefore I am.*

A FEW THINGS happen before I release the memory of Skip like a captive dove.

For one, I scrutinize my body. This is hard, considering I've never been the kind of girl to bend backward over a handheld mirror. I have always been too shy, even alone, to give myself the monthly breast exams my doctor always explains with pamphlets. But before I shuffle down the hall to the dorm bathroom to take the symbolic morning-after shower that I've seen in too many movies, I force myself to do a thorough once-over. I pull my hair up off my face. I smell my skin. I check my inner thighs for bruises. Since I've never had sex before, I don't know what signs I am looking for.

The only thing I know with any degree of certainty is that I feel violently ill. My digestive system feels more off-kilter than ever, like organs are writhing and backfiring inside me, and I feel a squeezing stomach pain like someone is standing on my abdomen. I don't know whether it's nerves, or a hangover, or withdrawal from some date-rape drug that makes my heart flutter, but I am so unsteady on my feet that I have to sit on the floor of the bathtub under the shower spray. Between shampoo and conditioner, I bend over the drain to vomit. It's stomach fluids, the acidic yellow froth you spit up when there's nothing else in you.

Next, I avoid my mother, who has been calling as though she's psychic. She has been worried, she says, when she gets me to pick up the phone three days later. No doubt it's because I haven't returned her calls, but in the throes of my remaining paranoia, I'm convinced it's because she knows something that I don't. I think she must have had a premonition about Skip in a dream. Hot tears stream down my face halfway through our talk, and I have to put my hand over the receiver so she won't hear my voice tremble. I pick a fight that makes her hang up before we say our good-byes.

Last, I talk to Elle and get what I can of the details.

I do it while Elle and I sit at a picnic table outside of the university's food court. It's our favorite spot for heart-to-hearts and last-minute cramming, where the wind flips the pages of our notebooks and we ingest the eight-inch-tall cups of well-sugared coffee that we count on to fuel us through our hangovers.

Elle is wearing fingerless gloves and a puffy down vest that looks like a life jacket. She is straddling the picnic bench, hunched over notes on something difficult. Elle negates the myth that smart people don't binge drink—she's one of a handful of female physics majors, and the sharpest person I know. Her mind teems with a hundred mathematical theorems that she calls on to explain just about everything.

I am absently staring at the same notes on Ideological State Apparatus that I've had open all day, when I look up and ask her what happened.

I don't know how she answers because I still can't concentrate on anything external. Inside, I feel mental interference that is almost electrical. It is a deep static that is hard to hear over. Still, I hear Elle talk about how she left me at the party, where I was talking to Skip. She didn't want to go without me, but I was like the donkey that resists the force of the reins with its full weight. I threw a tantrum when she wouldn't let go of my arm. I told her, "I'm fine. Just leave. Just leave me the fuck alone." She has no gauge for how drunk I was because she was drunk, too.

Still, when Elle tells me, her face screws up in a look of guilt, and I can tell she's sorry she left. She is averting her eyes, pulling the cotton strings from the holed-out knees of her jeans, and questioning, I'm sure, if she could have done more. No doubt, she is feeling that female-specific remorse that happens when we think we haven't adequately mothered one another. It is the same remose I felt when I lost Natalie in Ocean City. It's the same remorse my mother will tell me she felt in high school, the night I was taken to the hospital. I think the world as I know it is a massive web of feminine guilt. We all mourn and make up for not just our own catastrophes, but also everyone else's.

Men don't do this. When men drink, they help each other, but they don't feel personally responsible for one another's catastrophes. Three years from now, when I'm living in New York, three boys I knew in college will crash at my apartment after a night at a nearby bar. One boy will turn up barefoot, and his face will be smeared with street sludge. The other two will let him sleep the entire night on my bathroom floor, without showing the slightest remorse about it. In the morning, when he's scrubbing puke off of his shirt collar, neither of them will tell him, "I shouldn't have let you get that drunk."

Yet my girlfriends and I do this all the time. We play God to one another. We are the omnipresence that won't let our friend Eve reach for that third apple martini.

I tell Elle, "It's fine. I think I'm fine."

It starts to snow, and I don't even bother to pack up my books. I turn my hands over on the table, so I can catch flakes on my inner forearms. I let them dissolve on my skin because I want to feel icy.

Elle says, "Whatever. If you can't remember it, it never really happened, anyway."

SOMEHOW THE word *whatever* has outlasted slacker culture. It is the one artifact that has survived all those movies from the mid-1990s, in which high-school dropouts and college graduates embraced Doc Martens and too much flannel, formed grunge bands with obscene names, went grocery shopping with their parents' gasoline cards, got drunk, got high, slept with their best friends, and challenged the system that would have them believe that doing nothing wasn't something in itself. Over the course of the past fifteen years, *whatever* has become one of those linguistic sneezes that transcends partisans. It is there in almost every facet of American culture, a ready-made column and comic-strip name for every would-be satirist. The word is scrawled under as many pictures in my high school yearbook as *Peace and Love* is in my parents'.

Girls were especially keen on the word from the start. From the moment Alicia Silverstone injected it with a shrill note of sarcasm in *Clueless,* it became immediately obvious that anytime I said something a little off-key, some eighth-grade girl would use her thumbs and index fingers to form a giant *W* to wag in my face, while she rolled her eyes and said "What-ever."

But Elle is right. Saying "whatever" is the best way I know to change the subject. It's a ready-made one-liner, a phrase that is devoid of control, responsibility, or ownership, with the capacity to mean anything, or everything, or nothing at all.

I decide that whatever happened with Skip meant nothing at all.

At school second semester, I assemble a steady team of drinking buddies from the girls I see every night at the campus bars. We are the sorriest girls I know. I am one of the lucky ones—among the girls I slug vodka with on the steps of the school chapel are several victims of rape and abuse and girls who have abusive boyfriends, divorced or dead parents, mothers in rehab and fathers in mental-health facilities. Some have half-siblings they've never met.

Together, we drink until we're batty enough to tick off our

disappointments, to cry, and to comfort each other the way girls do. It's like group therapy, only instead of helping me feel less disturbed, our meetings only push me deeper into depression. They make me more convinced that life as we know it is some kind of purgatory, in which everyone suffers and is punished, and every one of us is licking her wounds. All our talks turn back to suicide—who has tried it, and who has thought about trying it. Everyone knows how and under what circumstances she'd pull the trigger: if she had AIDS, if a sister died, if she were too irretrievably crazy.

By January 2000, I've felt sadness creeping into my daily routine. It's like a dampness, that cold, clammy feeling you get during a hurricane, when moisture seems to permeate your hair, your towels, and your sheets, even though the windows are closed. Some mornings, I wake up and snap immediately into crying. My whole body hurts like a bad joint that aches when it rains.

By winter, even good news makes me cry because I feel it has a swollen underbelly of human truth. Tears start running down my cheeks during class lectures. My eyes water in the laundry room, on the treadmill, and during student-union screenings of slapstick comedies. One night, Tess finds me sobbing during the health segment of the evening news. Scientists have discovered scarred cells from cardiac arrest fall away over time, and she can't understand how sadly hopeful that is. To me, it means that the human heart has the capacity to heal itself.

It's hard to say what is responsible for the change in me. For the most part, I blame Chris, who won't date me, or the fact that my father was laid off. And once in a blue moon, I'll fault Skip. It doesn't occur to me that alcohol might be unhinging me, that drinking at the rate I am can induce depression, impulsive behavior, and symptoms of bipolar and borderline personality disorder. Experts suggest that drinking when you feel low is like taking speed if you're feeling jumpy: It heightens the ailment instead of remedying it.

There is no reason that that would occur to me. Alcohol is still the one elixir that can remedy my glum moods. And when my blood buzzes on beer or hard liquor, it doesn't feel like a downer. The times that I am drinking are still the few when I don't feel anguish. After a few jiggers of vodka, the heaviness in my chest buoys up, and I feel light, and light-headed.

Elle and I start spending every spare moment together, and we are a match made in Bellevue. Afternoons, we sip coffee over our copies of *The Daily Orange,* smoke Marlboros in the carpeted corridors of Watson Hall, or share a joint in the stairwell at the library. We spend nights at a campus bar ordering shots of "Blood and Sand," or spilling Bombay on her roommate's bedspread while we mix nightcaps.

We are together so often that some of the drunken frat boys at the campus bars start to lean in and ask, "Are you dykes?" And even my mother, in a much less explicit way, asks during our weekly phone calls if I have *something to tell her* about my relationship with Elle. The rumors only get worse when a visiting beer promoter persuades us to peck on the mouth, and posts the picture on a popular college-party Web site.

But, for maybe the first time ever, I don't care what people think. I admire Elle. Her sadness has a great, booming quality. You can feel it approaching before she does, like the glass of water that ripples in *Jurassic Park* before the tyrannosaurus roars onto the screen.

Elle refuses to dress up her hurt for other people's sake. Save for the bars, Elle refuses to get dressed at all. She goes to class with eyes smudged with liner from the night before, wearing pajama pants and confrontational T-shirts, the type with HELL HATH NO FURY and STILL ILL lettered across the chest. Elle's moods are as gory as surgery shows on TV. Her every torn heartstring is displayed like payback for the world that inflicted the injury.

Some afternoons, Elle and I drink on the quad in plain view. We share a thermos filled with something gamy she mixed up, and swallow the capsules of St. John's Wort I've begun to carry in my book bag. I've been following the directions printed on the side of the bottle, but the six pills I take every day do nothing to cure my feeling of imminent doom.

As we drink, we share headphones. We each have a plastic earpiece stuffed into one ear; we listen to Elliott Smith's "Everything Means Nothing to Me," and The Beatles' "Yer Blues," and The Smiths' "I Know It's Over" on repeat. Sometimes we fall asleep there, with our heads on our balled-up sweatshirts. CD cases are spread out between us, along with the journals we use to store morbid collections of quotes and the suicide letters we call poetry. I wake up in the dark and the grass, head pounding, when the lampposts switch on outside Machinery Hall.

In many ways, a glass in your hand is an outward expression of pain. It will take me a good number of years to realize it, but drinking is a visible sign to the world that you're hurting, in the same way that starving and cutting are for some girls. In a movie, drinking is one of the best ways for a hero to convey despair without a voice-over. All he really needs to do is walk into a bar, order a shot of tequila, and stare at it resolutely before he slams it back and orders another.

Later, I'll wonder if I hoped someone would catch me during this period. I'll think maybe I wanted someone to notice that I was always blue, always thirsty for another glass of beer, and ask me who or what broke my heart. I don't want to use the phrase "cry for help" because I don't think I wanted to be rescued. Disaster was still too moving. It was a challenge of psychological and bodily limits that seems risky but not wholly dangerous, like skydiving or bungee jumping, any extreme stunt you have to sign a waiver for.

What I really wanted was empathy. I wanted the company of women—it could only be women—who understood how it feels to be emotionally bombed, blasted, capsized, toppled, clobbered, damaged, dismantled, all the totally destructive adjectives people use in place of *drunk*.

That is exactly what I get from Elle. Together, we are like war veterans. We both feel horrifically wounded.

ELLE AND I start to steal things.

At first, it's nothing big. We'll be rotten drunk at a bar on Marshall Street on the night of a university basketball game, and some local guy with season tickets will grab the seat of Elle's jeans. She'll remark about the wedding band on his hand, and he'll make a move like he's going to hit her. And we'll finally pinch his vintage Zippo or pack of cigarettes, or whatever else he has laid out on the bar, to settle the score.

Sometimes we swipe tips from the bartender who urges girls to donate their panties for free drinks. Other times, we lift cocktail glasses from one bar and drop them at another just because it feels like anarchic disorder. When we bar-crawl, we carry full drinks in our purses so as not to waste them, vodka and fruit juice spilling over our wallets and room keys.

We know no one misses the goods we lift, but scoring them becomes a type of game. It is a challenge to see just how much we can steal from the men who steal from us: the bar owners who take so much of our money, the beer promoters who come to our campus and try to convince girls to flash them for T-shirts, the guy at the end of the bar who thinks that, because we drink, he can paw us.

And we're not the only ones on campus who take things when we get drunk enough. On campus, almost every dorm room bursts with theft's prizes. Kitchenettes are stocked with soup cans and cracker boxes, food that was lifted from house parties in purses and pockets, when the going was rough. Some boys have whole bottles of booze that they've stolen from bars, ashtrays and pool cues, plus police barricades and traffic cones, things they picked up off the street during the walk home. At the campus bars, there are even people who steal wallets. They linger behind the mass of people ordering drinks, scouting for someone drunk enough to accept help counting their bills. One morning after a vast bender, Elle and I wake up to discover that our cash and credit cards are gone to the dogs.

The contents of fraternity and sorority houses are particularly fluid. Pranks are ongoing. Seemingly as old as the organizations themselves is the members' drive to break in to rival houses and make off with a composite photo, a paddle, a plaque. Between fraternities and sororities the theft is a type of hair-pulling. At Zeta, we keep two ongoing lists: one of the items we have missing, and one of the items we have stolen and intend to return. Our three-digit door code changes weekly, yet the Sigma

Taus always crack it. They break in, screeching drunk at two A.M., looking for the plaques we have hidden in the laundry room, and taking a bronze cup off our mantel as quid pro quo when they can't find the goods. Romantically, we never progressed beyond junior high. Aside from being drunk, being abusive is still one of the only ways we know to communicate interest.

I have my own reasons for wanting to steal from fraternities. It is the year of the fraternity asshole: At Dartmouth College, Zeta Psi is publishing the *Zetemouth,* a fraternity newsletter that chronicles the brothers' sex lives. It prints sexy photos of women the brothers claim they slept with, and categorizes them as "loose," "dirty," "guaranteed hookups," and "sure things." They are releasing the "Manwhore Edition," in which one reporter writes that so-and-so "strikes again," and "she's dirtier than ever . . . if she hooks up with one more Zete, I'm going to need a flowchart just to keep up." Another article promises to deliver "patented date-rape techniques" in a future edition.

After Skip, I've decided that fraternities and the boys in them are hazards. At universities, they are the last booby trap that women have left to dismantle. They are the self-flooding sprinkler system that would drive us violently away. I think fraternities should be dismantled. When you crack open the fraternal system and see it clearly, you realize how outrageous it is, in this day and age, that organizations still exist to protect the interests of white males—namely, drinking and sex.

No structure needs to further these boys' advancement. They have gone as far as the game goes. They have collected all the Monopoly money, and earned the title of all-time champions. Any funds fraternities raise for charitable organizations, all the Habitat for Humanity houses they can build, will not compensate for their utter destructiveness. They take far more than they give. They've had their cake, and eaten ours, too.

I know I sound militant. I don't know whether it's because drinking squashes my inhibitions or boosts my courage, but lately, when I'm drunk, I feel a hostility that I've never known before. It is a tension deep in my gut that makes me want to yell until my face is red, knock over glasses with the back of my hand, and kick people I don't know in the shins.

It is with that thundering rage that Elle and I start breaking into fraternities to steal things. We feel it's our job to steal back everything that has been confiscated from us. It is an act of revolt against an invincible adversary. We want to rupture the walls of any space that would keep us out. Our assault on a frat house is a hostile takeover: We want to explode it, seize it, smash the framework of the institution, make it true, at last make it ours.

IT IS A Monday night when Zeta's president charges Elle with the task of returning a composite photo to Skip's fraternity.

It is a mistake from the start. In the frame, the brothers look dapper as ever. Every one is accounted for in his navy blazer, white shirt, red-and-blue-striped tie. They are the photos that are taken every spring, when a man from the local Budget Photo makes his rounds with a tripod and a gray muslin backdrop, snapping portraits that make everyone look hungover, so puffy and sallow that a third of us opt not to be photographed.

This one was stolen during a Zeta scavenger hunt, which was someone's sorry excuse for a party. Pledging has gone dry, and the new girls are grumbling that running around campus, gathering trophies, dining-hall forks, and copies of *Playgirl* is no substitute for drinking.

Of course, Elle won't just go knock on the door and hand it back to them; that's not her style. And I won't let her recruit someone else to do it for her because that's not my style. We've been mixing vodka tonics since five, and listening to "Hate and War." In many ways, The Clash is like alcohol: It feels like something we've stolen from boys. And while we were attempting to harness its power, we fell in love with it. It has seeped into our souls.

The drinks are invigorating. The taste is raw, and the vodka fizzles. And suddenly, the opportunity for reprisal feels just too sweet to pass up. I want to stick it to those guys in their Brooks Brothers ties, by turning their composite photo into conceptual art. I am making dumb jokes about how we should cut the penises out of the *Playgirl*s from the scavenger hunt and tape them atop the guys' necks because they are supreme dickheads. And next thing I know, we're actually doing it. We are drinking more and more vodka while we work, until the whole project has a frantic intensity. Time is snowballing from eight o'clock to ten o'clock and beyond, and we are sticking dicks all over the glass until we're out of tape. By the time we're done, the whole piece looks like Brigid Berlin's cock book from the 1960s. On the backside of the frame, we scrawl TO: THE BIGGEST PRICKS WE KNOW in red lipstick, with a drowsy, crooked hand.

We shouldn't deliver it. In our right minds, we never would. But under the armor of hard liquor, we feel unconquerable. So, I find myself cowering behind a pillar on the front porch of the frat I swore I'd never go back to, while Elle steals in through the unlocked door to hang the photo on an empty nail in the foyer.

The second she screams I know they've caught her, and when I inch up to the door to see what's going on, some jock in a dirty ball cap grabs me by the arm and pulls me inside, too.

A couple of boys have trapped Elle in the kitchen. Having peeled off the black sweatshirt she put on earlier for night camouflage, one boy is spraying her with the long hose of the kitchen sink, while another holds her wrists tightly behind her back. Even as she throws her shoulders, she can't worm loose. Another guy is dancing on the tiles in front of her, as though to provoke her, yelling, "Aww, wet T-shirt contest!" She is kicking her legs wildly at the knees and trying desperately to spit in his face.

The guy who pulled me inside has me in the type of wrestling hold that they never make girls learn in high-school gym class. His elbows are hooked under my armpits, and his palms are pushing hard against the back of my head. I am immobilized and woozy. My chin has been driven to my chest, and it is impossible to focus on anything above my shoelaces. I can't see the brothers who are filtering downstairs as they hear the commotion, but I can hear them. They sound like bellowing whales in my ringing ears.

The pressure on my neck is so great that it drives me to my knees.

It's hard to say what happens next. The hose from the kitchen sink is spraying me hard and cold in the face, and with my hands trapped behind my back, I can't reach up to push the strands of wet hair out of my eyes. I can hear Elle alternating between laughing and screaming. It is the sound that my mother outlawed when my sister and I were young, on the basis that she couldn't tell if we were hurt or playing. Similarly, I can't tell if we're playing. The boys are smiling like the whole thing is a joke as they slap me across the cheeks, tickle my sides, and spank me. And I am feeling the biting frustration that comes from being restrained, from shouting "TIME OUT," and having it fall on deaf male ears.

Whoever has been pushing his thumbs into my elbows finally lets me go. He is a short, red-haired senior in boxer shorts and a tight undershirt that clings around the muscles of his chest. He moves into my line of vision to say, "You're the girl Skip had sex with."

His words are the ipecac that instantly makes me feel like I'm going to be sick. It doesn't mean anything conclusively; I know that boys lie all the time about their exploits. I can still mentally "whatever" it. But it causes me the kind of hurt that makes me want to hurt someone else. I move a little to my left, to a bucket of varnish I've had my eye on. I grab the handle of the brush that's been stewing in it and shove the bristles as deep as I can into the redheaded boy's ear.

Someone tosses us our sweatshirts and instructs us to "Get the fuck out." Elle and I put our heads through our sweatshirts as we move for the door. The fabric fuzz of them is wet, we think, with kitchen water. Tomorrow, we will realize that a brother emptied his bladder on them.

It doesn't end there. I am crying, and Elle's telling me, "Goddamn it, don't cry."

Instead of going home, we trudge in the rain to a campus bar, where the owner seems pleased to see us. We sit with him in a corner booth and tell him the whole story. He nods and says, "You have to get them back."

It's a slow night. On campus, everyone knows that only people with alcohol problems go out on Monday nights. Tuesdays, Wednesdays, even Sundays are fine. Thursdays, Fridays, and Saturdays are universal. But there's no getting around the fact that drinking on Monday is desperate. Only a handful of people teeter on bar stools, spinning quarters and lighting cigarettes. The owner gives us free glasses of wine. The table is a clutter of smudged glasses, emptied of everything but ice. I feel myself drifting in and out of consciousness like someone going under ether.

Elle and I will piece together the rest in the morning. We will be sitting opposite each other on her bed, where I spent the night because I was too down and out to go home, and doing our best to fill in the blanks from the piles of clues that are scattered around us. We cover our mouths with our hands when we realize just how humiliating they are.

We did go back to Skip's fraternity to "get them back," as the bar owner had suggested. Sometime after two A.M., after the bars had closed, we circled the house three times, testing every locked door and latched window. It was during a thunderstorm; because our clothes are still streaked with wet dirt. The light blue sweater I have on has a muddy footprint across the chest.

While we were skulking in the bushes, Elle found an unlocked basement window and dove through it. It was a four-foot drop from there to the floor of the basement, which was the same space where my blackout had happened three months before. Elle stood underneath with her arms spread wide open to catch me.

From there, we proceeded to clean them out. I don't exactly remember snatching books from the bookshelf, and balls from the pool table, and picture frames off the walls. But I know we did because it is all here on Elle's floor in a massive heap. There are plaques and trophies, a stuffed animal, a television remote, an alarm clock, an umbrella stand, kitchen mitts, an oil painting, candlesticks, and *three* 40"x 30" picture frames. It is thousands of dollars' worth of junk, and I have no idea how we could have carried it all between the two points. I ask Elle if she remembers making multiple trips.

It gets worse. When Elle spots a thirty-pack of beer on the floor, we start to remember the rest. Our raid on Skip's fraternity had not satisfied our appetite for destruction, so we crossed the street to Chris's fraternity, where the brothers and their dates were passed out upstairs after a date party. Elle popped open one of the house's front windows, and we proceeded to wreak havoc there, too, picking up the leftover beer, along with a few more plaques and baubles. We found our way to the basement, where we discovered a can of Benjamin Moore paint, and overturned the whole can onto the floor. We laid in the spill and made snow angels.

Anxiety usually accompanies a hangover. It is just part of the equation: Your stomach turns over, your head beats itself like a drum, your hands jitter, your muscles feel drained, and you feel nervous. But this is a whole other level of panic. There is campus security to worry about, plus Zeta's president. But more than that, we are ashamed of our anger, and what appears to be superhuman strength. It means we are not well-behaved or well-adjusted. Normal women would be more composed, far less seduced by an excess of booze or emotion.

As for the plunder, Elle "borrows" Brianne's car, without asking, and we unload the whole rain-damaged cargo on the fraternity's driveway. We pull down the sun visors to hide our faces as we peel away.

ELLE AND I lay low for the rest of the semester. We stop trying to compete with men when we're drunk because Skip's fraternity has taught us that men are brawnier, that they can hurt us in ways we will never be able to hurt them. Men have the shut out; we will never beat them.

We try to stop getting drunk so much. We try to stop being *so much* in general. We tone down the P.D.E., meaning public displays of emotion. Elle loses herself between the musty stacks in the physics library, in an ongoing chain of extra-credit assignments and study groups, where she and ten men sit bent over graph paper and calculators, arguing and laughing and jotting things down. My transfer papers go through, and I delve into the required classes for my new journalism major. I spend whole evenings in the school graphics lab, fiddling with newspaper layouts in QuarkXPress, with the clip art and dummy text that refuse to line up.

I also start dating a photography major who fills my blank nights. He is perfectly arrogant, another twig-armed, potty-mouthed meth-head. And after Skip, I am extra afraid to let him touch me.

SPRING COMES again to Syracuse, and it isn't easy. There are girls everywhere, still tan from spring break, sunning their legs on the quad, sipping Chardonnay in the outdoor cafés on Marshall Street (they switch from beer to wine come bathing-suit season). Girls are wearing ridiculous sunglasses with pastel-colored lenses, puckering their lips while they smoke light cigarettes. Painted toenails curl over their sandals. Cleavage heaves out of their sundresses. Everyone is exquisitely happy.

On the other hand, I want to knock them all off, execution-style. I can't help but think about my favorite part in *The Bell Jar*: when Esther Greenwood is sitting around a conference table at a New York fashion magazine with a dozen other nineteen-year-old interns, thinking, *I'm so glad they're going to die.* In fact, I think that image is what makes me start to work on my own exit plans. Not plans to take my own life, but to take a summer internship. It is an almost-desperate measure.

People with substance-abuse issues like to think that changing physical states is the equivalent of changing emotional states. We like to think that removing ourselves from the craziness of the city, the suburbs, the house, the workplace, the campus, will remove the craziness from us, too. And why wouldn't we? Everywhere we look, instant gratification is alive and well. It is the concept that drives consumerism, manifest destiny, and the American dream. Somewhere inside all of us, particularly women, lies a ruby of hope. It is faith that once we find the right skin product, or piece of real estate, or cocktail, or car, or lipstick or diet, we will, at last, feel good about ourselves. The void will fall away and we will feel complete. We are willing to pay out the ass for it. And I am willing to spend the summer alone in New York, where I expect to find it.

My parents seem almost happy that I won't be spending the summer at home.

Years from now, they'll admit just how much I ruptured their routine during the summers I stayed home. My mom was working fifteen-hour days, constructing department-store displays. My dad was doing consulting work from home. And my sister, who was obedient then, was earning Girl Scout badges and memorizing vocabulary words at the kitchen table.

When I was home on break, they had to worry about me. At night, they had to listen for the whir of the garage door, a sign that I had made it home safely from a party. Midnight would come and go. So would two A.M. Then five A.M. My father would drive over to the party in his slippers, spot my car still parked in the driveway, and sigh a breath of relief that I hadn't wrapped it around a tree on Route 117, that I'd only passed out and stayed the night. He would scrawl a note on my windshield that said, We were worried, call when you wake up, and drive home.

Summers in a small town are sweet. There is iced tea, and black-eyed Susans. Kids still buy penny candy the way they did some fifty years ago. There are sparklers and group hikes. The dog pokes at a suspicious toad in the driveway, and deer creep up to the house to rub their heads against the dining-room window. All this is lost on me, so I take an internship at a small trade magazine in New York City.

NEW YORK is the ideal destination for the drunk and the downtrodden.

Even four years from now, after I've worked hard to shake both depression and booze, summers in the city will still make me sad. The urban landscape is a paragon for the one inside. The increased sunlight just distills the grayness. Everything looks bleached out. Inside, lobbies smell like sweat. Outside, garbage is more putrid. Sidewalks marinate in the smell of urine and warm beer.

When I arrive in May 2000, I think it will be the other way around. Clomping down Sixth Avenue on my first day of work, I think, *This is a vast improvement.* Here, in a city of eight million, I think whatever temporary afflictions I am experiencing will feel scaled down. I expect to evanesce in the rush-hour crowds, to feel dwarfed by the tall buildings and tall women, teetering on their four-inch-tall heels.

And if not, I think I will feel commiseration.

New York is like the crisis hot lines that tell potential suicides,

"You are never alone." Here, you really aren't ever alone. Everywhere you look, there is someone to remind you they are there. There they are, crossing against a light. And there, catching your hair in the corner of their open umbrella. And there, letting their fluffy, white poodle crap in the middle of the sidewalk. Everywhere you turn, there is someone else to remind you just how miserable they are, too.

I find out quickly that this doesn't help. If anything, it only reminds me how disconnected I am. After a few weeks, I can ride eight stops on the number 6 train with one person's hand on my ass and another person's sour armpit two inches from my face, and still emerge through the sliding glass doors unruffled because I'm troubled by something bigger. Even in Midtown, among the throngs of people that shoulder by me, I feel the thump of loneliness. From the outside, it's hard to imagine life can exist inside the mirrored skyscrapers, when I walk by and all I can see is my own pained little face staring back.

When I feel sad after work, and I usually do, I call Josh, a friend from a summer I spent at Columbia University during high school, who has a summer sublet a few blocks away on Carmine Street. Josh spends his days earning five times the wages that I do, reading biographies about Virginia Woolf for the founding editor at one of New York's top publishing houses, and calling me to say how much I remind him of her (in terms of psychosis, not talent). Together, we drink vodka tonics at cavernous bars in Chinatown and argue through half-open eyes about which one of us is more hopeless.

Plus, I make new drinking buddies. My next-door neighbors in a Washington Square dorm are boys who live there year-round. They are the privileged city boys I've heard rumors about.

Half of them are the sons of screen actors, in town for the summer to make up the classes they failed and to hunt for East Village lofts. They never rest from drinking. Their compartment-sized rooms are packed with guitars and amps and turntables, gourmet food they ordered from errand-running services, jugs of wine, bottles of Jim Beam, upside-down Frisbees heaped with cigarette butts. They tell me that I come visit them at four A.M. some mornings, drunk as a skunk after a night out with Josh, to smoke cigarettes, do more shots, and share intimate details about my life. I tell them I don't remember stopping by at all.

At work, I throw up in the bathroom so often that a coworker asks if I'm bulimic. But I'm never the only one who is hungover. At work on Friday mornings there are dozens of people, from assistants to managers, who look haggard after launch parties. They congregate around a dripping coffeepot, smoothing their unwashed hair and cracking jokes about how wasted they got last night. Looking back, it should have been my first indication that excessive drinking doesn't automatically stop after college—you don't just quit relying on alcohol as a mode to connect you to people.

I meet a twenty-three-year-old advertising assistant named Glynn. She is my kind of girl, a former literature major who rents a tenement on Avenue B. We spend a few nights together after work, smoking a joint in her apartment or bar-hopping below Houston, drinking beer at Brownies and nodding along to the chords of a friend-of-a-friend's band.

There are yuppie friends to make, too. The dot.com bubble hasn't burst yet and media layoffs, while always at hand, aren't as frequent and vicious. It is three months after *New York* magazine published a feature about Manhattan's poverty elite:

the twentysomething media planners who make $24,000 in annual salary, but $100,000 in corporate perks, like cruises on the Forbes yacht and all-expenses-paid ski trips, tickets to the MTV Movie Awards, and all the drinks they can drink. I make friends with two of the male club promoters who are featured in the story, and every weekend they put Josh and me on their parties' guest lists.

The boy I was dating back at S.U. is spending the summer at NYU, too, in one of the one-bedroom apartments on Union Square that the school manages to pack kids into in fours. We go on a few forgettable dates before he stops returning my calls. I can only remember one of them: We went to a Creole restaurant in the Village, where he ordered melon balls, and the owner's cats freely wandered the tables, turning loops through our legs. Even topped on vodka and melon liqueur, I was as mute as a stone, and about that animated.

When the boy stops calling, I quit eating. It seems like the natural thing to do, partly because I've picked up on the fact that I'm ugly, and partly because food turns my stomach, which is already squirming with sadness and nerves. For a month, I eat two bananas and a carton of yogurt per day. Sometimes I'll eat the frozen, low-fat, low-calorie chemicals that pass for ice cream. In a flash, I've lost ten pounds. At work, my pleated skirts slide down off my hips. Josh drags me to dinner on Spring Street, in an attempt to force-feed me. But I ignore my thirty-dollar plate of pasta and suck down red wine by the glass.

I also quit my weekend job and quit going to night class, instead wandering for hours through the East Village, sweating through clothes that are too heavy and black to wear in the summer. One day, I meet a French photographer. I drink cold beer with him at a bar called The Library, follow him down to Pitt Street, and pose for his photos. I lean against door frames with my jeans unbuttoned while he snaps the shutter and calls out, "Look drunk," and I let my face slacken into a look that I know well.

Drinking becomes my full-time summer occupation. I devote increased hours to it. I give it increased effort.

THE WEIGHT I've lost makes up for the tolerance I've gained. Pretty soon I am lying down in the backseat of a cab every time I go out, telling Josh, "I'm going to throw up," while the driver speeds faster down Second Avenue in an effort to get me out quick. Every hungover morning, I am sitting on the ledge of the window overlooking East Fourth Street, smoking a cigarette with the screen up, trying to decide if I'd break my legs or my neck if I jumped.

And I'm not the only one who has these destructive thoughts while I'm wrecked. My phone hums constantly at four in the morning. One of my drinking buddies is always on the other end, stewed to the gills and sobbing hysterically. One says she just dragged a knife too deep across her shin, and she's scared because it won't stop bleeding. Another girl, who is at S.U. for summer sessions, says she just walked over to Lawrinson Hall, the twenty-one-story dorm, for the explicit purpose of jumping off the roof. It seems that alcohol, which has always given us the courage to dance in public or be close to men, is giving us the fearlessness to abuse ourselves, too.

Elle's self-batter is the most terrifying. She calls at ten P.M. one Saturday, to say she is lying in on a hammock in her backyard. She has downed eight beers and ten sleeping pills, and she can't move her legs. Her parents are at a party, and there is no one to check on her, so I make a frantic phone call to the poison control center to find out if ten is a lethal number. A frosty operator tells me, "Anyone who swallows ten of anything needs to go to a hospital." I don't know Elle's address, or the name of her town, so I call the state police and leave her phone number.

Later, Elle will tell me her father was awakened by three cops who said they were there investigating a drug overdose. His denial was so earnest that, even after it took him twenty minutes to shake Elle awake, he still believed her when she said it was a friend's sick hoax.

I, too, make midnight phone calls. My friends and I call it "drunk dialing" because some nights when you're drunk enough, your phone seems to dial the numbers on its own—especially calling ex-boyfriends with whom your subconscious secretly wants to make contact. One night I drunk-dial my mother, sobbing with an anxiety attack. I tell her I can't breathe, my throat feels as tight as a tourniquet, and the walls of my dorm room are lurching out at me.

It will be the only time of emotional turmoil in which I remember asking her for help, rather than snapping at her defensively and running off like a wounded animal. It is probably a testament to how frightened I am. Lately, charging along the sidewalk in the rain on my way home from work, feet slipping around in my sandals, I feel as unstable as my umbrella—I get the feeling I could be blown inside-out at any second. The wind might break me in half.

My mother must sense it, too, because she books an express flight to LaGuardia the very next weekend.

· · ·

EVEN THOUGH I know my mom is coming, I'm still surprised by the shrill *eerrrr* of the intercom. It's been three hours since I made it home from my promoter friends' party, a ridiculous affair at which I remember drinking thirteen-dollar drinks called "red devils," and burning a woman with a cigarette while I was trying to convince her to go on a date with Josh. In the VIP room, I'd introduced myself to the man who was on the cover of a recent *Rolling Stone,* as though I were someone worthwhile. I'd called home from a pay phone to say I might be hungover when my mom arrives.

Still, the damage is worse than I thought. Through the fog of a hangover, I can see that I am sleeping fully naked, which has been happening a lot lately, when I pass out before I can finish changing for bed. When I knock into the bathroom, there is red-stained vomit all over the sink, the hand towels, the toilet seat. It looks like the scene of a homicide. In the mirror, my face is bloated and yellow. My eyes are half-moons of smeared mascara. My hair is knotted, matted, and sticky with liquor and puke. I try as fast as I can to wet my face and wipe down the bathroom. I hide the dirty clothes, ashtrays, and empty bottles that have been lying in piles on the desks and the beds ever since my roommate moved out.

When I finally take the elevator downstairs to meet my mom, both she and the female security guard cry "Good God" as I round the corner. There is no denying that I am a wreck. But my mother humors me. She makes up the spare double bed with sheets that she brought from home, while I shower. She pages through my stack of *Village Voice*s while I run the water in the sink to muffle the sound every time I throw up.

My mother is a creature of habit, content always to stay at

home with her tea, her dogs, and her cable TV, and I feel deeply guilty for being fucked-up enough to make her come to New York. Later, the thought of her that day, struggling with my dad's rolling suitcase, stepping out of a cab with no idea whether she was on Washington North or South, wearing the flowing black dress she specifically wore because she heard me say, "Everyone in Manhattan wears black," will always make my eyes well up.

My eyes do well up as I walk her down the street, past the park. I am describing landmarks in fits and starts, and I trail off every time I try to tell her about Henry James's house, or the chess shops, or the dog that sometimes sits in the fountain and bounces tennis balls off its nose. We sit at an open-air table at The Grey Dog's Coffee, and I drink strong coffee and eat hummus on toast, and then I toss it all up in the toilet of the charming, dried flower–filled bathroom.

As we continue to walk it becomes clear that my system is intensely out of whack. Every few blocks a buzzing noise starts in my ears, and my stomach cramps. I have to tell my mom, "Give me a minute." I say, "I just need a minute to rest here on the steps of the Angelika." Or "against the doorway of Mercer Kitchen." Or "on the curb."

My mom tells me the story about how she once threw up in the bushes the day after a big party in Texas. I know she's trying to make me feel better, but it only makes me feel worse, knowing it was the only time she's ever been hungover, and I feel the same headaches and nausea every weekend.

At a corner grocery my mom buys me the only hangover medication she knows, which is aspirin and bottled water. It doesn't help. I can't keep the water down. I have to stoop over the sidewalk and vomit all the way down West Broadway, in front of all the high-end boutiques my mother and I are too intimidated to go into to browse. She keeps asking if I need to go back to the dorm and rest. And I keep assuring her, after every spit-up, that I feel much better. I tell her, "This was definitely the last time."

When I throw up on the corner of Canal Street, some of it splashes my mom's shoes, and a man walking by shouts out, "Rough night, eh?"

It is too much for her. She shoots her arm up from the shoulder to hail a cab, saying, "We *will* go back to the dorm, and you *will* sleep this off."

Back in the dorm, we curl up in identical double beds, pulling down the shades, though the room is still as hot and bright as the August afternoon. I sleep until six o'clock at night, dimly aware of the sound of my mother hanging up my clothes and scrubbing the bathroom with the only cleaning supplies I have: Febreze and toilet paper.

A few times she comes over to stroke my head or put a glass of water on the nightstand. She tends to me like a sick person. Which, it's becoming clear to both of us, I am.

ABUSE

ASCENT AND DESCENT

THE LIFE OF a young drunk is not a continuous fall into the pit of abject alcohol abuse. It is a herky-jerky evolution. You slip, you trip, and you tumble into the habit of drinking when you are afraid, or enraged, or heartsick, and every so often, you hit a ledge from which you can see how deep into dependence you are. Every so often, you feel so lost in the hollow of your own need that you decide to try to hoist yourself out of it.

And you think you should be able to clamber out. You should be able to rise above your voracity for vodka because there are people everywhere, reminding you that this is a life-stage behavior that every girl eventually outgrows. But that kind of climb is not easy, it is not even possible, when you have no other reserves of strength. When all of your endurance is tied up in drinking, there is nothing else that can hold you. Without it, you tire in no time. You get scared, you surrender, and you slide even deeper into drinking.

I BEGIN junior year with a neat little pack of birth-control pills that, lengthwise, look like candy dots, sorted as they are into rows of whites, greens, and blues. They were prescribed to me by my Dorothy Hamill–looking, chronically pregnant pediatrician (yes, at age twenty I still see a *pediatrician*), after I burst into tears during the depression-screening bit of my yearly physical, when she asked me if I felt "hopeless about the future." She'd wheeled her stool up too close, and said, "That's your menstrual cycle talking." She wrote a prescription for the oral contraceptives meant to harness my hormones and give my black moods the dependability of modern medicine. It mattered little to her that I've never—that I remember—had sex. She didn't ask me how often I booze.

I also move in to the sorority house, which statistically ups the likelihood that I will pickle myself, since studies have found that nearly three-fourths of sorority-house residents are binge drinkers.

My dad drives up to Syracuse to help lug my boxes up three floors to my bedroom, which I will share with two other girls. The room is shaped like a bottle: It is rectangular with a windowed enclave, like a bottleneck, that is wide enough for a bed. Since I am the first to arrive, I set up camp there. I position the head of my mattress so it looks out over Comstock Avenue, so that even in my sleep, I will hear the sounds of people staggering home from the campus bars. They will be fighting, singing, shrieking, and knocking into things. Here, I will be surrounded by people who drink as much and as often as I do.

I start the semester off hopeful. Pictures show me still gaunt and muscled from the summer, in combat boots, dilapidated jeans, belts made of chrome bullets, and the boys'-sized T-shirts I picked up at thrift stores. My hair is stick-straight and blonde from a bad dye job that I embraced, hoping it would help me lighten up. There is a soldier-like resolve about me, like I came back prepared for a fight.

I start picking up assignments from the entertainment editor at *The Daily Orange.* He is a boy with whom I exchanged vows at a wedding-themed party last year, although we never acknowledge the fact that we got drunk on tequila, kissed, and woke up on the couch the next morning, flecked with thrown rice.

I start to forgo nights at the campus bar in exchange for nights of researching stories at the city courthouse, for interviewing HIV bug-chasers I've met online, or a local coven of witches who let me sit in during their ceremonies downtown. On the days that my stories run in the newspaper, I feel as happy as I do at any bar's happy hour. I turn up at the student center at seven A.M., when the papers are delivered in stacks. I trip around campus, joy-filled at the prospect that someone, somewhere, is reading something I've written.

Drinking also shifts to my mind's periphery when I enroll in a reporting class with an adjunct professor. She is a health reporter from the city newspaper who looks motherly but is tough as nails, and she likes me for no reason at all. When the state fair comes to town, she gives me an assignment to write about the professional BMX riders who spend days somersaulting their bikes over a cement half-pipe, and I approach it with a surge of ambition that I haven't felt since eighth grade. I spend the day drinking plain old iced tea. I fill notepads with bits of conversation, and ride fearlessly over potholes in my seat on the backs of their bikes.

For the first month of school, writing is its own upper. Pounding on my computer keys feels like playing the piano, like arranging words into harmony that sings back to me. I can work for thirty minutes on a single sentence, reading it aloud and listening to how one word can change the whole tune, making it sadder, or sweeter, or more melodic. Sometimes, my roommate April asks me what I'm working on. And when I read the words out loud to her, I am filled with an inner heat that feels almost like pride. It feels almost as good as the cinch of confidence that I get from alcohol.

Alas, the buzz won't last.

I blame the house. Summer drops off into fall almost immediately, and the off-campus atmosphere has Gothic terror. The trees around campus seem to skip the foliage part completely, and in the light of the lampposts their bare branches reach out, broken and skeletal. At the fraternity next door, the boys roast the corpse of a pig for what they call their annual "home cumming party," and the smoke from the charred meat slithers in through our closed windows. Sigma Alpha Epsilon stakes crosses painted with girls' names on the lawn of every sorority, which is their way of acknowledging who has been invited to their yearly Paddy Murphy event, but it looks like three blocks' worth of gravestones of girls who are already dead.

In Zeta, things start to break. In the middle of the night, someone turns over all our patio furniture, and smashes beer bottles against the side of the house. The kitchen door is mysteriously splintered. Our drinking glasses vanish as people carry them up to their rooms to mix drinks or to use them as ashtrays, so we have to eat in shifts. The chef starts coming to work drunk and has to be fired. Our housemother, a woman who we used to see once a semester when she passed out room keys, meets a man and disappears altogether. The sisters walk around with the stunned eyes of the stoned.

Even by college standards, the house teems with erratic behavior. For starters, the sisters don't eat, ever, unless they do. There are always girls leaning over the industrial counters in the kitchen, hollowing out bagels with spoons and mixing liquid diets in the blender, screaming at the new cook that "There is too much fucking oil in everything." And yet they are back there at three in the morning, drunk and high, devouring meat loaf, egg salad, and pizza doused with salad dressing, leaving the floors streaked with peanut butter and empty bags of cookies. Someone is always getting ready to go out to the bars, or roosting on the fire escape, smoking the joint that our president forbids on the basis that the administration can revoke our charter if we're caught with drugs. Plus, there is always someone who has gotten *too* drunk, who is bawling in the house phone booth or passed out on the floor of the bathroom, who needs to be tucked into bed.

My room is particularly weird. Even though my roommates and I are all oddballs, we have nothing in common. April stays awake all night by the glow of a book light, smoking cigarettes, praying the rosary, typing in frenzied bursts on her laptop, and then sleeping for days at a time. Selene does tai chi every morning while French records chirp in the background, and she teaches English as a second language to middle-aged students, whom she brings back to our room to smoke pot.

And then there's me. I start plastering the ceiling and the walls around my bed with disturbing photos from art magazines, and with handwritten passages that I've copied from books. I work with manic energy until I've cleaned the school store out of poster putty. People who visit our room gasp with disbelief when they see my psychotic scrapbook: the layers of photographs, fabric, newspaper, clumped paint, and poetry scratched onto scrap paper. At the time, I don't know why I am preoccupied with the project. But years later, I will think it was because I needed something immoderate to compensate for the fact that I wasn't drinking excessively. I'll think I worked wildly to fill my vacant walls because I suddenly had vacant needs.

I CAN'T pinpoint the exact moment that I slip back into hard drinking. I know it has something to do with the house, which is always stirred up. There are a million activities that I feel obligated to mix myself into. The owners of the campus bars dream up new drink specials, and the girls I live with start going out Tuesday and Wednesday nights, too. The door dings with boys delivering invitations to date parties. The house's phone line rings with sports teams calling to schedule a party. The fraternities next door are spinning records and playing kickball on their front lawns every afternoon. Every night, some sister I barely know is knocking on my door, pleading with me to go with her to a party because she doesn't want to show up alone.

The month I took off doesn't slow down my drinking at all. Pretty soon, I am grappling with the security keypad every night. I am staggering up the stairway while I grip the railing with both hands, watching the oriental patterns on the stairs recede and wobble under me, until I make it to my floor, my door, and pass out in my clothes on my bed.

In the morning, there is too much absence to define my blackouts by the events that are missing. There are more things I can't remember than things I can. A night is no longer a solid sheet, interrupted by fissures. Instead, it is a gaping hole, scattered with fragments of conversations and episodes, like a night sky punctuated by planes disguised as stars.

BIRTH-CONTROL pills have an adverse affect on me; they always will. In the years to come I will repeatedly try them in what the doctor assures me is the lowest possible dosage, and they will bring me to depths of anxiety and depression that I have never known. But in the fall of junior year, the combination of oral contraceptives and liquor unglues me.

For starters, the drinking weight I never put on before starts to amass, and I can feel it bubbling out over the waistband of my pants and under my chin. In pictures, I look like my own stunt double. I am a tough and meaty version of me, with shoulders that roll forward and a mouth that never smiles, unless it is in the accidental flush of drunkenness, when my cheeks are as round and red as hothouse tomatoes. My eyes, when they are not relaxed into a state of rolling, squint in disdain. I look mean.

I start to act mean, too. After a few cups of something hard, combativeness, which is something I haven't felt since Elle and I raided Skip's frat house, comes back to me. Only this time, my anger is completely irrational. Nothing external provokes me. I can be lying on the tiles of Zeta's bathroom, my head can be swimming with half a liter of Smirnoff, and I am still overcome by the urge to punch something, even if it's just the toilet-paper roll. This time, I am beating off the lances of my own thoughts. I am fighting an invasion that is coming from my own head.

Eventually, I find something material to duel. I find out the boy I was dating during the summer was also dating a girl in the sorority next door. And, as a couple, they give me a target at which to throw the sharp darts of disappointment inside me.

When I see them together, I feel a hatred that curls my toes. It is a tension in my chest like a wire tugged hard from both ends. I have contempt not just for her, but for her whole sorority. I don't detest only him, but men everywhere. When I drink it all comes unhooked and takes flight like a shot rubber band.

One night at a campus bar, the girl is fingering her hair in the bathroom mirror while I am dabbing at the grenadine stain on my jeans with a wet wad of toilet paper. I can see her glancing at me through the bathroom mirror, and my scorn is biting. I've never hit anyone before, but I clench my free fist and promise myself that I'll imprint my knuckles in her jaw if she doesn't stop staring at me. I'm a liquor-crusted mess and I know it, and the fact that she is here to see it only makes me want to pulverize something. When I start wavering toward the exit, she says, "Bye." She is smiling, and the corners of her mouth draw into an effortless bow, like she has such a surplus of smiles that she can give them away to just anyone, for any reason; she can give them away to me. Before I swing out the bathroom door, I reply, "You're boring," and the words taste like vinegar.

What I really mean to say is, she has a stark elegance that I envy. We had a poetry workshop together a year ago, and we will again a year from now, when I'll realize that she is really fantastic. Every day, she wore headbands and pea coats and checkered scarves that didn't smell like liquor, or cigarettes, or vomit. She sat tall in her chair, unlike those of us whose hangovers gave us curvature of the spine. And when she spoke to say, "I love the way this poem captures both the inane and the deep," her voice was crisp and unshakeable.

She lives in the sorority next door, with whom the Zetas have a long-standing rivalry. From our end, it's no contest. We are the Zeta Alcoholics, and they are the Alpha Babes. They are all white, all blonde, all members of the university dance team. One day after happy hour, it is easy to recruit a few Zetas to join me on the roof, where we have a clear view of the girl and her fellow babes, who are trickling out onto the sidewalk after a chapter meeting. The whole pug-drunk lot of us leans over the edge of the roof and pelts them with eggs. Every scream from the sidewalk quiets me. Each splattering sound makes me feel a little lighter.

The boy doesn't deserve my best efforts, but I can't see that when I've been slurping vodka cocktails for six hours, and feeling my rage *rat-a-tat* through me like seeds trundling around inside a dried gourd. So one night, at a party where a group of us are slurping wine from the bottle, and Elle slips and overturns the whole thing on a cream-colored couch, I find myself sitting opposite him on the carpet, giving him a piece of my mind. I have my finger pointed gun-like at his chest, and I push it into his sternum to accentuate my points. I push it in over and over, like I'm ringing a doorbell that no one runs to answer. Elle will tell me later that I droned in the slow singsong timbre that only drunkards have. I said, "Your photos are for shit, all of them are flat and ill-lit, and you are not nearly as handsome as you think you are."

I start a relationship with another man. I will call him X because he is a variable that changes constantly and means something different every time.

Sometimes X has authentic feelings for me, though I can't ever believe it enough to return his phone calls. He is the rugby player who wants me to come watch his games, or the film major who lets me sleep in his feather-light bed when I am too drunk to go home—the one who kisses me once and then exhales, saying he can't believe he found the courage to do it.

More often, X is a boy who pushes me up against the wall at a party while I'm loaded and looking for the bathroom, the one who says nothing before he makes a move to cup my breasts through my shirt. X is the boy who walks me back to his place and doesn't offer his hand when I slip while stepping over a guardrail and cut a gash in my back. He is someone's ex-boyfriend, who pulls me down onto the torn couch in the smoking room. He is my date to a semiformal, the boy who hails a cab with the fifteen dollars he borrowed from the bartender while I was throwing up in the bathroom. Occasionally, X is Chris.

EVEN AS my tolerance for alcohol goes sky-high, I am not considered one of the house's loose cannons. In Zeta, there are girls who drink seven nights a week, whereas I drink five. They can handle four Long Island Iced Teas, whereas I'm tap-shackled after two. Plus, there are narcoleptic drunks: One of the sisters passes out behind a Dumpster on East Adams Street and doesn't wake until the next morning, when she hears the *psst psst* sounds of a concerned homeless man. There are humpty-dumpty drunks too: One girl tumbles down the fire escape and breaks her front teeth. Another girl runs into a door frame and breaks her nose

By comparison, my drunken disasters look minimal. When I write to Chris years later, asking him if, during college, it was clear that I had alcohol issues, he'll say, "No, we all drank as much as you did. Plus, there were people far crazier . . . Don't you remember your friend Elle?"

The sisters of Zeta seem to think Elle is a cataclysm. Elle sets people evacuating when she whirls into the den after dinner, shrieking and pulling her hair, with her breath hinting of whiskey. They scramble to pack up their textbooks and coffee mugs and bottles of nail polish, as though she were a class-four hurricane, like the force of her drunkenness has the capacity to blow out the windows.

In Zeta, the secret to getting piss-drunk is to not piss anyone off while you do it. You can down all the Gin-and-Gingers you like, as long as you can still manage to keep your blouse on in public and avoid kissing some sister's boyfriend. You can also drink wildly when everyone else does, and bank on the fact that your blackouts will line up.

For instance, I wake up wincing one morning when I remember the way I ran around a party the night before, wearing the heavy, ceramic head of a fraternity's dog-shaped statue. But at breakfast, when I see half a dozen hungover faces, recoiling from the smell of cooked eggs, I realize the squinting faces are trying hard to recall their own acts of embarrassment. No one can possibly remember mine.

The key is to not humiliate yourself irreversibly. It is okay to be the girl who passes out in the hallway or pukes on the porch; there isn't a girl among us who hasn't done that stuff. We make up for it the next morning by cracking jokes over the basket of bagels and eradicating the evidence with the garden hose. Drunk, we allow ourselves the space to cry or hide our heads in our hands. We even permit ourselves the freedom to call one another names like *psycho, bitch,* or *slut.* These things are familiar. They are passive-aggressive, which is feminine.

But may the Lord help the girl who gets drunk and belligerent: the one who throws punches and demitasse cups, or puts her fist through the wall of the laundry room. Her drunkenness is scary. It sends us all tripping up the stairs, where we huddle together to watch from the safety of the second-floor landing. We watch her the same way we'd watch a lion tear through steaks behind Plexiglas at the zoo.

Drinking confirms men's gender role, whereas it diminishes women's. We are meant to believe that men who drink heavily are men's men. Beer ads play strongly to the idea that men drink because they like shooting pool, watching ESPN, and bonding with other men. And they drink because they appreciate women —particularly, big-haired, big-chested broads in '80s-style bikinis.

By contrast, a girl's drinking makes her less feminine. The sisters think of the aggressive drunk as brutish, and as a result her penance is long and difficult. She is nicknamed "Fight Club" or "DUI Hard" or "Hit-and-Rum." For weeks, she is the punch line at dinner, when someone will lean over the leaves of her salad to say: "Hit-and-Rum walked into a bar . . . Ouch." A whole month passes before the sisters speak to the sophomore who got butt-wasted, belted out Queen, and emptied shampoo bottles on the floor of the bathroom.

I HAVE never been frightened by Elle's excess because its breadth has always been just as wide as my own, and beneath it has always been the same woe, the same bitterness, the same pang. I like that Elle doesn't subscribe to the rules of girlhood. I like that she is rowdy, and spontaneous, and intimidating. I like the way she'll hiss at the girls who get in her way when she's grappling with four beer bottles in the campus bar. Sometimes, she'll lurch forward and bare her teeth like she's apt to bite them.

Later, I will be one of these girls. I will look down at my shoes if I stumble into Elle in an empty bar bathroom. My hands will tremble, and I will be afraid that she might bludgeon me among the tampon dispensers and cigarette-stopped sinks, where there is no one around to protect me. But for now, I take a secret pride in the way Elle can ruffle other girls. She turns them entirely to stone, save for their eyelashes, which flutter like they've been poked in the eyes. Standing next to Elle, I almost feel cocky; it's like having an all-state linebacker on the field with me.

But all of that changes the night that we are set to initiate a new group of pledges into full Zeta sisters.

THE INITIATION is scheduled for three A.M., and rather than setting our alarm clocks for that ungodly hour, Elle and I decide to go to a party and drink rum, which always keeps us awake and electrified clear into the first streaks of sunup.

The party is like any other, except as I've gotten older, everyone I drink with has begun to look younger. The drinks are too weak, and the music is trite. The crowd of boys and girls who are milking the keg looks babyish. Elle goes upstairs to smoke a joint with someone from her physics classes, and leaves me to stand in a doorway, where I bite the rim of my plastic cup and watch the clock.

I don't know how long I lean there, with my head against the door frame. I am not drunk, and I feel acutely frustrated as a result of it. There is no use filling my cup. My tolerance is huge, and the watered-down beer doesn't affect me.

Everyone else is drunk, and the fact that I'm not makes me feel left out, as though I've failed to grab a seat in a game of musical chairs. Girls lope by carrying cups full of foam. A boy who is careening through the crowd singes my arm with his lit cigarette, and it blisters immediately into a perfectly round sore. Eventually, a boy who works with Elle at a campus bar, where he checks IDs and she stamps hands, sees me waiting and talks to me.

Three A.M. rolls around. Elle still hasn't come back, so I climb the stairs to go look for her. My heart sputters as I turn down hallways and peer into bedrooms because this reminds me of the way I lost Natalie in Ocean City. Five years later, experience has taught me that any time a girlfriend disappears at a party, it means something bad has happened. Eventually, a boy who is zigzagging down the hallway, holding a blue bottle of vodka, tells me Elle left for Zeta an hour ago.

It doesn't make sense that Elle would just cut me loose in the party's living room and duck out the side door without me. But for the time being, there is no time to figure it out. I am late. The other sisters are already shimmying into their hooded black robes. Pledges are lining up outside the house's secret entrance. I am running through the park toward the house. My boots are breaking through the frost on the ground, and I can see my breath's fog. At least I know where Elle is.

ELLE IS the first person I see when I tramp into the room where the other sisters are already beginning to line up to start the ceremony. She is balled up on the floor of the chapter room, weeping, and the black polyester of her robe is spread out around her. She looks like a puddle, and the sisters are snickering.

Zeta's president pulls me into the kitchen to say, "We don't know what's wrong with her. She won't put her arms through the holes of her robes. Someone saw bandages on her wrists, and started telling people that she cut them."

When I go back into the chapter room to kneel down next to Elle, she won't turn to face me. She sinks deeper into the carpet. Her shoulders convulse. Every time I try to put an arm around her, she swats it off.

The initiation lasts five hours, and I spend the whole time watching Elle cry through her teeth, and running the night over and over in my head, trying to figure out what I did wrong.

SHE AGREES to meet me the next night, on the concrete steps outside of Bird Library. She takes pulls off an extra-long cigarette, and starts by saying, "it was melodramatic and silly and I never would have done it if I weren't drunk."

Then she goes on to tell me things that I've already sensed. I've already felt them in my blood. I already know that she left the party to put notches in both her wrists. I learn that she did it first with a razor blade, but the business of cutting was harder than it looks in movies. The edge of the blade wasn't sharp enough, and it wouldn't slice deep enough, so she traded it for a steel chef's knife. Sometime later, her roommate walked in and saw the knife, the blade, and the bloody kitchen rags on the counter. Together, they bound her wrists with strips of gauze and packing tape.

Snow is drifting from the sky, in a way that is calm and airy. It is collecting in the long, black fibers of Elle's hair in a way that makes it look like she's wearing a pearl headdress. It is early evening. The breeze is gentle, and the moon is muted behind a thin drift of clouds. As usual, I hate the universe and its irony. The world looks too pretty for this moment. It doesn't fit this talk, which is too sad, and biting, and ugly.

My whole face is damp with tears. I keep saying, "Show me, I want to see," but Elle shakes her head *no*. I lurch forward anyway, and she doesn't fight me off. When I roll back one of her sweater sleeves, she sits very still, and her face stays expressionless. She is wearing a black-leather bracelet that has two silver snaps I have to pop open. Under it, there is thick cotton gauze rolled halfway up her forearm.

She tells me it was my fault that she did it, because I was talking to the boy that she works with. She says, she's liked him for months, and I *knew* that, and yet I let him put his arm around my waist, anyway. It doesn't matter when I tell her I was just glad to have someone to talk to while I waited for her to come back for me. The scars will stay with her and, in her mind, they will always be my fault.

Elle says, "I don't want to be around you anymore."

I can't think of a thing to say. I mop my nose on my jacket sleeve. I bend forward and cradle my own wrists in my lap, as though they were hers. I am not used to pleading my case. In the past, Elle has been the one to speak for me; she has always argued on my behalf when I have felt this indefensible. I look up at the flat face of the library. My mind is blank. I don't have a shred of certainty.

I tell Elle, "I'm sorry." And I mean it.

For years I will mean it. I will add her injuries to my running list of ruination, right alongside whatever happened to Natalie in Ocean City, and whatever happened to me with Skip, and all the other destruction I hold myself liable for. In the future, even after addiction counselors translate the term *alcohol abuse* for me, even after they say "It is improper use of alcohol, like drinking to medicate your moods," the word *abuse* will always make me think of these kinds of maltreatment. It will make me think of the ways we emotionally battered each other while we were wasted.

I almost wish Elle had pummeled me instead. A black eye would heal far quicker than this emotional wound. It will take me years to absolve myself of the blame she has assigned to me. It will take me years to see that Elle blamed me because it was easier than blaming alcohol, and alcohol-induced depression. We were best friends, but her relationship with alcohol went deeper; she had been allied with it for far longer.

AFTER MY friendship with Elle dissolves, I stay on the periphery of house activities because I don't want to see her. I hide in the third-floor phone booth when everyone filters downstairs for chapter meetings. I spend a long time studying rows of numbered spines in the library and dropping hurried notes of apology in the president's mailbox.

I show up for rush because I have to; it is a requirement. Shirking it means removing myself from Zeta for good and putting my name on a waitlist for a spare cot in an underclassman dorm. I drink with April the night before rush, and I am hungover for its duration. My hair is unwashed, and my clothes smell of cigarettes, and my thighs pimple with itchy hives I can't shake.

Still, sisters steer their rush crushes to me. They are the quick-witted girls, with clean skin and mod glasses, who everyone wants to join Zeta. The fact that I'm charged with persuading them is a compliment; it means the girls I live with think I have retained some semblance of stature and intrigue. I do my best to woo the recruits, the same way that the sisters baited me, by clattering on to them about our parties, our drinking, and our drugs. I sense the girls are looking for some other source of enthusiasm, but I don't know what it is or how to give it to them. In the end, we lose every last one of them to other sororities.

One Tuesday night in November, I get bullied into taking a role in a house skit. It is part of a fraternity's week-long philanthropy, and I join the troupe the night before the competition because I'm not stealthy enough to avoid their committee meeting on the second-floor landing. They assure me I can hit the open bar before I have to go onstage.

The night of the competition, we rehearse in the dining room of the boys' fraternity while they mix cocktails to take the edge off our stage fright. I drown a glass filled two inches high with vodka and topped off with cranberry juice. It is all I need to go runny.

My beer tears begin while we are walking to the bar. They persist while I'm showing my ID to the doorman, while pledges whose names I don't know ask me what's wrong, and while someone's boyfriend keeps bringing me shots, which only make me sob harder. I am the kind of dead-drunk where I can hear my voice vibrating in my throat, and my breath is bumping in and out of me hard and fast, but I can't hear what I'm saying. I don't know who or what I am mourning; it might be Elle, or Skip, or Chris. These days, there are too many sore spots that trigger tears. I can't name just one.

When it's time to take our place onstage, I stand inert in front of some three hundred people, forget that I'm supposed to deliver lines, and instead just totter and weep openly for the full four minutes. It is as though the alcohol I am funneling into my body is leaking back out the ducts of my eyes. If someone licked my face, I'm sure my tears would taste like Barton vodka.

I stay in bed the whole next day because I don't want to face the Zetas downstairs. Were I to untwist myself from my comforter and slog down the hall to the bathroom, I would have to face girls who know me too intimately. They would look up from blow-drying their hair or brushing their teeth with looks that are too knowing. They've seen me cry, and they know I have private afflictions. I think if I'd stripped my shirt off on stage, I still wouldn't feel this exposed.

THIS KIND of self-loathing used to be the reason that I drank in the first place.

I swilled vodka to flip over humiliating experiences, like someone who turns stained couch cushions to avoid looking at smudges. I drank to forget the spots in time when someone snickered when I stood up to speak, when a boy ignored me, when a woman eyed me from top to bottom and stopped curtly at my boots. I drank to forget fights with my parents, the nights when they had the misfortune of calling during one of my hopeless moods, when I cut their questions short and later felt guilty, when I fell asleep convinced that my mother must hate me. I drank to turn these memories over because I couldn't bear to look at them.

But skit-night proves that my drinking has become its own tarnish. Drinking to quash the past won't work anymore because the past has welled back up. Every awful feeling bobbed back up under the alcohol and burst open. Now I feel doubly bad, on account of the things that have been bothering me and the emotion that I've neglected to control.

After lunch, Hannah comes to sit on the side of my bed. She says, "Don't worry. It was just beer tears. The sisters understand. At one point or another, we've all gotten drunk and sobbed senselessly."

I draw my knees toward me and watch the tent they make in the sheets. I nod. I tell Hannah, "I know." But deep down, I sense that the tears were not meaningless. I think that crying was an honest reflex, an involuntary reaction to some inner pressure point. They might have been my body's way of telling me that something is wrong inside, that six years of drinking is catching up with me. It is contorting me into some different girl, a new person who I can sometimes see in pictures, behind my glassed eyes and in the down-turned corners of my mouth. This new girl is sad and secretive and volatile. She is me, and I am in trouble.

Second semester of junior year is a drop in the bucket. Two-thirds of my friends and acquaintances leave to study in Europe. Their postcards arrive weekly and get pinned up in the sorority mailroom. There are pictures of plazas and palazzos, the sun setting on London Bridge, the sun rising on Notre Dame, the brown-and-white–trimmed canal houses in Amsterdam that look like short stacks. The cursive in the back boxes is minuscule, in an attempt to squeeze in descriptions of every pub, hash restaurant, live sex show, and weekend Eurail ride to Ibiza. Every girl has a favorite corner café, bridge, pub, discotheque, and strong brand of cigarettes. Everyone has a new understanding of culture.

I, too, had put in an application to study in London, and even made arrangements to temp at my favorite British women's magazine. But at the last minute, I defected. I decided to stay in Syracuse because I didn't want to fall behind on my course load; the prospect of spending an extra year making up graphics classes was just too horrifying. Instead, I interview for a job at Syracuse's weekly newspaper, where I slump at the intern's desk, typing out human-interest stories of low quality.

Suddenly, I am among the oldest girls living in Zeta. Once the girls my age take British Air flights to new flats in Camden, a crop of nineteen-year-olds moves in to take their place. April stays put with me. But Selene takes her records, her bong, and her yoga mat to Paris, leaving a vintage map tacked above her desk for us to remember her by. In her space, a bubbly eighteen-year-old named Eva unpacks teddy bears, Ralph Lauren sweaters, and a clear vase filled with Christmas lights that serves as a night-light.

Eva surprises me. I would have guessed she was too prim and prissy to slug Jim Beam. Every bit of clothing that hangs in her lopsided armoire is pastel-colored. She has more powder-blue sundresses, pink sweaters, and T-shirts in shades of rubber-duck yellow than there are in the infant section of any department store. She speaks with a baby voice, too, which is high and whiny in its

Long Island accent. But sure enough, within the first week of living with us, Eva wakes up with a boy in her bed and can't remember ripping open the condom wrapper on the nightstand; she bounds downstairs to eat French toast, telling me "Sex is really no big deal." Another night, she staggers home soaked in beer, after a girl she got into a fight with poured a cup over her head.

The new girls make me uneasy in their wildness, particularly my "little sister," Hailey, who acts as though she's demonized by the same sadness and rage that held me captive last semester and the summer before it. For a month Hailey chews shyly at dinner, while the girls around her shout, gossip, and smack the table hard enough to bounce the silver. That is, until Smirnoff transforms her overnight into the house's constant source of theatrics. Come three A.M., she is always in the phone booth making prank calls, or in the kitchen filling water balloons. Sometimes she is hanging out the second-story window, flinging beer bottles at her ex-boyfriend's window in the fraternity next door.

Hailey upsets me the way my real little sister does when I see her doing something moronic that I sense she learned by observation. Three years from now, I'll be able to see an icky younger version of me in my sister when she comes home from her freshman year at college. There, even in the heat of her southern university, she'll wear my old five-inch-high shit-kickers and concert T-shirts (now twice dilapidated), and stay out in bars past four A.M., fermenting herself. After a time, it will be hard to be around either of them. They remind me of the me I am trying hard not to be.

These girls, in no small part, are the reason I try to pull myself out of the trench of my alcohol abuse in winter of 2001. Once I am alone in the house, living with girls who are two and three years younger than I am, it occurs to me to start acting older. I realize winter is sliding into spring, which will slide into summer. Junior year will fall off into senior year. And beyond senior year, real life looms as ghastly and gargantuan as a nuclear mushroom cloud. I think that after three years of college, I should try to grow up, and outgrow the life-stage behavior of binge drinking.

ONE NIGHT in the library stacks, I run into a boy I haven't seen since he gave me a piggyback ride home from a party freshman year, and resolve to start dating him.

Years later, I will think it must have been more organic than that. I must have felt some romantic spark worth nurturing. But in retrospect, it escapes me. I can only see him for what he eventually becomes: a long distraction from the inevitable.

My boyfriend fills the blank box of time until May. He is kind, if grating. He likes what I let him see in me, which is not much. And as a result, he treats me like Any Girl. It is the way he thinks a girlfriend should be treated: He buys me jewelry based on my birthstone and brings me bunched carnations that make the sisters say, *"Awww."* I say "me, too" when he tells me he loves me. I give up my virtual virginity, not because I feel desire, but because I don't think I'll ever feel grown-up until I do.

We take trips together that enable me to get away from the house, and from the girls who reel home dished from a night at a frat party. We take his station wagon up Route 5 to Skaneateles and sit under the gazebo, holding coffee in foam cups and staring at the ice on the lake. We coast down I-81 to Ithaca, and then over to Cornell, where he rings the bell at their chapter of Zeta, even though I scream at him not to. We take the New York Turnpike home to my house one weekend, where my dad snaps a picture of us on the porch swing, and my mom attributes "selective serotonin reuptake inhibitors and a good man" to the bright change she sees in me.

After three months of abstinence, I feel so changed that I go to a party as a test to myself. It is a "paint party" at Chris's fraternity, where everyone pours big vats of water-based paint over each other's heads, as though the theme were abuse itself. I think I will only have a couple glasses of the punch the boys call jungle juice, but it tastes rich and syrupy, and I get obliterated without any effort. The paint that splashes over my shoulders and down my arms feels cool, and I don't even care that it's stained me everywhere. I twirl around under the blue spray of a squirt gun, and the room keeps spinning after I stop. I am lax enough to let some boy pick me up and toss me into a crowd of people on the second-floor landing, where I slip through everyone's paint-slick hands and hit my back against the floor with a crack.

When I weave through the third-floor hallway, dragging one Crayola-red hand along the wall, Chris is there to grab me by the shirtwaist. I have no sober sensibility to stop me from kissing him. I forget that I have a boyfriend. I forget that I am trying to be a grown-up, and dependable, that I am trying to stop abusing other people with my drunken whims.

There is nothing to stop me from standing on my toes to whisper in Chris's ear. I tell him he's the only one I've ever wanted. He just looks at me. I notice he has a blue streak across one cheek from where I held his face with my hand, and there is something like a flicker in his eyes. It's a look I don't know how to interpret; behind it might be anything from affection to resentment to drunkenness. My relationship with Chris is just as fitful as my current relationship with drinking. I plunge into it, I feel frightened, and then I try to pull myself out. I feel passionate about him, and yet I am terrified by that passion. I am afraid my need runs too deep.

Before Chris can say anything, a sister comes over to say that my boyfriend is waiting in the foyer to drive me home. I leave Chris standing in the hallway, and it is the last time I will see him before he graduates. I go back and smear my paint-stained self over the pillowcases of my boyfriend's bed.

IN MARCH, I go to Cancun for spring break. I committed to it last semester, when Elle convinced me to go with her and Brianne, plus six people I know in passing from the campus bars. Though Elle pulled out at the last minute, after our fight, I go because our all-inclusive package—which includes airfare, lodging, and a big packet of all-you-can-drink tickets—is dependent on a group of eight, and we have already called our travel agent with too many substitutions.

I immediately regret my decision to go. Our charter flight out of John F. Kennedy Airport is delayed for more than twenty-four hours due to technical problems, and the terminal is awash with three-hundred jocks getting drunk on duty-free liquor. There is an air of anarchy. People are hooting and running around barefoot, emulating some spring-break insanity they've seen on MTV. One of the girls I barely know gets drunk at the airport bar and has sex with a man in the public bathroom before we even board the plane. I take a sip of Brianne's cup, filled with Gatorade and vodka, and fall asleep with my face in my knapsack.

Spring break doesn't work for me, and it doesn't work with me in it. During the flight, the smell of the Bloody Marys coming off the seatbacks all around me turns my stomach, and I feel offended for the pretty flight attendant when a thunder-mouthed frat boy puts his hand on her ass. We land at midnight, and I am too cranky to rejoice at the novelty of buying Coronas on the airport shuttle. But I crack open a bottle anyway, while a tour leader blathers into the bus' P.A., and try to sip it between bumps in the road.

I don't know what I expected, but even in the prime of my excess, the amount of drinking that goes on during spring break would be too much for me. The heat is insufferable the first day I try to endure it hungover; when I unroll my hotel towel on a poolside chair, my head pounds, and my chin beads up with perspiration. All around the perimeter of the pool, girls are tied into bikinis by strings that reveal no tan lines. They sit on the tiled stools of the hotel wet bar, smoking Camels and ordering bottles of Bud, unaffected by heat or hangovers. I, however, am morose, sallow, and turning more lobster-red by the day. Every glass of beer saps me of energy. I can feel myself dehydrating like a sun-dried berry.

As the week goes on, I realize that no matter how many all-inclusive Creamsicle-flavored cocktails I down, I can't get drunk. The bars must have realized that packing the drinks with handfuls of ice, to displace the real liquor, forces us to order twice as many. Our drink levels plunge dramatically after we pick out the ice cubes and toss them into the sand, afraid that the dissolving water will give us Montezuma's revenge.

While the girls I came with still manage to get afflicted, I just get a headache. I keep thinking that if I were drunk, perhaps I wouldn't feel as insulted by the lewd promotions going on at every beach and in every bar: people flashing their private parts and tonguing shots off one another's necks; men nibbling cupcakes off of girls' laps to win bottles of liquor; girls sucking suggestively on frozen bananas for the sake of free T-shirts. A booze cruise drops us at an island for three hours of watching simulated sex contests, in which the winners actually fornicate onstage. Sober, everything I see makes me livid.

The girls I share a room with don't share my objections to spring-break culture. On the stretch of beach outside the Oasis Hotel, they get blighted on Alabama Slammers and enter the hotel's infamous wet T-shirt contest, which sounds misleading because the girls don't wear T-shirts at all. They dance bare-chested under the spray of a garden hose, while men pack in by the hundreds to watch their breasts bounce in circles like blown pinwheels. One of the girls I came with wins a Bacardi key chain as her prize for third place. We all assure her that she would have won first, had she not slipped on the wet floorboards and tumbled bare-ass-over-elbows off the stage.

Together, the girls meet men from state universities and reality-TV shows, with whom they exchange cell-phone numbers so they can meet them later at La Boom and Senor Frogs and share margaritas from yard-tall plastic tubes. At five A.M. every day, I am vaguely aware of the door handle clicking as someone struggles with the key. I hear the low whispers of a man as he knocks into the bureau, followed by my roommate's inebriated giggling. Then comes the dragging sound of someone pulling back the sliding glass door to the balcony, where the next day, she'll say they had sex on our wet beach towels.

After a few days I stop hanging out with them altogether. I go to the beach alone, while everyone sleeps off the night before, and float facedown in the impossibly blue water to see just how far down the beach the tide will carry me.

The night before we fly home, I finally drink my fill of tequila at an open-air bar, where I meet perhaps the only art-school boy in all of Mexico. He is so pale and rail-thin that one of the boys who came with us will, in an ongoing joke, call him Powder, after the bald, albino boy in that Victor Salva movie. Powder and I share a pitcher of sangria and yammer at each other the way drunkards do. He is not really listening to my talk about poetry, and I am not really listening to his talk about photography or sculpture. Yet my hand is on his shoulder, and his hand is on my thigh. And I feel lit up like a punched-tin lantern. That morning, while the sky is lighting up to a sherbet-colored orange, we walk to the beach. Someone steals my handbag while we're stretched out in the sand, kissing.

I make it back to New York because I had the foresight to store my passport in the hotel safe. But in the process, I got into a brutal screaming match with Brianne, who insisted on being in charge of the safe's key on the day we checked in, when we stuffed it with drink tickets and traveler's checks. When I burst through the door that morning, she was keg-legged, too, lying in bed with the quarterback from a Midwest university, and she was not pleased about being interrupted. She shoved the alarm clock off the nightstand and said she didn't see how my lost purse was her problem.

While I'm figuring out how to get back to school without a ride from Brianne, and in the absence of cash or credit cards, I ring up eight hundred dollars' worth of collect calls to my parents. They call my cousin, who lives in Manhattan and offers to help. She sends a car service to pick me up when I land at JFK. I spend two baffled hours at the terminal's curb, trying to figure out which of the numbered black town cars is intended for me, before I give up and take a cab to the studio apartment she shares with her fiancé. It's two A.M. when I coil up on their spare futon for a few fitful hours of sleep.

The next day, my dad lands me a ticket on a commuter flight to Syracuse. It puts them out another few hundred dollars that they don't have to spare, and makes me wonder if I wouldn't have done less financial damage if I'd just gone to Europe. It occurs to me that my abuse has continued right where it left off—I am still mistreating everyone in the throes of my drinking.

The light coming through the plane window is too bright. I can see the ovular splotch of it even with my eyes closed, and it sets off some delayed hangover, a sickness that's been waiting until we were someplace over the Catskills to strike like a gong. The woman next to me looks alarmed when I extract the paper barf-bag from the seat pocket, to hold on my lap, just in case. I decide to ascend, again, from drinking as the plane descends on Hancock International Airport.

LIQUID HEART

SINCE MY ALCOHOL abuse has always been social, it only makes sense that I become antisocial in my self-reform. I associate abusive drinking with parties and bars, with spring break and the sorority house, which are the types of places where people convene for the sole purpose of getting shitfaced. I think I'll be good as new once I escape mobs and mob mentality. If I can stay away from other students until I graduate, holing up in my new, off-campus apartment like it's the Fortress of Solitude, I can stay clear of confusion and emptiness, and thus alcohol.

During the summer before my senior year of college, I turn twenty-one, and my boyfriend drives to Massachusetts to celebrate with me, even though I tell him not to. My parents take us to dinner at the restaurant where we used to spend every Christmas Eve when I was young. It is the place where my sister and I would barrel down the corridors in our patent-leather shoes and matching taffeta dresses, throwing pecan rolls at the geese on the patio, and playing "Joy to the World" on the restaurant's piano.

But on the night of my long-anticipated twenty-first birthday, I am not festive. I am still trying to abstain from alcohol as a result of my disastrous spring break. But at the same time, I feel conflicted about the fact that I am not sticking to prototype. Another girl would be off taking twenty-one shots right now and forging from bar to bar in a T-shirt reading BARELY LEGAL.

My mother prods me to order a glass of white wine because she wants me to experience the ritual of being carded, but I clench my jaw and refuse. There is no way to tell her that the ceremony holds no thrill. I have been carded for years. I have passed off dozens of fake IDs to waitresses and bouncers, and the fact that the transaction is now legitimate doesn't make a damned bit of difference.

I gloom through the soup, the salad, and the fish course, ignoring the wine menu that my mother has set in front of me like a place card. Just when I think I've escaped the pressure to drink, a waitress sneaks up behind me and delivers a slice of Chocolate-Merlot cake topped with a candle. My boyfriend starts to hum "Happy Birthday to You." I close my eyes and wish for a new life.

Two WEEKS before classes start in August 2001, I sublet my apartment in a complex that's just off campus. I do it because the building stands among the fraternity and sorority houses on Walnut Park, and I have no desire to be anywhere near Greek row since I withdrew my membership from Zeta. I sense that the series of town houses, laid out in a three-sided square, will be awash with the type of drunken disorder I am trying to avoid. Nine months later, the apartment's management office will send me a laundry list of what looks like drunken destruction by the women who took my place on the lease, including stained floors, cigarette-burned carpets, and shrubs that someone lit on fire.

Instead, I move into a ground-level apartment on East Genessee Street. I bring the terrier puppy that I adopted from the local animal shelter in July, when it occurred to me that having something to take care of might force me to act responsibly.

The apartment's location is terribly ironic: Not only does it position me as far as possible from the campus bars and senior housing complexes, it is also equidistant from Crouse Hospital's psychiatric and rehab facilities—about one block from both. On the mornings that I walk to class, I'll have to sidestep a mass of people smoking cigarettes and slugging coffee as they wait to be let in for their morning AA meetings.

I live here quietly for two months like someone in the Witness Protection Program. Later, all I will remember from that time is a cold stone of fear in my stomach. The threat is bigger than the apartment's dangerous location, bigger than my upstairs neighbors' nightly dish-throwing ritual, or the parking lot outside my living room window, where an attendant is robbed and stabbed while I'm watching prime-time TV.

It is almost as if I expect someone from the past to come find me. I am afraid to see the people who I have abused, and the ones who have abused me. Chris and Skip have graduated, but I am afraid of Brianne and Elle, who narrows her eyes when she passes me on the campus sidewalks. Even when I dye my hair an inconspicuous shade of black, I don't feel unseen. I call Bell Atlantic twice to confirm that my phone number is unlisted, and I still jump at night when dark has blacked out the windows and I can hear someone's shoes crunch outside in the gravel. Whenever there is a knock at the back door, I glance through the peephole, heart bumping, even after my boyfriend announces, "It's me."

Two months blow past. During the day, I boil water for tea and walk the dog up the hill to Thornden Park. He, too, is fundamentally opposed to leaving the house, and when I fasten on his leash, he hooks his claws into the carpet. He is anxious, anti-social, and clingy, and my mother jokes that I have projected my personality onto him. I start skipping classes for his sake because, in the rare hours I leave him alone, he rips the stuffing from my bedspread and chews the stringy, white stuffing like gum. I ditch at least two classes a week to stay home and toss his rubber ball to him across the sloped kitchen floor.

The only class I attend religiously is my poetry workshop. It is comprised of only eight students, most of whom I recognize from my hard-drinking past, including an ex-X's roommate, one of the campus bars' bouncers, and the Alpha girl I used to throw eggs at. For workshop, I submit a series of creepy poems about Catholicism that are wholly out of character. Years later, I will see the struggle for abstinence in the lines, which are constructed entirely around the poles of good and evil, right and wrong, and all or nothing. Loads of people write poems about getting drunk.

Our professor entertains them all. She reads every drunken ballad aloud with the same fervid energy. Instead of the affected drone of most poets, who hold the last word in a line like the challenging note of a song, she reads from the belly. Lines sputter out of her like clips from a machine gun. Occasionally, one like, "I got drunk and listed everything from this girl I loved to my first car and entitled the list: 'all the shit I got drunk and fucked up,'" will pitch her forward in her chair, to laugh and slap both hands against her desk.

How could she instruct us to write on some other subject? She was a woman who had devoted some six hundred pages to family addiction. Better than anyone, she knew that liquor could shoot a good life dead, and inspire in its place a most moving eulogy. She photocopied for us a copy of Franz Wright's poem "Alcohol."

I STAY sequestered until Halloween. That's the night when the foil-wrapped candy and teenagers in face paint remind me of the first time I got drunk, and my boredom gets the best of me. The tedium of life in my apartment overshadows my fear of seeing people from the past. Like a big guy who forgets his own strength, I forget how easy it is for me to get violently drunk. I go to a campus bar on the arm of my ghoulish boyfriend.

Once I am packed inside with the crowd of bodies, already belligerent, I change my mind and want go home. The bottle of light beer that I allow myself tastes buttery, and it does nothing to calm me against the boys dressed in orange waste-disposal suits who use their elbows to push through the bodies around the bar. I have forgotten how the air in these places is sticky. I've forgotten the way the smell of the smoke hovering in the light fixtures seeps into your hair, and stays even after you've washed it. The wire end of a girl's angel wing pokes me in the eye. I feel strangulated. My dull boyfriend is lost to the men's room, but I am desperate enough to leave without him. When I start to shoulder through the doorway's gossamer spiderwebs, I run into Vanessa.

Vanessa is one of the girls I used to slug vodka with during sophomore year. She is a statuesque, Scarsdale-bred redhead who rebels against her wealthy family by binge drinking and dating working-class men. Tonight she is dressed in gloves, a tiara, and cat-eyed glasses for the purpose of being Holly Golightly from *Breakfast at Tiffany's*.

We talk as we wait for a spot at the bar. Vanessa is back after a semester in Paris, and she tells me all about the winery laborer she met in the Southwest of France and was briefly engaged to, while she takes drags from the wand of her foot-long cigarette holder. She buys us rounds of her favorite shots, called "Redheaded Sluts," and charges them to her dad's American Express Platinum card. We are slamming back the mixture of juice and Jägermëister in big swallows when she convinces me to part with my unlisted phone number.

ONCE I begin to re-liquefy, or return to a vodka-based state after a period of solid abstinence, I think it will be a prolonged homecoming. When Vanessa calls two days later to invite me to a jazz bar downtown, I think I will have to reacquaint myself with booze the same way I will have to catch up with her. We will slump down on one of the bar's velour couches, and it will take some effort on my part to drink flavored martinis. I expect re-liquefying will be like drinking for the first time ever. Like a shelved game that you have to set up and start all over again, I will have to review the tactics and the rules. Stoli will taste and smell too strong. My tolerance will be next to nil.

But it doesn't happen that way. Instead, I pound three of those raspberry-colored suckers. Rather than feeling drunk, I feel nourished, like a starved kitten clamped down on its mother's tit. The warmth that sparks in my sternum and creeps up to my cheeks feels familiar. It runs in tingly explosions, like bubbles rising in a glass of champagne.

Vanessa is going on about an ex-boyfriend's emails and her new boyfriend's motorcycle, and asking do I remember Tuesdays at Harry's, when we used to order carrot-cake shots by the tray? I listen, leaning down to sip from my glass in its space at the table, rather than lifting it to my mouth, taking care not to let one precious drop slosh over the mouth of the V. After we pay the bar tab, we drive to her boyfriend's house to play Trivial Pursuit and drink beer. And after that, I wobble home to my apartment and pass out plumb numb in bed, while the dog licks my face.

I also expect to be able to limit my drinking to just a few nights a week. But that won't work out, either. One of the campus bar owners realizes that he can supplement his slow nights—Sundays, Tuesdays, and Wednesdays—by designating those nights "for seniors." It's a ridiculous concept, considering that seniors, for the most part, are the only students of legal drinking age, anyway. But the gimmick works on us. Vanessa and I turn up early in an effort to score a table among the pack of people that pushes in around the bar, holding out their "beer tour" passports for the bartender to stamp. A certain number of ink marks is required to have one's name listed on the bar's annual plaque of seniors, which hangs on the wall like a drunkard's yearbook. We go to happy hour on Fridays, even though five hours of chain-smoking, pitching playing cards, and pouring light beer from plastic pitchers is a big-time commitment, since people come straight from classes and linger until midnight. On Saturdays, we go to dive bars in Armory Square, where we have to orbit the same three blocks to find a parking space, and one drunken night Vanessa puts two separate dents in her parents' Mercedes.

Less than a month after our reunion, Vanessa and I are hunched at one bar stool or another, sucking down Blue Hawaiians by the strawful, five or six nights a week.

It's not that Vanessa convinces me to give up abstinence altogether, she just persuades me to postpone it. She says we will have plenty of time to dry out and stop killing brain cells once college ends. But until then, we should take advantage of the fact that we don't have to wake up for work every morning. She says, "This is your senior year, and you'll regret missing out on it." It's as though she knows my fear of omission motivates me to do just about everything.

One night in November, I break things off with my boyfriend while I am still pie-eyed from happy hour. I do it because I associate him with not drinking, the same way I used to associate Chris with drinking. And now that I've decided that abstinence means little to me, I decide that this boy, who has dated me for ten long months, means little to me, too.

When I come home after a night out with Vanessa, I don't dread tottering up the steps, feeling for the light switch, or stumbling over the dog, who likes to execute figure eights through my legs. What I dread is the prospect that my boyfriend will be sleeping in my bed, that he might reach out to touch my back in the dark. Just as I used to, I prefer booze to boys. Nights, I now want to roll into unconsciousness undisturbed. I want to enjoy the rocking sensation of falling asleep plastered, which feels like sleeping in the gully of a drifting canoe.

It's snowing outside when we return each other's apartment keys. Fat flakes of it are clinging like starfish to the window screens, and part of me is glad because it means he has to walk home in it. For a mile, all those specks of snow will slap him cold in the face. "Sorry," I say, "I'm in no shape to drive."

Vanessa and I are in each other's pockets the way that Elle and I used to be. Together, we can make a drinking game out of anything: infomercials or Scrabble or the pattern of traffic trickling down Ostrom Avenue. I spend the time between and after classes at her apartment, where we tip back in matching sling chairs and drink bottled Labatt's. I wake up often in that chair, to the sensation of my own head pulsating like a human heart. When I glance over at Vanessa, her mouth is knocked open in a way that makes her look like someone in a boxing movie, like she's just been hit with a slow-motion left hook. Hours have passed. My dog has been busy chewing the spines off her roommate's textbooks. And my station wagon, which is blocking the complex's driveway, has half a dozen angry notes stuffed under the wipers.

Vanessa's boyfriends are the only force that can break our routine. During our nights downtown, men heave themselves into her as though by magnetic force. One moment, we will be gesturing with lit cigarettes and ordering glasses of something hard and syrupy, and the next, the man Vanessa has been smirking at will crisscross the room and wedge between us at the bar. A guy from her study group, or a married lawyer, or the waiter she meets one hungover morning at T.G.I.Friday's can drop her out of my life for weeks at a time and leave me to my own devices.

I have my own magnetic fields, which repel romantic interaction to a safe distance. So I spend the time alone in my apartment. I start up a pen-pal-variety relationship with Chris, who graduated last spring and has since progressed into the realm that those of us who are still studying Greek epic in English translation call "the real world." I spend nights drafting emails to him, looking for the combination of "best words, best order" that Stephen Dobyns says poets ought to strive for. The dog perches on my lap through every round of edits.

Once I start re-liquefying, I have an avenue through which to see Chris again. Even if I hadn't had a boyfriend during the months that I wasn't drinking, there would have been no way to see Chris without alcohol. For years, our interaction had been limited to parties and bars. I'd learned that waiting on a bar stool, downing shots, and peeling the labels off of beer bottles, was the only hope I had to spend time with him. Experience taught me that he would cross the room at last call to wordlessly follow me home.

When Chris visits campus during homecoming weekend, he calls me from the road to tell me which campus bar to meet him at. I haven't seen him in nine months, but when I spot him through all the bodies and cigarette smoke, his look is so familiar that it makes my breath catch, and I have to drink big gulps from my glass to keep my tongue from tying.

When he crosses the room to hug me, the moment is crushingly brief. After he steps back from the embrace, he is gone to his friends, who are sardined in a booth pouring beer pitchers and igniting napkins with cigarette lighters. I fall back into the same routine of waiting. I hole up on a bar stool, drinking rum and watching the bartender knot a cherry stem in his mouth, using only his tongue.

So much time passes while I'm waiting for Chris that my drunkenness burns off. By the time we make it back to the couch in my apartment, I am experiencing the same old hesitation. I sit a good foot away from him, with my hands crossed in my lap, until he grabs me by one elbow and pulls me next to him. When we kiss, it is not as easy as I remembered it. Instead, our mouths are timid and halting.

In the black space of my bedroom, Chris asks, "What do you want to do?"

When I say "Everything," the space between his eyebrows seams, as though he doesn't understand where the word is coming from. He wants to know why—after two years of passing out in his arms or recoiling from the closeness—I have the sudden desire to do everything. And in the moment, it is too hard to explain that my expectations for sex, which I waited and waited for, have been lessened by the boyfriend who I did not love and by not knowing what happened with Skip. I can't tell him that sometime during the past two years, the idea lost its glitter and became a drill, a procedure to get through.

Everything is fumbling and uncomfortable. But, in a backward way, I like the awkwardness. There is a shy tenderness to it that is different from the other nights I've spent with Chris, when alcohol made our bodies too eager and unfeeling for doubt. It occurs to me that he isn't drunk, either, and the few moments before I nod off to sleep feel like a breakthrough.

I don't know he'll be gone in the morning. I don't know it will be six months before he writes to me again.

I AM STILL mourning Chris's disappearance on New Year's Eve. Vanessa and I forgo invites to the Harvard Club to stay in our respective hometowns and go to parties with people we knew in high school. I am at a party that's being thrown by a girl who was my best friend for six months in fifth grade, when we would play dress up in clip-on earrings and Lycra miniskirts and apply mascara to our eyelashes in goopy coats.

Words can't describe how heinous the scene is. All the snot-nosed ex–student council members have put on their best grown-up faces. They are clustered in the living room, in front of card tables stacked high with saucers of coconut-crab dip and plates of mini-quiche. Our gracious hostess asked everyone to bring *two* bottles of wine and *two* trays of hors d'oeuvres, and the resulting bounty looks like the Last Supper. The boys are discussing whatever post-graduation jobs they've lined up at American Express or General Electric, and the girls are yapping about their secrets for getting their anchovy puffs perfectly puffy.

I am in the kitchen, slumped against the counter with the stoners, who still strike me as having more conviction than I do. I come to find out the boy I had a crush on in high school has been hopping freight trains for a year, stopping only long enough to find work harvesting avocados or alfalfa in order to finance a trip to someplace else. A girl I passed out next to on a coat-bed last year tells me she's moved from Chardonnay to cocaine as casually as if she were telling me she'd transferred colleges.

Through all this, I am standing at the kitchen table mixing my hundredth glass of cranberry juice and Malibu rum. I brought the bottle, which is an opaque white color, so I can't chart how much of it I've poured.

It was a Christmas gift from my parents. My dad had asked me if I wanted anything before his holiday liquor-store run, which was when he bought enough wine to keep the relatives too paddled to bicker during Christmas dinner. I'd told him "Malibu," which I loved for its artificial coconut flavoring. I'd opened it on Christmas morning; it was wrapped up among the usual boxes of winter sweaters (to keep warm) and books (to keep smart). My parents gave it to me because I was newly twenty-one. My dad had joked with me about the bottle's utter girliness. It looked like a bottle of sunscreen, he said, with its picture of twin palm trees in front of a half-set Caribbean sun.

I am drinking Malibu as hard as I did that night in high

school when I had my stomach pumped. I've had five years of boozing experience since then, so I ought to know better. By now, I should know that you have to give each viscous glass a few minutes to absorb before you pour yourself another, that you can't expect to immediately feel all mops and brooms. But I do. I am deeply frustrated by the fact that all the Malibu I am sipping isn't having any effect on me. I feel like I'm trying to evoke a genie; I'm rubbing the bottle 'til my palms start to burn, but I can't stir up the sensation of drunken comfort. That hot flush of confidence stays plugged up inside me.

Later, I'll wonder if my childhood friends have always awakened my wholehearted desire to be comatose. I can feel the Yalies in the living room eyeing me as they molest bowls of bean dip. A girl whose name I can't remember studies my haltered pantsuit and describes it in two mouthed syllables that I can make out from clear across the room: *Uh-gly*. An ex–English teacher's daughter tumbles over to give me hug, and to apologize for that time in high school when she wrote KOREN IS A HO-BAG SLUT on the wall of the locker room. I feel that if I were wasted immediately, it still wouldn't be soon enough.

Drunkenness doesn't creep up on me softly; it comes up behind me and shoves. When I look up from my glass, it's midnight already. The TV is all snow, and our countdown lacks any degree of precision; 2002 begins when some tin-hatted jock howls "Happy New Year." I have funhouse–mirror vision, in which people look like squiggly lines. Their features bulge outward or cave inward, depending on the angle from which I look at them. Party hats are hitting the ceiling. Boys are lifting girls up by their waists. People are making moves to hug me.

He appears behind me when someone switches on the stereo. He is the hostess's brother: older by a few years and handsome, if you like that type. I suspect he is very drunk, too, but I am at the vanishing point where I can't gauge how far-gone anyone else is. In ten years, he has never breathed a word to me, unless you count a ski trip I took with his family when I was ten, when he leaned over during dinner to tell me that my sweater, which was stitched with yarn-haired horses, was *gay*. I'm confused by the fact that he has now pulled me into him. I have no clue why he is trying to dance with me with both hands cupped tight around the contours of my ass.

I don't want to dance, for two reasons. First off, I feel woozy. Odds are, my head is wobbling around on my neck, the way Vanessa always tells me it does when I am a real wreck—*bobble-headed,* she calls it, after the sports figurines with spring necks that make their heads wiggle and nod. Second, every time this boy tries to pull me close to shimmy and shake, the Yalies shit themselves laughing. Even half-shot, I am aware of people judging me. I won't be humiliated.

And so it goes like this: I start to break away, and he grabs me by one hand and snaps me back into him like a yo-yo. In my head, it looks choreographed that way, like salsa dancing, like the moment the woman turns away from her partner and then spins, top-like, into his chest. But I know, fucked-up as I am, it can't possibly look that civil or smooth.

Later, friends will tell me that I wobbled up to them repeatedly to say, "Please rescue me" or "Please make him leave me alone." But they also say that the moment he scuttled up behind me and caught me around the waist, I collapsed in his arms and seemed more than content to let him kiss me.

. . .

THE NEXT thing I know, I am lying on his daybed. In retrospect, I'll know it's almost morning because the room has a weird light about it. Sun must be coming in through the pores of the red curtains, and as a result, everything looks dark and orange, the way I imagine things must look in the womb. The light makes me think of the album art on Nirvana's *In Utero,* the anatomic illustration of a winged woman, looking wide open with arms outstretched.

I'm naked, even though I don't want to be. I let my halter suit slide off the bed because he promises that I won't have to do anything. Without clothes on, my body feels cold and snail-like. It always feels this way when I'm drunk. The sensation of bareness usually sobers me right up. Usually, it's like a cold shower that sets me turning over bedspreads to find my under-things.

Tonight, though, I can't feel nakedness anywhere near that intensely. In fact, as time passes, I can't really feel anything at all. It's like my body just dissolves below my neck. My body parts seem to exist independent of each other, like there's nothing stringing them together. I, as a person, don't seem to exist anymore. I feel like a car that's been scrapped for parts.

They are parts I am only aware of when the boy taps at them, first with his fingers, like a metal pointer, and later with the half-slack slug of his dick. I'm just lying there, thinking about that sketch on the Nirvana cover. I know I'm saying, "No, I really don't want to," and trying to say, "You said we didn't have to," though it only comes out "You said, you said," the way a kid reminds you that you said she could have an ice-cream sundae after some boring errand, like a trip to the furniture store.

But for everything I say, I can't physically unload him from his space on top of me. Tonight, my drunkenness is heavy. I feel as though I am lying under the lead apron the dental hygienist pulls over me every time she photographs my wisdom teeth. All I can do is implore him to dig a condom out of the nightstand drawer, and then lie quietly for a few more minutes before getting up to put on my clothes.

Standing up is not an improvement. All those syrupy glasses of Malibu have transformed the approaching hangover into something like an insulin crash. It's not the usual headache I feel, which is a low, aching pain behind my forehead. No, this is a sharp, light-headed pain, like the one you would get after hanging your head between your knees for twenty minutes, and then suddenly sitting up. I almost can't make it down the two flights of stairs to my car, which has taken it upon itself to change location during the night. My knees give out and my ears buzz, and I'd probably sit down to take a rest, were the boy not walking with me.

When I sink into the driver's seat, he says the words that will stick with me. It's an apology that will be there every time I wonder if I really was wronged, if maybe I was too dazed to remember things accurately. Before I turn the key in the ignition, he leans down to kiss me on the cheek. And to say, "Sorry about the whole sex thing."

At home, I lie in bed, facedown, and my skin feels prickly. I can't let myself feel abused. He was drunk, which makes him less blameworthy; and I was drunk, which makes me more so. I don't need anyone to explain this equation to me. I just know it, the same way that people just know how to grieve. My stomach bucks. My head thwacks. In its hangover, my body reminds me that I am at fault.

BACK AT SCHOOL, it is a particularly brutal winter. The snow is so continual that we can't help but feel like the sky is pushing in on us. Sometimes it flutters down so hard that the clouds buckle and split open with lightning. From a distance, it's hard to tell the snowbanks from the slush-colored sky.

There are reminders everywhere that the end is near. On TV, car commercials are set to the tune of "Pomp and Circumstance." The campus bulletin boards are all pinned with flyers auctioning off extra tickets for commencement. And instead of making my great escape feel more imminent, it only makes my jaw lock up in a panic attack.

I can't believe I am about to graduate, and that isn't yearbook rhetoric. I don't mean it in the wistful *where-has-the-time-gone* sort of way. I literally mean that I don't think I am going to fulfill the requirements that are compulsory to earn my bachelor's degree. Even on the day a woman draws a tape measure around the crown of my head to fit my mortarboard cap (broadcasting an impossible girth of twenty-three and a half inches), I have to go home and reexamine the registrar's letter that I've taped to my refrigerator. It is the semesterly memo we have all come to live by, which keeps an ongoing countdown of requirements: one more foreign-language class, one intensive writing, two more natural science and mathematics. Only this time, on the line for remaining credits, the office staff had drawn a flat, blank-faced "zero." That zero has the gravitational field of a black hole; in a matter of weeks it will be the plug pulled out of my cosmic bathtub drain; it will suck down life-as-I-know-it.

In the months after New Year's, I have been blinking drunk almost every night. I no longer know whether I'm drinking to generate new stories or to forget old ones. And in a way, it doesn't even matter; the quality of my drinking is that dreary. It has all the daily excitement of cooking spaghetti or washing my face.

If ever the slogan "I drink, therefore I am" was applicable, it is to describe me, now. I drink because I always drink. I drink to feel the liquor vapor clear out my sinuses, or to hear the smoothed-over sound of my own voice. These have become the sensations that convince me I'm still here. I drink now for the dullness of it. There's no passion or exhilaration left. Taking a shot of vodka is like kissing a lover I've touched lips with for seven straight years.

In the throes of daily rum withdrawal I am wracked with anxiety. In addition to nightmares that a failed term paper costs me my diploma, I have recurring dreams that I've stolen cars, robbed grocery stores, or committed some other act of treachery and have SWAT teams pursuing me. Nights that I come home stupefied on what the bartender calls "Bloody Brain" shots (a testament to just how many brain cells the drink seems to kill), I dream I hear helicopters and see searchlights. I imagine that a hundred uniformed officers wait outside, their pistols aimed at my apartment's sad little door.

It began in late February with something I saw on *Dateline*. A federal judge had overturned the murder conviction of Paul Cox. Paul had been convicted of a double murder in White Plains in 1988, when in the midst of an alcoholic blackout, he broke into his childhood home and stabbed the new tenants to death while they slept. At an AA meeting, he'd confessed that he'd woken up with blood on his clothes after a bizarre dream about killing his parents. And though the judge ultimately ruled that the information was privileged, like coming clean to a priest, it was the first time AA had ever broken its code of anonymity.

I was sorely hungover while I watched it. I'd dragged my pillows and bedspread onto the floor in the living room, where I liked to create my own recovery unit. The Brita pitcher was on the floor near my head, along with a box of saltines, which I had taken to buying in bulk at Sam's Club. The dog, having long since decided my sick days were his favorites, had wadded himself up under my armpit.

The music on *Dateline* has always terrified me. It's the same synthetic chiming used on *Unsolved Mysteries.* It used to make me bury my head under the blanket on the nights I slept over at my nana's house, when I could hear Robert Stack's voice down the hall, narrating how police had uncovered the body of a girl just like me. But when I heard the Paul Cox story, my head was still hissing. I still had to force myself to drink water because its clear color made my mind drift back to vodka. That day, the tinkling music set my spine shivering for a whole new reason. It occurred to me that Paul was living in an eternal state of hangover, just like me.

For the first time ever, I felt an affinity for the killer as well as the victim. It occurred to me that, like the suicides in Dante's *Inferno,* Paul's crime was committed in a single moment of blind passion. And I was willing to bet he'd repeat the hell of it every moment to eternity. I couldn't imagine how anyone could go on living after that kind of murderous bender. I imagine that the memory of life before the incident must hang daily in front of you, like the carrot that taunts the donkey. It must be a lasting reminder of the good life you've cast away.

I'VE STARTED driving everywhere I need to go, mostly because the sidewalks outside my apartment aren't shoveled, and the only way to walk to campus is in the ruts left by cars swerving down University Avenue. I can't make the hike. My almost-daily drinking has brought me to new depths of sluggishness, in which any task short of brushing my teeth physically exhausts me.

So I drive everywhere. When I go to class, I park illegally in

Thornden Park, digging one of my parking tickets from the glove compartment and pinning it to the windshield as a lame decoy. When I go to the campus bars, I parallel-park the station wagon among the stretch of open meters on South Crouse Avenue.

It is a four-block drive from the campus bars to my apartment, but most mornings when I wake up, I can't recall making it. I have to part the bedroom curtains to make sure my car found its way to the parking lot. Some mornings it turns up missing, and it takes me some time to remember that I walked home because a bartender insisted on it.

After a night like that, I circle the wagon as inconspicuously as possible before I drive it again. If the lot attendant sees me, he probably thinks I'm dusting off the night's snowfall. But I am actually hunting for evidence of a gruesome, life-altering accident I might not remember. I push the inches off the headlights and rearview mirrors with the fists of my sweatshirt; my fingers are balled up and shaking in the sleeves, probably as much from nerves as from cold and withdrawal. I'm panicky at the thought of uncovering a dented fender from a run-in with a parking meter, or worse, the remains of someone's house cat on the tires.

Coincidentally, I pick up a job driving my poetry teacher's teenaged son home from school on the days she teaches graduate classes. Rent, combined with big bar tabs, has left me flat broke. Plus, I failed miserably at my previous part-time job as a beer vendor at the Carrier Dome (I was meant to carry water bottles, but a sleazy manager decided that having a young gal sell beer would be more profitable). I walked out the first day, still wearing my change apron and Michelob Light hat, once I realized that my unformed biceps couldn't possibly lug thirty cans up and down hundreds of bleachers.

On the days that I pick him up at school behind a line of yellow buses, I accelerate slowly, as though the road I travel is a perpetual school zone. It is a relief to be carrying "precious cargo," which was the term my parents always used with the people who carted me around in high school. It's a sensation I don't get when I am driving alone, flying down Route 5 like I'm trying to break the sound barrier, having long since stopped caring if a car wreck claimed me, and often hoping for it. Often, as the kid sits in my passenger seat, I get a weird sensation that he's older than me, like even as he studies algebra and prepares for PSATs, he understands more. Other times, he just scans the alternative radio stations like any other teenaged boy, as likeable and levelheaded in person as he is in the poem my teacher publishes in *The New Yorker*.

I make a mistake the day I tow Vanessa along.

I agree to drive her to Peter's Groceries after I drop the son off at home because her parents confiscated her car after seeing the dents she drunkenly put in it. She is sitting in the backseat next to his book bag, and through the rearview mirror, I can see that she is wearing her hangover sunglasses, the really opaque ones through which you can barely make out the outline of her eyelashes. The current of air howling through the open window has her red hair fanning her face. Neither the son nor I are big talkers, and the trip is generally silent while we watch traffic or tap our fingers in time to the radio. But Vanessa is a socializer, and I can see that the silence is killing her. Eventually, she leans between the front seats to ask my teacher's son what grade he's in, what sports he plays, and whether he dates. He politely responds, saying "Ninth, lacrosse, no."

I am still driving with DMV-test precision, stopping for a full ten seconds at STOP signs and the like. But I almost veer into oncoming traffic when she asks him, "Do you drink?" I'll wait until we are wandering through the store's cereal aisle to ask what in the hell compelled her to bring up alcohol in front of a boy who was only fifteen. And she'll respond by saying "What's the big deal? We started drinking at fourteen."

But the boy is unphased. He might even be intrigued by the question's honesty. He twists around in his seat to look at her, and chronicles three generations' worth of addiction as briefly as he can before the car turns his street corner, ignoring the fact that she would know all this had she read his mother's books. Before he clicks the car door closed, he says, given his family history, trying alcohol is just too risky. He runs the chance that he might get addicted.

It will forever be the most informed argument against underage drinking I've ever heard. And it's far more honest than all the bullshit kids get dished about drunk driving and peer pressure, or even drinking moderately and responsibly. At the time, this is lost on me. I am six years older than he is, and neither my friends nor I think of alcohol as an addictive substance. To us, dependence is pinned only to drugs, like cocaine (maybe even pot, if you buy those public service announcements that say, "It's a lot more dangerous than we thought"), and cigarettes, which we resolve to stop smoking post-graduation.

I won't know until much later that a quarter of all college students have family histories of alcoholism, or whether I find myself among that demographic. Who would think to approach their parents to ask how much or how often their parents, or their parents' parents, drank, and whether they experienced hardships as a result of it? I have no idea whether the women my mother keeps framed in our living room, yellowed photos of great-aunts and great, great grandmothers wearing lace bonnets, might have a bearing on my present. Nor can I see how close my own addiction looms. I already *need* alcohol, not physically but certainly emotionally; my relationships, self-image, and ability to cope fluctuate with my blood-alcohol content.

GRADUATION FALLS on a weekend that's inconvenient for everyone. My dad flies in alone on Friday night, coming directly from a business meeting in Miami. My mom and sister wait to drive in at four A.M. the next day because my sister has her junior prom on Friday night.

Like everyone else wearing a black, polyester poncho, I've long since accepted the fact that the ceremony is for my parents' sake, not mine. If I had it my way, I would have gone home a week ago and waited for my diploma to arrive in the mail. Still, that obligation to my parents doesn't make the slow procession onto the football field any less agonizing. I am severely hungover, and when the tassels ahead of me move forward at a snail's pace, I start to wonder if I can make it to a folding chair without fainting. My hands are shaking even as I lace them in front of me. And when I catch my family hanging over the dome's third-tier railing, it takes all my energy to look happy and accomplished, to wave one hand high above my head and blow my mother a kiss.

The smell coming off the robes all around me is flammable. As I enter a row, an usher stops me short and scolds me for entering the aisle from the wrong direction. (No one I know attended the graduation rehearsal because it fell during happy hour.) I plant myself beside my old roommate, April, and her boyfriend, and they are the only people in the immediate area who don't smell of tequila. Everyone else looks as sallow and nauseated as I do, as anxious to get the hell out of Dodge, to throw their caps up into the rafters and run out before the black mass hits the Astroturf.

As I sit through the speeches, I think *It is time for this madness to end.* In the rows ahead of me, there are too many ex-Xs to name. There are boys I've cried in front of and passed out next to on couches. There are boys who have backed me into a corner in someone's apartment, seized my arms hard enough to leave marks, and refused to loosen their grips when I tried to wriggle away. There are too many reminders of sticky kisses that have not blossomed into real romance, despite my most heartfelt affections. There are boys I have told afterward, in no uncertain terms, to "go fuck themselves."

There are girls, too, standing on their chairs in order to get a clear view of the stage. In the rows, I can make out so many of them who I once slugged wine with. They are girls who sat rolling drunk with me at three A.M. in Walnut Park, sharing drags off a joint and telling stories that I swiftly forgot. They are girls who meant the world to me, and then, after a time, meant nothing. A few, in these final months, have reeled up high on Heineken to say "I've missed you" (like Elle), or "I want you in my life" (like April). More have cornered me in bar bathrooms, loaded and angry, looking to throw a drink. Some (like Hannah) have called in the early hours of the morning to say they saw me drinking Bacardi with their ex-boyfriends, and to kindly ask me to stay away.

Perhaps my only consolation is the fact that I made it.

I think of graduation the way the devout think of the apocalypse. For months, people have talked about this day like the fiery flames of hell engulfing the planet. Graduation will absolve us of our sins. After today, our addictions will drift away like all the world's islands. We will stop drinking, stop dieting during the day and eating pizza at three A.M., stop relying on pot with TV and cigarettes with coffee. Our drunken abuses, like mountains, will fade away and never be found, and we will only have the stories to recap. We will tell of our near-misses with wonder and gratitude.

Yes, when the chancellor says, "Allow me to present the class of 2002," we will fly clean out of our robes and ascend to our destiny. We'll find paradise in the "real world," where there are men seeking meaningful relationships, jobs in media, and cheap and spacious lofts in major cities.

THE END HAS NO END

I MOVE TO Manhattan two weeks after graduation. Everyone I know does, with the exception of the people who grew up there, who instead migrate west, to Los Angeles. Everyone regards her sixth-story walk-up as a triumph, regardless of its sludge-streaked windows, the alien insects in the bathtub cracks, and the flickering light fixtures, which turn everything the blanched color of oatmeal. Everyone feels redeemed by urbanism, as if change were as simple as getting a new zip code. No one expects the past to run into the present. We don't know it will seep down on us like leaks from an apartment upstairs.

I move because my old boss has a new job as the publisher of a men's magazine, and when I call him on my twenty-second birthday, he says that, eerily enough, his assistant quit ten minutes ago. Two days later, I am taking typing tests in the human resources department. Two days after that, Vanessa and I are wheezing up the stairwells of a dozen Upper East Side apartment buildings before we land ourselves in a roach-infested pre-war building in the east Seventies.

Vanessa moves to New York with me because, she says, she doesn't want our friendship to ebb under the stress of new jobs and so many miles. She doesn't want our nightly cocktail hours to give way to weekly emails. I suspect I am also the springboard that catapults her closer to her latest boyfriend's Brooklyn loft. They broke up not more than an hour after we returned our graduation gowns to the rental company, on the basis that he didn't want a long-distance relationship.

We don't unpack for a month. Our CDs and desk lamps and scented candles stay snarled in the wastepaper baskets we used to transport them. Our clothes stay crumpled in our suitcases. A box filled with books stays in the alcove that we call a living room, and we'll use it as a coffee table, a cardboard surface on which to rest drinks.

Between interviews at TV production companies, Vanessa picks up a job waiting tables at a neighborhood café. She works the night shift. Most nights, when I turn the key to the apartment, the only traces of her are nail polish bottles on the windowsill, T-shirts hung to dry on the shower rod, and refrigerator shelves filled with the foam take-out containers she brings home from work. In order to see her, I have to walk down to the restaurant and sit at its bar, where she sneaks me martinis so I will stay long enough to distract her between customers.

Before I moved to New York, I'd never had a martini in my life. And, even though the V-shaped glasses Vanessa brings me are free, I hate the yuppie cliché of them. I hate that the hangovers they cause feel like heroin withdrawal, that the dry vermouth makes my mouth feel mucusy, and that I can only force them down when I am already drunk. I drink them because shots no longer get me sufficiently drunk, the way that before shots, sugary rum drinks didn't get me sufficiently drunk, and before those, beer, then wine coolers, then wine. I don't like martinis, but I succumb to them, the way drug users who hate needles succumb to mainlining because they need a stronger, new high.

On martini nights, I teeter out onto the street when Vanessa's dinner crowd picks up, into the overlong summer light. The sidewalk always tilts. I feel extra impaired, weaving between strollers and leashed collies and couples linking arms. I have always hated being drunk in the daylight, which gives the sun the sick glare of a fluorescent bulb. It makes the simple fact of being drunk look much uglier.

THE UPPER East Side is college-town Manhattan. Compared to other parts of the city, its rents are among the cheapest, and as a result, recent college graduates pack fourfold into its one-bedroom apartments. In the months that I live here, not a day goes by that I don't run into someone I knew in college: In a booth at Ellen's Stardust Diner, an old campus bartender eats pancakes; on the number 6 train, a boy who once backed me against a bar's pinball machine ducks behind his copy of the *Post;* at a corner on Eightieth Street, a sorority sister wants to play with my hair and relive past parties. I can't scuttle past a neighborhood bar without spotting a familiar pack of frat boys streaming out of a cab like circus clowns.

There is something like three bars on every block outside our apartment. Every night of the week, I can hear the sounds of alcohol abuse from my window. My dreams are filled with shrieking, with base lines, with names shouted long and loud down Second Avenue. The smell of beer and cigarettes that rises from the sidewalk pervades my bedroom window and gets into my sheets. Within a month of moving in, Vanessa has made our introductions with every bartender in a one-mile radius, and they are all friendly with her parents' not-yet-cancelled platinum card.

We have not yet implemented the plan to curb our drinking. We've postponed it because it is summer, and what is summer if not for picnics of lousy wine and crackers, beach coolers gorged with beer bottles, a ten-speed blender pulverizing ice cubes and vodka for frozen lemonade? We can't afford cable or Internet access or air-conditioning fixtures on my starting salary and Vanessa's tips, and we are too hot and hesitant to invent new ways to pass the half-lit hours after work. We don't know about free films on rooftops in Brooklyn. We don't know Friday nights' admission is "pay-what-you-wish" at the Whitney Museum, just four blocks away. We don't yet know to pay attention to bills and flyers, to stand at newsstands while we thumb *The New Yorker,* to run our fingers over *The Village Voice*'s club listings until they come up blackened. Instead, we drink, and vow to cut back in September, which still feels like the start of a school year.

During the week, I am limited to a couple of glasses of beer or wine after work, when I sit in a warped lawn chair on the apartment's tar roof with whatever college drinking buddy stops by to visit. Sometimes we stay up there past sundown, pitching cards and looking through the lit windows of a nearby high-rise, trying to figure out what's on TV. I suddenly understand why so many people pour drinks after work: A bit of alcohol is enough to make me feel less defeated and lightly sleepy.

While I am enslaved to my alarm clock, which is fine-tuned to account for morning rush hour, Vanessa still tours bars with other waitresses after they cash out for the night. She befriends brusque women with oddly spelled names like Hollee and Kym, and I start to feel as though I am losing her to them, to the blueberry martinis they drink and the bars with red-draped ceilings where they kill time. When Friday nights come, I want to reassert my friendship, which makes my drinking determined and frenzied.

An average weekend finds Vanessa and me in whiskey bars where the air is dank and the light is grainy, or in dive bars where the walls are papered with pinups, or in college bars with fenced-in patios that waft beer breath onto the street. We drink budget beer or matter-of-fact shots, or, sometimes, chichi cocktails with offensive names (one night a man offers to buy me a drink called "a miscarriage," which I kindly refuse). I spend every last dollar in my wallet, no matter how much cash I bring out.

After the bars close at four A.M. and the owners begin sweeping the sidewalks, I trail Vanessa and her latest love interest into all-night diners. I sit with them at counters while they eat omelets and I knock over sugar shakers. My head bows forward, my eyes burn with the strain of staying open, and I know that if I let myself, I could pass out on my swiveling stool. Still, these greasy spoons are crowded with people as drunk as I am, a faint beer vapor hangs over the smell of burned toast, and the owners seem to appreciate our business. One night, I find myself nodding as the mustached manager tries to teach me Portuguese; I parrot words that Vanessa shrieks and says translate to "I am a drunken little whore."

Weekend afternoons are consumed by my hangovers, which are among the most violent I've known. Summer sun streams through my windows like light through a magnifying glass, and

I toss and kick down the sheets, writing like an ant doused in lighter fluid. I vomit most mornings, but sometimes, I also spit up black specks that remind me of coffee grounds, and I don't know they are symptomatic of stomach bleeding. Sometimes, my feet are muddy when I catch them poking out of the covers, and I realize I walked down Third Avenue with my shoes in my hands.

ALL AT ONCE, the sun cools and stops filtering down side streets. A breeze kicks up and pulls discarded newspapers into traffic. The dogs start wearing sweaters; the mannequins in window displays are stripped naked and redressed in tweed; and the downtown bus is crowded with mothers transporting their children to school. It occurs to me that it's fall, and I still haven't cut back on alcohol.

It doesn't take me long to realize that the adult world will never present me with a good reason to stop drinking. If anything, it invents new incentives. At work, my email is jammed with appeals to "save the date" of a going-away party or a department happy hour. At home, my answering machine blinks with half a dozen messages, all of which are alike: Five seconds of shapeless music and conversation, followed by a bumping sound like the phone is being juggled, and then a vaguely familiar voice coming on the line, shouting, dispatching me to a dive bar downtown.

I do save dates, obsessively, in the day planner that I tote around in my big, brown satchel. The agenda eases me. The more I have scrawled in the column marked IMPORTANT MATTERS the less I worry that my college friends will recede into the city's millions and leave me alone. I remember from past summers how easy it is to feel isolated in New York, what with large laughing parties at outdoor cafés, women gossiping on the subway, and old friends blocking the sidewalk with unexpected reunions. I attend every party because I fear missing one will cut me out of the program. If I missed one, my message machine might fall mute, traumatized.

Even if I wanted to abstain at these post-college get-togethers, I'm not sure I could muster it. Even if a hard drink weren't the only thing that could comfort me upon seeing old pals wearing the wounded expressions of aspiring-screenwriters-turned-mailroom-clerks, I don't think I could pass on the rounds of tequila shots that are always circulating. Someone I know always ends up groaning, "Come on, Koren, come on." Someone is always holding a shot glass a few inches from my face, like the childhood bullies who held their palms just far enough from your skin to sing, "Not touching, not touching."

Drinkers are a tribal gang. We have our own lexicon, our own nicknames, and our own list of virtues that we drink to. If we are pounding mimosas at brunch, we expect everyone else to pummel them, too, because there's nothing worse than having someone lucid in the presence of our third chorus of "Peace, Love and Understanding."

Abstinence is particularly hard in New York because there is no ironclad excuse for it. The city is awash with designated drivers, so you don't have a potential D.U.I. charge to fend off whatever friend or colleague is moving in to fill your glass. Here, as long as you can slur your address to a cabdriver, you can't escape generous refills. Unless you're pregnant, or nursing, or taking medication that has fatal side effects when it's taken with booze, it's hard to explain why you won't have a drink.

In the post-college world, I notice an overwhelming assumption that everyone wants to drink. At twenty-two, the age when you can responsibly make it to work on time and pay bills almost on time, people assume you know how to drink responsibly, too, as though we can all find that balance with the same degree of precision. As a result, we look with astonishment at the person who abstains. I know because I'll experience it constantly after I quit drinking; someone will hold a bottleneck the way a butcher holds a dead chicken, and ruffle their brows as they say, "Koren, are you *sure* you don't want any?" When people are of legal drinking age, we assume that they *want* to drink, and look for a reason why they *don't,* rather than assuming that they don't want to drink and probing for reasons why they do. We assume that the person who won't accept just one glass of wine has a "problem," like alcoholism, a reason that they *can't* drink, even though they want to.

Also after college, alcohol transforms into a status symbol. All at once, I become aware of the way people look at me in the liquor store when I veer directly for the wall of cheap wine. I notice the faces that waitresses make when I don't order a drink with my pasta; they are pitiful looks that suggest I can't afford one. Like everything else in New York, drinking is dictated by brands. People are conscious about drinking the best wine and the most premium vodka, about ordering liquor by the bottle instead of by the glass. The change is disheartening. Alcohol feels like an old friend that's begun to act too good for me.

Of course, drinking has been a symbol of fashion and taste since the Roaring Twenties; that is, since long before TV celebrities started pulling open their refrigerator to display two-hundred-dollar bottles of Kristal champagne. But I've never thought about it that way—at least, not until I landed myself in a city that served fifty-dollar cocktails topped with liquefied gold. Now, I am at bars among drunken investment bankers and advertising executives. I meet men who don't just stagger, swear, and say "bitch" to the woman standing in their way of the bar, but also feel proud and justified in doing so. Their benders, in addition to being symbols of their masculinity, are markers of their affluence. I meet men who boast that their bar tabs are equivalent to my one-month's rent.

AT WORK, more of my expectations for the real world burn out and die hard.

For starters, women are just as catty as they were in high school. I'll be clipping down the long hall from my desk to reception, my worn-down heels clicking on every patch of hardwood floor, when, for no reason, a woman from another department will turn and narrow her eyes like I just stole her boyfriend.

I notice the other twentysomething assistants are an organized clique. They have marked off a windowside table a few feet from my cubicle, where they convene to gossip and eat lunch. While I type spreadsheets, I can hear them whisper about my new haircut's curious wisps or the eyesore that is my old, moss-colored cardigan. Together, they awaken my deepest social anxieties, the ones that only the highest-proof whiskey can quell. I walk around wearing a worried and apologetic expression. I leave interoffice voicemails that start, "I'm sorry to ask you" or "If it isn't too inconvenient . . ." I spend a lot of time trying to figure out which one of them I offended, and what exactly I did that was wrong.

The decorum that so many professors had me coming to expect doesn't exist beyond the executive level. There are few neckties at work, and no panty hose. Instead, everyone has dirty hair and nicotine-stained fingers. Most of the office twenty- and thirtysomethings blow into meetings wearing rumpled jeans and suede sneakers. They curse constantly, even passionately, because every task is urgent and *fuck* is the most urgent expletive. Every day, the lunchroom is filled with girls tallying their daily Weight Watchers points and talking of cutting food calories for the sake of drinking more booze.

I am an advertising assistant. This means it is my job to aid the magazine's mostly female sales reps, and it is their job to go to product launch parties after work, to sample the latest brands of flavored vodka and sweet-talk brand managers who might buy ads in the September issue. The women for whom I photocopy things are all blonde, and striking in their caramel-colored pantsuits and five-hundred-dollar heels. They swallow diet pills that they disguise in vitamin bottles and store in their desk drawers. They break for bikini waxes between appointments. These are women for whom martini lunches still exist. After lunch with executives from a liquor company, they skip in with flushed cheeks and collapse into their chairs; they push their bangs off their foreheads and say, "Whoa, I'm tipsy." The associate publisher, also female, laughs often and praises them for their drinking stamina, for their ability to keep up with male executives from a Scotch whiskey company.

It doesn't take me long to realize how much business is done over drinks. Of course, no one would dare say that outright. No boss could reprimand you for not attending a staff party where the magazine's music editors smoke a joint in the boardroom and the soon-to-be director of marketing downs enough 7&7s to do a red-faced rendition of the general manager. But when the stomach flu forces me to miss an office party, my bosses assure me I missed a hell of a time. In a way, I feel left out as a result of it. I can tell margaritas bonded the people that sit in adjacent cubicles. They are gossiping over email, discussing in the pop-up boxes of their computer screens the magazine's celebrity founder, who got drunk and fell off the stage during his speech.

I find out that I will never get promoted without networking, and networking is what happens when the women I work with are drunk off their saucers. The few times that I clink glasses with my colleagues, they tell me about the magazines they've worked for before and the interviews they're going to on the sly. They confide in me about their ex-boyfriends and ex-roommates, and they look to commiserate about the people who make waves for them at work.

Still, in the year that I work at the magazine, I'll go to just one corporate party.

It is a celebration for the advertising and marketing departments, held at the Connecticut home of one of the magazine's publishers. Work ends promptly at five on the Thursday of the party, which is rare, and the whole staff piles into three buses for the drive up the Bruckner Expressway. During the ride, we lamely discuss clients, ad pages, and overdue deadlines.

But something changes once we arrive and begin ordering cocktails from starch-shirted caterers. Each glass of liquor loosens some collective tension, which I think I can chart by the slipping knots of men's ties. By the time the sun plunges into the tree line and the mosquitoes come out, the office's notorious control freak is twirling in front of the band and keeping time on a tambourine. One of the male sales reps grabs me by the hip and slurringly asks if I like Led Zeppelin. I sip two glasses of white wine with ice cubes, which is not enough to make me any less anxious. The women I work with shake their hips and make wafting gestures that mean *come and dance with us,* but I only last for a few minutes of tambourine-thumping before I get embarrassed and scuttle back to my lawn chair.

I suppose I should feel relieved by the prevalent drinking culture at work. Hanging about at the bar across the street from the office, I ought to be in my element. I ought to drink Cabernet and let it unfix me enough to play darts with my bosses, or let the IT technician tell me jokes, or feed compliments to the assistants who hate me. Instead, I drink very little, or not a drop. And after a time, I start inventing doctors' appointments and dinners with aunts. I make up reasons why I can't go out at all after work.

I surprise myself this way.

Years later, I'll think I avoided drinking with colleagues because alcohol had been my private passion, and it was charged with an eroticism that felt highly intimate. I'd never gotten drunk with adults, older people, relatives, even men. Those people always made me feel self-conscious and silly, as though I were drinking as a child or a female, or, as my women's studies professors always said, an Other.

Or I might shrink from it because I know I am at a high risk for humiliating myself. I don't want to suffer the same fate as the young female assistants at other companies. I don't want to be like the girls who puke or pass out in front of clients. They end up being the jokes of interoffice emails, until they get fired or their scandals end up on Page Six.

Either way, I only come unglued with my female friends, when our excess can't be pinned to a stage or an age. Mostly, I still drink with Vanessa because our alcohol abuse still has a comfortable symmetry.

In September, Vanessa gets a job as a production assistant at a cable network, and we get the idea to throw a celebratory party.

My old roommate April helps us post our invitation on a Web

site. Our apartment is too small to house the people that RSVP "yes," so we decide to throw the party on the roof. Vanessa goes to a hardware store to buy long-burning deck candles and strands of Christmas bulbs so we'll have light outside. I go to the grocery store to buy strawberries, obscene-looking shrimp, long ropes of French bread, and wedges of rank, gourmet cheese. Even as I buy it, I know the spread will look shabby and sad on the chipped pink plates that we use for platters. But it feels good to labor over a project outside of work at the magazine, where tasks occupy my hands but not my head, which wanders toward questions of romance or career, concepts that are deeper and more troubling.

On the day of the party, the only thing left to worry about is liquor, which Vanessa and I run to buy at The Bottle Shop. We spend a long time in the store, scrutinizing labels, unable to decide. If we buy vodka, we have to buy juice or tonic water. If we buy rum, we have to buy Coke. When Vanessa asks the salesgirl for recommendations, she suggests we buy Blue Curacao and Sambuca to make drinks called "Blue Smurfs." We chip in to buy the bottles, even though the drink name is dumb and redundant.

Before anyone arrives, we try out the recipe in the fat flower vase we use for a pitcher, and pour it into martini glasses we got as party favors at a Zeta formal. The drinks are the color of Windex, and they stain our tongues.

April is the first person to arrive. When she swings open the dented door to the roof, Vanessa and I are leaning over the lip of the building and looking for people we recognize on the street. I've already swallowed two Smurfs, and Second Avenue looks like an arcade game from six stories up. Cabs shoot by in both directions, charging on cars like Pacmen eating whatever it is that they eat. All at once, I feel a surge of vertigo. The cigarette I'm holding slides through my fingers and over the side.

Normally, two glasses of anything wouldn't waste me. Plus, the shallow glasses that I drank from held liquor in piddling amounts. But I haven't eaten in two straight days. Vanessa gave me a Phentermine pill that she ordered online from a foreign pharmacy, saying it would speed me through a long day at work. The diet pill stayed with me, turning my stomach at the taste of everything from toast to water, and without food in my system, the blue liqueur must have absorbed instantly. I am crouching on the tar roof, shuddering with my head between my knees.

The next thing I see is the emblem on the toilet that reads CRANE PLUMBING. Above the words is a blue cartoon heron that I watch while I vomit blue drinks. My precision is minimal and leaves stains that no grout-cleaner will ever get out. Either April or Vanessa is holding my hair, and trying to stop laughing. I am leaning so far into the bowl that the sides clear my shoulders. It probably looks like a portal I am trying to escape through.

The party starts at nine-thirty. Friends and acquaintances and love interests come from all over the city, plus New Jersey and Long Island. People bring snapshots from graduation and bottles of wine tied off with ribbon. A boy I like sits in one of the chairs on the roof, drinking beer in the glitter of the Christmas lights and eating my shoddy hors d'oeuvres. He tells Vanessa that he came specifically to see me, but it's been two hours since she tucked me, passed-out, into bed.

THERE IS no point to meeting men anymore. I've learned that no substantial romance can come from the bartender at a Greenwich Village taproom who scrawls his phone number between the pages of my journal. I don't expect real endearment from the graphic designers, booking agents, and freelance photographers who introduce themselves in bars; I particularly hate the way they slip me their business cards, which makes the transaction feel like one.

Whereas Vanessa continues to have spellbinding three-week relationships with the men she meets in pubs—imagining that each one is *the one* and picturing the princess-cut engagement ring, the Amsale gown, the ceremony at St. James the Less, and the sunset reception at Sunningdale Country Club—all romantic optimism is gone from me. I don't trust men, don't believe in them. And while I'll still find myself sitting on the lap of some principal dancer I just met, letting him nuzzle my ear and tell me there's elegant choreography in the way I hold a wineglass, I don't trick myself into thinking he likes me. Rejecting the concept of romance is almost as freeing as renouncing God. It means I can forget conscience, and do whatever I feel like.

I treat men more like anthropological specimens than love interests. I don't give out my phone number or make movie dates. I don't want their kisses or their false compliments. I just want their stories. In bars, I let men brush my hand because I want them to tell me about their hometowns and high-school teachers, their punk-pop revival bands and dead-end day jobs, their abusive fathers, drug-addicted mothers, and sisters in bacterial comas. I am only interested in men as voyeuristic opportunities. In public, I pay attention to the watches they wear, the books they read, and the food they pitch into their grocery carts. I study them because I want to understand them. I want to decide if they are the adversaries I think they are.

That is my goal when I agree to share a cab with two strange men after a three-martini night.

It's three A.M. and Vanessa and I are tottering out of a bar in the Meat-Packing district. I have decided to wear the strap of my purse around my neck, and she is trying to hail a cab with both hands held out in front of her, like someone groping through a thick fog. When one finally swerves to the curb, two men in black dress shirts cut us off and slide into its backseat. They have the sense of entitlement that I hate in men, and I thump the window with the palms of my hands. I am the brave kind of drunk, where I can feel my adrenaline rising, my heart pumping vodka. I decide I have no problem dragging them out by the stays in their shirt collars. Vanessa, however, doesn't have any male-specific scorn. She asks them to drop us off at home on their way uptown.

I sit up front with the driver, enjoying the reckless, late-night speed with which cabs always thrust up Park Avenue. When I turn around to face Vanessa, she is kissing one of them; her cheeks puff and contract like some slime-sucking fish. When the cab stops short in front of their apartment she wants to accept the men's invitation to go upstairs. And while I have no desire to spend time with either of them, I know I will have ample opportunity to study their bookshelves, DVD cases, and kitchen cabinets.

I realize how drunk I am when I swing open the cab's door. For a moment, the sidewalk is a raft that glides away from me as I step onto it, and I have to have to flap my arms to catch my balance. The building's lobby is a blur of plant leaves and lampshades that I lope through to catch up to Vanessa and the men. By now, I know better than to let her out of my sight. I don't trust strange, drunken men. Or any men at all, for that matter.

When we reach the apartment, the man Vanessa has been kissing wants to take her to his bedroom. But I say, "No way are you taking her anywhere, unless I come along as a chaperone," and so all four of us lean back on a brown suede bed with our heads on the pillows.

I rest my eyes while everyone around me talks. My body feels vegetative. I can feel someone's hand rubbing my calf but I don't care enough to move it. Vanessa is balled up next to me, kicking me in the ribs and saying, "Let's have a group back rub," and giggling. The last thing I remember is one of the men licking my foot and the other kneading the side of my thigh with the heel of his hand. Then my eyelids drop like the curtain at the end of a play.

The next morning, in that Fifth Avenue co-op, I hit my version of rock bottom. It isn't on a park bench, or behind a waste receptacle, or under the Triborough Bridge, but what can I say, except, to each her own?

I wake up in my clothes and feel thankful for them. I'm lying on my side, on that brown suede comforter, with no idea whose master bedroom I'm in. Vanessa is a few feet away from me on the king-sized bed, lying with her back to me. No matter how many times I hiss into her ear, she refuses to lift her head from the trough of the pillow. My own voice sounds amplified in my head, like I'm wearing earplugs. I would trade my firstborn child for an aspirin.

The men I vaguely remember from the night before have disappeared into some other cavern in this massive piece of real estate. Through the bedroom windows, I can see Central Park from what looks like fifty stories up, and the whole verdant mass of it smiles, foggy and green. I can see that the closet door is pulled open to reveal the limp arms of suit jackets. The pillowcases, which are soft in an expensive way, stink like cologne. It is a fruity scent that reminds me of schnapps and makes me breathe through my mouth. Down the long, white corridor, I hear a coffeepot gurgle. Silverware clinks as someone pulls kitchen drawers open.

I finally poke Vanessa in the armpit and let my finger wiggle there, until she opens her eyes with the startled look of someone who just heard a loud noise. But the halls have gone still and silent. Whoever was moving around has gone out for a jog or climbed back into bed. The first thing Vanessa says is, "Where the fuck are we?"

I roll back over to face the window. There's dew on the glass. Through it, I can see the park's band shell, a crescent-shaped pond, and green slopes with flecks of faraway people. The cold weather has turned the green trees yellow around the edges, like old broccoli. The view looks static like a stage backdrop, which it might as well be. We are the same characters in the same comic drama. Only the setting has changed.

THE STILL-TO-LEARN

THE GREAT THING about the information age is it allows me to seek help in the most passive and anonymous way possible. Email is a bottle I can fold my SOS into. I can chuck it into the vast ocean of humanity, and hope some sympathetic soul will read it and lob back a response.

And at the same time, seeking help is made difficult by the ambiguity of my relationship with alcohol. There are plenty of resources for alcoholics in search of addiction care. Web sites explain the subtleties of motivational enhancement therapy and supportive-expressive psychotherapy, plus the differences between inpatient, outpatient, and residential treatment. But there aren't any resources for young people who, in the fallout from college, have been adversely affected by alcohol but are not physically addicted to it. I don't know how to name that kind of drinking. I can't think of a thing to type into the blank box of an Internet search engine.

I do my research during downtime at work, and I find plenty of self-screening tests for alcoholism online. I spend my lunch hour in my unkempt cubicle, discreetly stooped over my keyboard, answering questions like: "How often have you felt remorse after drinking?" And "What is the greatest number of drinks you've had at any one time?" My results put me in a gray zone, defined as problematic drinking. Web sites tell me to seek further evaluation, but they don't say where. They advise seeking help, but they won't say what form that help ought to take.

What I want is someone who will confirm what I have always suspected, and always allowed friends and adults to nullify: This drinking is wrecking me.

Vanessa doesn't think our Fifth Avenue sleepover was a wake-up call. She can't see why it was a big deal that we slept in a house without knowing whose name was on the lease. Whereas I obsess on what could have happened—the fact that we could have been abused in any number of foreseeable ways, all the while not even having an address to give to a 911 operator—she fixates on the fact that nothing *did* happen. She arches her eyebrows the way she does when she thinks I am being hysterical. And when she finally says, "I see your point," it is with an air of aloofness. She only says it to appease me.

While I'm frustrated by Vanessa's indifference, I understand why it is difficult for her to understand my concern. For the most part, the change is in my head. Drinking in New York is neither more nor less dangerous than drinking in college. And, by the same token, the owners of the Fifth Avenue co-op were neither more nor less menacing than the college boys I'm accustomed to.

Only the location was alien. In college, I blacked out in familiar settings. Even if I didn't recognize where I was when I opened my eyes, I didn't think there was any real risk if I woke up and saw milk crates filled with records, spiral notebooks stacked on a desk, or a half-dead spider plant suspended from a hook in the ceiling. Just as watching a bullfighter take a horn makes you realize that the threat of a mauling has always been present, that Fifth Avenue apartment—in its urban opulence—made me see that my drinking has been tearing me apart all along. Perhaps I should have realized it with my first blackout, or my first drunken tumble, or my first stomach pumping. But these occurred at home or at college, where my drinking felt insulated, and I had the illusion of safety.

I feel that this event is significant, and yet I've never trusted the validity of my feelings. I go hunting for an expert to confirm them.

ON ONE of the alcohol-screening Web sites, I find the email address of an addiction counselor and decide to write to him. I don't want his advice per se. I don't want to know whether he thinks I should cut back or quit drinking entirely. I just want him to classify me. I'm not sure how to address the email in the subject portion, so I leave it blank, which always gives the impression of wordless despondency. Before I click the send button, I double-check to make sure he is headquartered in a different time zone. I don't want to risk the prospect of an in-person evaluation.

A few days later, I receive this response:

Dear Ms. Zailckas, In answer to your questions:

1) *I would classify your situation as alcohol abuse, and not alcoholism, from what you have told me. Abusers find the volition to stop when the reasons for abuse stop (such as graduating from college and getting a job, or getting away from a miserable situation) or when the consequences of the abuse make them realize they need to change.*

2) *Everyone should practice sobriety, which is not the same as abstinence. Sobriety is making important decisions based on reason and consideration. Alcoholics need to practice abstinence because they have a genetically based reaction to alcohol that makes them lose control and cause havoc in their lives. Abusers do not have that reaction, and so they can drink "normally" if they choose to do so.*

3) *I would recommend AA for anyone in an abusive drinking pattern because twelve-step programs are helpful for anyone trying to build a good life. If, after one has developed a good life, she discovers that she is not really an alcoholic, who cares? The good life is not going to be retracted.*

I do want a good life. More than anything, I want to be one of those people I see at sundown on weekdays. I want to be as laughing as the women who window shop with their girlfriends after the boutiques have lowered their steel security gates, or as lovely as the women who curl their hands into their lovers' coat pockets, or as self-possessed as the women who lope behind their sprightly black Labradors. I want their sound friendships, their romances, and their swollen self-confidence, and yet I don't know how to achieve these things without alcohol. These are the wants I always drank to fulfill.

I decide to take the doctor's advice and try an AA meeting. I call Alcoholics Anonymous, where I am referred to New York Intergroup, where a pleasant young operator reads me meeting times like movie times. I request AA groups in the East Village, which is more than seventy blocks from my apartment, so I won't have to worry about encountering alcoholics in the neighborhood post office or the produce aisle of the grocery store. Downtown, I also expect to find a younger crowd than the group of crusty old men that smoke Marlboro Reds in front of a meeting on East Eightieth Street.

Still, a curious thing happens when I show up at a church on Lafayette Street after work. The night is mild and the sidewalks are empty, save for the mass of people dallying under a sallow streetlight. They are all young, blue-jeaned, pink-cheeked, and tousle-haired. As I approach them, I can see they are calling out to one another and embracing. Some are dancing. More are blowing over the mouth-holes of their deli coffee cups. The scene is so kindly I panic. I don't know what I will say to this confederacy of cat-eyed extroverts wearing Army jackets and plastic earrings. When I reach the church entrance, I keep walking to the corner bookstore. I go inside and pretend to scan the racks for a rare volume of poetry.

After I chicken out of the AA meeting, I decide I have found the volition to stop drinking myself into blackout mode, and therefore can try to drink "normally." In my mind, this means drinking one glass of beer or wine when it is expected of me on a date, at a corporate function, or during a holiday dinner. It also means I will look for new ways to bond with Vanessa because as long as we are drinking together, I'm afraid we will never drink moderately.

I don't realize that something will shift when Vanessa and I stop drinking together. A fault opens itself in the floor space between our bedrooms, and it gradually becomes harder to cross. I don't explicitly tell her that I am trying to get a handle on my alcohol abuse. Instead, I start to invite her to bookstores and flea markets and tea shops rather than bars. Only our new outings don't function the same way our martini nights did: in the fiction aisle, she hears my false enthusiasm for choices; amid the boxes of old boots and belt buckles, I sense she is attacking my personal style. Together, we fall into vast lulls of silence over kettles of peach oolong tea.

I think back six months to college and try to remember some activity, aside from drinking, that Vanessa and I enjoyed doing together. But I can only remember beer while we bowled or wine while we cooked. Or else there was some residual hangover to talk about during the gray afternoons that we roved the trail around Green Lakes State Park. We don't like the same movies or bands or stores. We've been inseparable for the past ten months, but we don't have a damn thing, aside from alcohol, to talk about.

Eventually, our interaction drops off altogether. Vanessa camps out at her boyfriend's house for weeks at a time, and I close myself off in my bedroom with a tall stack of overdue library books. She still goes to bars with the waitress from her old job, or with her boyfriend from Brooklyn, who shoulders her up the stairs some nights. Sometimes I recognize her voice, drunk and baying, when I get three A.M. prank calls. When we are home together, our apartment reverberates with waves of passive aggression. Our only form of communication is about the outstanding electric bills we keep taped to the refrigerator; we are at constant odds about how much we owe each other.

I START dating a boy. Actually, he's a man. At least that's what April says, when she meets us at a sushi joint on Bleecker Street. She pulls my ponytail while we're conspiring in the ladies' room and says, "K, you've found a real man this time."

By the same token, I immediately know Matt is the type of man that I should have been dating all along. He is an intern at the magazine, and the sales reps fan themselves when he glides past our row of cubicles, purring and saying he has "bad-boy" appeal. I guess I can see that. Matt has the rock-star good looks that strangers regularly compare to Mick Jagger or Jim Morrison, anyone who is all eyes and hair. Women, particularly, have the idea that he smokes hand-rolled cigarettes and shoves over drum kits. But the truth is just the opposite; Matt will prove to be the kindest man I've ever known. As I get to know him, I'll find he's never had a cigarette or a cavity. He'll confess that he's only had three hangovers, ever, and two of them will follow nights out with me.

And yet Matt, in the beginning, tosses me right back into voracious drinking. He does it because I am faced with the same old romantic problems when I'm in his presence: I try to break the ice and steady my breathing, and I work to be bright and entertaining.

Alcohol facilitates our first date. At an Irish pub near my apartment, we sit under a blackboard where draft beers are spelled out in chalk, and I drink the first blond pint, which stops my nervous shivering. Then we hail a cab to an East Village bar, where I sip a tall vodka drink that enables me to pull a plastic rose from a vase and stuff it into Matt's shirt pocket as a boutonniere, my joke about first-date formality. Then we link arms and trip to the garden lounge on Avenue C, where we drink red wine and I lean against him amid the candles and throw pillows without feeling silly. Much later, Matt will admit it was four rounds of drinks that gave him the courage to lean over and kiss me while the cab bumped back up First Avenue, and I'll admit I was drunk enough to lose my cell phone between the cab seats.

Second and third dates follow. In windowless bars, where the weather inside feels overcast, Matt and I drink enough beer to get jelly-kneed and tug on each other's sleeves. I can't stick to a couple of bottles, nor can I restrict myself to beer or wine when hard alcohol is so alluringly disarming, when it gives me the courage to air sentiments like "You're wonderful."

But the pattern of drinking and confessing is just as confusing as it was in college. In graffitied bars, Matt calls me "sweets" and lets me mess up his hair, and I believe it when he tells me he wants to keep seeing me even after he goes back to a Philadelphia university for his senior year. But that certainty burns off the next morning, with my blood-alcohol level. Matt is quiet in his hangovers, and I wonder if his affection for me is wavering.

Our nights might continue in this cycle, but Matt leaves for college. On a Sunday in September, he drives over to say good-bye in a car bulging with boxes. We hug in front of the corner luncheonette. People are jetting onto the sidewalk after brunches of Bloody Marys, and the scene feels too busy and public. He says he will call me when he hits I-95, but I am skeptical. I wave good-bye and turn around before he pulls the car into traffic. I don't want my last memory of him to be his taillights rounding the corner of East Seventy-eighth Street.

But the phone rings a few hours later, while I am searching for a TV signal in the static, and his call is so prompt that I have to stop for an instant and make sure I'm not imagining it. It rings the next night when I am sponging down the refrigerator door. And it rings the night after that, by which time I've learned to snatch up the phone before Vanessa can answer it.

For a month, I talk to Matt on the phone every night until well after midnight, when the phone's battery dies. Another girl might have learned to do this in high school: roosting on the kitchen counter or the fire escape with the phone cradled against one shoulder, soaking up stories, and learning that not all silences are bad. But I've never exposed myself without the confessional catalyst of alcohol. Maybe the fact that I can't see Matt's expression makes it easier for me to tell him things. I describe for him the orchids that grow wild in my hometown, the argument I had with my parents on a trip to San Francisco, the way our house cat used to claw my sister and me when we tried to tie him into bonnets.

Months go by, and I save enough money to move out of the apartment I share with Vanessa and into a small studio in the East Village. Tompkins Square Park, with its women in top hats and men in eyeliner, is the perfect location to practice sobriety. The view from my window holds the promise of unconditional acceptance; in this part of town, cars are bedecked with glitter and baby dolls' heads, street activists pass out flyers that encourage you to "ban Republican marriage," and men slap shoulders outside of Doc Holiday's, where they compare conspiracy theories. Here, nothing is too kooky or creepy or off-putting. I can let the inner awkwardness I've always felt flower, and I can stop using alcohol as a mode of belonging.

Time doesn't pass while I'm living alone. Every day becomes

an ordered little compartment, in which I work, elbow my way into a subway car, buy milk at East Village Farms, mop the floors, watch pointless TV, and interact with no one other than the two-dollar psychic and people I give dimes to on the street. Thanks to caller ID, I can avoid the people I used to drink with, who call me, dead-drunk, from a nearby bar to see if I'll come down. I'm glad I had the sense to keep my address private, so no one buzzed can buzz my intercom.

I know I am making the same mistake that I made in college, when I mistook being reclusive for being sober. But I have few college friends beyond my hard-drinking-buddies, and my new friends from work won't make the fifteen-dollar cab ride without the prospect of a few rounds of beer. I'm often lonely, but I don't know who to invite over. I am hard-pressed to find other twenty-two-year-olds who don't drink.

I spend most of my time with Matt, who takes the train to visit me every few weeks. Matt drinks occasionally, but it means little to him. His relationship with alcohol doesn't run nearly as deep as mine does. We occasionally sip beer when we are together, when we're at a show with a two-drink minimum or an after-party where the beer is free. I try to intersperse glasses of water between beers, which everyone always says is the key to drinking moderately.

My new approach to "normal" and "responsible" drinking is to drink only while I'm doing something else, too, like watching a band, as opposed to absentmindedly draining Amstels because I've run out of change for the jukebox. The method is kind of like that old cliché of thinking about baseball while you're having sex; I rely on outside entertainment to distract me from the joy that alcohol brings me. Only it doesn't always work. Sometimes, when I'm already buzzed after the drink minimum, the feeling multiplies inside me like microbes and I feel a greedy desire to feed it two more beers so it will grow.

I AM NURTURING that kind of buzz on New Year's Eve, after four bottles of beer. Matt and I have spent the evening blowing paper horns, sneering for a disposable camera, and listening to a generally bad band that, tonight, sounded good. I am skipping down the street while the wind lifts the pleats of my skirt. Matt is lost somewhere behind me on the crosswalk. The people I pass on the street look out at me through the zeros of their 2003-shaped glasses, and their faces smear. The headlights of cars trail the way they would in a photo taken with a sluggish shutter in low light.

Every few steps, I turn around to tell Matt that I hate him. I've been saying it for many blocks, and I can't remember why. Maybe it's because a woman's name popped up in the caller ID box of his cell phone at midnight. Or it might be because he wants to stay out when I want to go home. Or it could be because my feet hurt and alcohol has resurrected my irrational hostility.

Eventually, I push into a bar on Avenue B, where the air is sweaty and the clientele looks as pissed off as I do. I decide I want to order more beer, to shift and twist angrily on my bar stool, and to give Matt the silent treatment. And when he asks me what's wrong, I want to slap a bottle off a table, so I do. He laughs and presses his forehead to mine, like I am acting for the sake of some joke. But my rage is real. I'll be able to see it tomorrow when we develop the night's roll of film. A picture will show me standing in the middle of Houston Street, flashing my middle finger for the camera, while traffic is stopped behind me for the red light. My smile will look wide and kidding, but

I'll be able to tell by the squint of my eyes that the fuck-you sentiment is genuine.

I decide to quit drinking for good before the hangover hits. I make up my mind during the cab ride home, when I feel dizzy and Matt lets me lie down and rest my head on his lap. My stomach pitches with every pothole on First Avenue, and when I look up I can see his face hanging over mine with ungrudging affection. I wonder how many people have shown his kind of faith in me, how many have made an effort to ally with me without alcohol. Probably no one has. His is the first honest friendship that I've had in years, and I don't want to spend my time with him drinking, sobbing, shrieking, and otherwise pushing him anyway. A rare truth falls over me like the glare from the streetlights. I know that as long as I keep drinking, I will drive back everyone who is good-natured. Only people who are as drunk and damaged as I am will stay.

In the year and a half since I've quit drinking, I'm not sure if I've found the "good life" that the addiction counselor mentioned to me, but I've certainly uncovered a better one. It's made up of good days and bad days, and they are sometimes grossly out of proportion. But I think that's the thing that makes abstinence momentous; it has a sweet-and-sour appeal.

I've learned that I will always be uptight. In the absence of alcohol, I have learned that I am not and have never been an extrovert. I will never be the kind of woman who dances at weddings, unburdens to hairdressers, or stops strangers to admire their shoes. Instead, I have a cautious carriage, an unwavering gait, and the kind of rigid shoulder blades that make yoga instructors grind their elbows into them. Like all escapists, I sometimes get lost in long moments of silence.

I've learned that my anxiety won't ever drop off entirely. I will always fear the outside chances: that a deadline will go unfulfilled, or an elevator will jam, or a mouse will scuttle across the floor no matter how many cubes of poison the exterminator drops behind the stove. Like so many people, I know I can't expect to stop feeling anxiety during a time in history when there is actually a device for measuring it—the terror-alert level, which in New York always hovers at orange. Without alcohol, it is harder to hide from my fears. Instead, I have to close my eyes, shake out my hands, and try to get a handle on them.

Likewise, I will always have emotional hot spots. Memories of drunken disasters tend to flood back to me at the most inconvenient moments. In Central Park, when I see teenaged girls unloading beer cans from their backpacks, I catch a glimpse of what I looked like ten years ago, and I have to look away. My breath seizes up while I'm watching a Brooklyn-based band because the percussion section is so violent it returns a hangover-like heart-thumping to me. Some part of me still feels distrustful of men; when I walk home with my hands bound up in plastic grocery bags, I feel the stab of panic when a man on the corner leans in too close to say, "Hey, pretty." I've learned that the deeper I examine the past, the less it wages war on my consciousness.

I've learned that I can't jolt myself out of sadness. Just as I couldn't do it with alcohol, I can't do it with naps, herbs, or rigorous exercise. I think I will always be more vulnerable to it than some people. I will always be moved to tears by an animal-rescue show, or a certain Polish poet, or some bit of advice from my mother. But depression, the feeling that I was slow-motion falling into my own imminent madness—or worse—ended when hard drinking did. Today, bad days have a bottom to them.

I've learned that romantic love adapts to life without alcohol. Once Matt and I stopped wasting whole hours in the bar below my apartment, our time together became less haphazard and more deliberate. We used to talk while we drank beer and played pinball at side-by-side machines. Now, we do it while we sit on a hill in the park. We cluck at squirrels and tell stories until we've missed the movie that we planned to see.

In the end, Matt elected to stop drinking as a show of solidarity. And though I am thankful for his support, I know my decision to abstain began as an individual choice, and I know it has to stay that way. I have to believe that it is easier for me to hold fast to what I want without alcohol. It makes it easier for me to know who I am, and to accept it.

I've learned that if my friendships have any hope of surviving, they can't have their roots in commiseration. As for the female friends I have cried in my beers with over the years, the women I loved so completely—for their sadness manifested as madness, or madness manifested as sadness, for their electric instability and profound pain—I have lost touch with every last one of them. Without alcohol, our friendship seized like an engine without oil. We could support each other through tragedies, but not through good days or even average ones.

In the wake of it all, I think I've learned what it means to be authentically glad. These days, I'm grateful for a hazy afternoon when the man behind the counter of the grocer remembers how I take my coffee, when the guy in the long tunnel of the Sixth Avenue subway station is still playing "A Hard Day's Night" on guitar, when the park is filled with strangers laughing as their dogs try to mount one another. I like picking up a roll of developed film at the corner photo lab and discovering that the world inside the prints confirms that, for a few brief moments, the world was as handsome as I thought it was. It convinces me that my efforts aren't useless. I think I've found some meaning here.

I know that I don't want to be bell-jarred by alcohol. I don't want to spend the next ten years waiting for alcoholism to fall like an ax, nor do I want to spin through any more cycles of hard drinking followed by abstinence, in which every lap picks up speed and tailspins me into more depression, aggression, and accidents. I have no desire to sacrifice more years to rebuilding and recovering. I refuse to watch life-as-I-know-it dissolve into a series of disasters transcribed into memoirs. I won't be a case in point for any more issues of self-ruin, or have solidity that's that cheap and flimsy.

OVER THE course of writing this book, I've learned that if any of us, girls and women, want true strength born of stability, we need to find a more productive outlet. Drinking, like all forms of self-destruction, isn't a valid art form because it allows the world to rejoice in our weakness, the inferiority that it has always expected of us. Rather than turning our dissatisfaction inward, allowing ourselves to be thwarted by gender stereotypes and the burdens to achieve feeble feminine goals like thinness, rather than allowing our frustrations to be wasted and to waste away inside of us, I think we should use them as ammunition against the world they were borne of. We will never really free ourselves of our inhibitions in dank bars. But I believe we can shed them in our projects. In our music, in our films, and on our canvases, we can be wildly immodest.

By the same token, I think it's time that we allow ourselves to experience real anger as women. And I don't mean that passive-aggressive dance that we've employed for too many years. It's not real anger if it is implied or a few degrees removed, if it takes the form of whispering, or cold shoulders, or silent treatment. Real anger is what popular culture would have us be afraid of, based on the fact that it is not courteous, elegant, or *feminine*. Since I've stopped drinking, I am perpetually angry: I am enraged by the alcohol industry, which alternates between pandering to women and using us to bait men. I'm sick of ad campaigns by Svedka vodka, which picture women kneeling to support trays of men's martinis, or holding glasses of vodka between their naked breasts. I'm sick of Wet gin by Beefeater (surely a liquor that was named with women in mind), the print ads of which read, "Your head is telling you to stay dry but your heart is shouting Wet! Wet! Wet!" as though alcohol were a necessary lubricant, the very ingredient that makes desire possible for women. I am insanely tired of Anheuser-Busch, which insults women's intelligence by playing to cultural stereotypes about body consciousness. I hate the fact that they think they can sucker us by marketing low-carb, low-calorie beer.

I've also had it with *Girls Gone Wild* producer Joe Francis, and with the thousands of aspiring home-movie makers he seems to have spawned: the men who linger on the sidelines of nightclubs like vultures, watching for the girl who totters on her feet and slurs her words, before luring her to pull up her skirt. In a 2002 *Rolling Stone* interview, Joe Francis actually said of the typical girl he convinces to flash her chest, "It's like the girl who says she's not going to have sex with you and then does. She goes, 'I shouldn't, I shouldn't,' but you know she's going to," which sounds to me like date-rape logic. And I'm frightened by the thousands of abusive men this Mardi Gras culture has made way for, the ones who actively seek out drunken girls for smash-and-grab sex.

I'm pissed at the government that would, through its allocation of dollars, have us believe that drug abuse is either a bigger issue or a more worthy one than underage drinking, neither of which is the case. And I'm sick of the ignorance that that lack of funding has generated, of the fathers who approach me at dinner parties with their four-year-old girls clasped to their pant legs and say, "Yeah, but studies say kids can buy drugs more easily than they can buy alcohol." To which I always respond, "I guess that means you keep heroin in your liquor cabinet?"

I'm tired of the world that won't rescue girls until we're long past the point of saving. We live in a culture that expects teenaged girls to cry for help by acting out in ways that girls are conditioned not to. Too many people rely on outward signs of aggression to indicate their daughters or girlfriends or sisters have problems with alcohol. They wait for fights, or D.U.I. charges, or destruction of property, when girls who drink are far less apt to break rules in overt ways. As a gender, we are far more likely to turn our drunken destructiveness inward, to wage private wars against ourselves, to attempt suicide, to be pinned down by fear and depression.

More than anything, I've had it with a world that has created a generation of women who are emotionally dependent on alcohol, and then demonized us for our lack of feminine control.

TODAY, IT occurs to me that there is one thing that can bond women more than a tray of cocktails: It is the way all these forces have splintered us.

Our first step is to stop being ashamed of our missteps. There are too many of us, women and young women and girls who are too dependent on liquor, for any one of us to be wholly at fault.

While I was writing this book, women emerged in astounding numbers to tell me their stories. I've heard about the sixteen-year-old girl in an alcohol-induced coma, whose parents had to switch off her respirator. I've heard from grown women who, in their youth, hid dozens of empty bottles in bins under their beds, and nightly slept over them like Hans Christian Andersen's princess on the pea. There have been parents who have driven through the night to be with college-aged daughters who got drunk and broke arms or legs. Every new story makes me think of Sylvia Plath's "Mushrooms." It finds me marveling, "So many of us!"

The devastating hours that women share with me bond me closer to them than happy hours ever would. I want to know them all because they make me think Plath's words might apply to us, too: "Our kind multiplies: / We shall by morning / Inherit the earth." In retelling our stories, our foot's certainly in the door.

This first occurs to me one night at a Midtown hotel. I'm forty-five minutes late for a corporate party in the hotel lounge. I've taken the wrong bus. The people I work with have left multiple messages on my cell phone, asking "Where the F are you?" And by the time I'm slipping up the steps to the bar, I've been walking in the rain for ten blocks, and my umbrella has blown inside-out. My shirt is clinging to my ribs, and my hair is wisping out at weird angles.

It's a bizarre pageant upstairs, where most of my coworkers are already worse for wear. They have formed a tight circle, the way girls used to at recess to play slap-clapping games. They are whispering, raising glasses of champagne, and swiveling their hips to lounge music. People are drunk enough to quit whining about diets and eat what appeals to them; everyone is carting around cocktail napkins loaded with pork crepes, deep-fried shrimp, and crackers coated with garlic dip. The sales rep who flew in from California is on his fourth mojito, saying he's still on Pacific Time and asking "Where's the closest strip club?"

On a corner banquette, the other assistants drink cautiously, or not at all. For the most part, they look bored or mortified, like drinking with these regional directors of advertising is about as appealing as drinking with relatives. Their chins are in their hands. They stealthily eye the time on their inner wrists.

I sit beside one of the twenty-year-old interns in my department. She is sweet and outspoken, with a bouncing gait that makes men peek out their office doors when she bounds down the halls with her arms full of packages to be messengered. Before I quit drinking, we had many wild nights together, during which we sipped cups at downtown performance spaces, got lit enough to keep drinking after the bands had packed their equipment, skipped up Second Avenue to dive bars, shared cigarettes and halves of Xanax, met impossibly handsome men who wore women's T-shirts, felt our eyelids get heavy, hugged, and staggered home to our respective neighborhoods.

Tonight, she has a stunned look about her. She's sitting with her feet tucked under her in a way that reminds me of a bird warming an egg. When the waitress comes by to say, "Anyone need anything?" she orders club soda, but lets the glass sit on her thigh and hiss lime-twisted bubbles. Without prompting, she says, "I promised my mom I wouldn't drink tonight."

No one has asked her why she isn't drinking vanilla-infused vodka or Tanqueray Ten; the people we work with are too busy supporting one another on their feet. Many of them have disappeared down the steep incline of industrial stairs, and the rest are shouldering into their overcoats and making plans to share cabs. The caterers are clearing the hors d'oeuvres table of nibbled strawberries, moist napkins, and lipstick-smudged stemware. Someone has dimmed the lights so the room has a gauzy, gold glow. I am the only one to notice she isn't drinking because, in my early abstinence, I'm like a starving woman on a diet: I make mental notes of what's in everyone's glass.

When she sees that I'm not drinking, either, she lowers her voice to say, "I'm recuperating. I was really messed-up last night."

All the executives we work for have vanished, and our little roped-off corner of the room has given way to hotel guests, mostly businessmen and their hookers. The bar is windowless, but I'm certain it is nighttime outside, the dense dark of midwinter. Here and there, I can make out women scrutinizing the leather-bound drink menus, and see one who is dabbing her shirt where she dripped a white-chocolate martini.

I ask her if she is okay.

She tells she me had her stomach pumped last night. She confesses it like a crime of passion, a murder she hadn't known she was capable of. She'd been downtown, nodding out time while a band played, drinking no more than usual, and then, who knows? She came to lying on a cot at the hospital, still queasy with a hangover, or maybe because of the onslaught of the suction pump.

For an instant I am sixteen again. I remember everything from the morning in September: my breakfast poker face, the aches in my arms, and the vacuous space in my head. It occurs to me that this is what so many people say recovery is. Through the exchange of war stories, we learn that our failings aren't only personal, they are cultural.

Once I start to pay attention, I overhear women everywhere telling my story. The woman folding T-shirts in the back of the thrift shop is saying, "Alcohol just makes me want to say what I mean." The girls walking in front of me on the sidewalk are talking about their weekend plans to "drink their way down the Lower East Side." Women on the F train are debating the best first-date drink. I've had these conversations a dozen times before. I could finish their sentences for them.

I've spent a lot of time trying to put a face to drinking. I've scrutinized too many beer commercials and liquor ads, trying to decide who personifies the way alcohol looks in my head, whether it's someone male or female, young or ridiculously young, thin or voluptuous, fair or bronzed, model-like or real-looking.

In the end, I see alcohol like a man who has courted us all. Alcohol has been the first love of so many of us; it had us believing we were desirable and challenging in its presence alone. It let us think it would take us away from small towns, stressful studies, tedious jobs, or unproductive relationships. We have been terrifyingly devoted to it, and it's left too many of us heart-sore.

Tonight, in the hotel lounge with another young woman who's known the hand of vertigo, the dead space of the overdose, the smell of self-induced sickness, I feel a fellowship with her that's more happy than sad. It's the privileged information that bonds women over all types of assholes. I'm thinking of women who find one another's phone numbers balled up in their boyfriend's sock drawers, who meet over tea to compare notes on various provocations—his dysfunctional family or bad sweaters or sexual inadequacies. Maybe that's just the stuff of movies. But even so, I'd like to think it's possible that ex-mistresses make the best friends. I love the idea that that's the valuable union—it just might be our exquisite revenge.

As we gather our purses, I slide my arm through her hinged elbow and say, "That happened to me, too."

ACKNOWLEDGMENTS

THIS BOOK wouldn't have been possible without Erin Hosier, my agent at The Gernert Company. Thank you for seeing the possibilities, for reading every word, and for guiding me every step of the way. You helped me find my story and, by extension, myself.

Molly Stern, my editor at Viking, taught me how to write a book when I was just a girl who wrote poems, and it's been the greatest gift of my life. Alessandra Lusardi, also at Viking, has been a smart voice and a reassuring presence throughout.

I owe everything to Mary Karr, "goddess." Thank you for being the Midas of inspiration, for touching everyone and turning all of us into writers. Thank you for saving me from the life I thought I wanted, from stale jobs and a hard heart. Without you, I would never have tried.

Thanks to Shari Smiley at Creative Artists Agency for the chat about books and drinking and music. You helped me find an end to this book before I'd even begun it.

I will always be grateful for the day I met Kevin Martinez. Thanks for being a wise voice, a kind boss, and an electric personality. Thank you for bringing me to New York, forgiving my slip-ups, and giving me math lessons.

Thanks also: Jody Kivort, for bearing my camera shyness. Michael Pirrocco, for making my manuscript look most photogenic. Dave Itzkoff, for the advice you gave me on the fire escape. James T. Hamilton, M.D., for the diagnosis. The Media Education Foundation makes the smartest media documentaries in existence; I am thankful they loaned me *Spin the Bottle*. Harvard School of Public Health College Alcohol Study has given the issue of college alcohol abuse the analysis it deserves, for which I am grateful. I have to thank everyone at Tinkle who made Sunday the most blessed day of the week. Windows 95 has been indestructible. Thank you Carl Barât and Peter Doherty for songs that pull my heartstrings and keep me company every workday.

I'd be a really rotten person were it not for my first writing teachers, Donna Lanza, Amber Smith, Judith Mandelbaum-Schmidt, and William Glavin, Jr.; thank you for the lifeline. My first editors, Molly English and Jill Johnson, never kept me on the bench.

I'd be lost without: David and Joan Lehmann, thank you for the long, scenic walks, for joking about "another chapter," and for always making me smile. Matt Chamberlain has given me unshakable support; you have been my mouse-catcher, my week-planner, my ass-kicker. Thank you for choosing me. My sister, Nikki Zailckas, is the love of my life; thank for your candidness, for your monologues, for your mania, and for being my little muse.

Most importantly, my parents have spent the last year answering my questions, quieting my panic attacks, reminding me to wash my hair, and FedExing my manuscript when I forgot it in their kitchen sink. I couldn't have made it without your courage and trust. Your love has been my oxygen tent.